A Movie Lectionary—Cycle B

LIGHTS CAMERA... FAITH!

A Movie Lover's Guide to Scripture

By Peter Malone, MSC with Rose Pacatte, FSP
Foreword by Chazz Palminteri

Pauline
BOOKS & MEDIA
Boston

Library of Congress Cataloging-in-Publication Data

Malone, Peter.
  Lights, camera...faith! : a movie lectionary. Cycle B / by Peter
Malone, MSC with Rose Pacatte, FSP.
      p. cm.
Includes bibliographical references and index.
  ISBN 0-8198-4492-6 (pbk.)
  1. Bible. N.T. Gospels — Criticism, interpretation, etc. 2. Motion
pictures — Religious aspects — Christianity. I. Title.
  BS2565 .M27 2001
  261.5'7— dc21
                           2001001422
                           Rev.

Cover design by Helen Rita Lane, FSP

Printed and published in the U.S.A. by Pauline Books & Media, 50 Saint Pauls
Avenue, Boston, MA 02130-3491.

www.pauline.org

Pauline Books & Media is the publishing house of the Daughters of St. Paul, an
international congregation of women religious serving the Church with the
communications media.

1 2 3 4 5 6 7 8 9   10 09 08 07 06 05 04 03 02

Contents

ADDITIONAL CELEBRATIONS

Foreword

Certain events in life leave an indelible impression. My first such event was when my mother took me to see the movie, *Around the World in Eighty Days*. I remember the wonderful swirl of colors in that dark theatre and watching all the countries fly across the screen before my eyes. For a boy from a little Bronx neighborhood, this was magical. I remember my mother smiling at my excitement. That was my first taste of falling in love with movies, and I've been searching for that feeling throughout my life. When I saw *To Kill a Mockingbird*, I felt that way again. That movie taught me about the way people can be treated because of their color and race. It helped me to understand how wrong it is to judge someone on the basis of race. That's the incredible thing about movies. They can teach you lessons you never dreamed of, and take you to emotional levels you never imagined.

Much later, when I wrote *A Bronx Tale*, I wanted to create a similar experience for people. The story explores the different worlds of the working man and the Mafia through the eyes of a nine-year-old boy. Lorenzo tells his son, "The saddest thing in life is wasted talent." Since its release, many people have told me that these words have touched them in some way. That's very rewarding to hear. And that's the power of movies. You can walk into a dark theatre and come out a different person.

The essence of any great movie is the struggle between good and evil. Many of the films featured in this book, such as *The Godfather, Life is Beautiful, To Kill a Mockingbird*, and *The Lord of the Rings*, do this brilliantly. Life is the same way. We are constantly confronted with evil in our everyday lives. A movie allows us to live, through its characters, certain situations that we may never experience personally—and still gain some personal knowledge. Movies teach us about ourselves and other people. They show us the world as it was—or as we might imagine it to have been—at any specific time in history. They are the world's home movies for generations to study.

As a grown man, I still search for the feeling of excitement I experienced as a young boy in that Bronx theatre. Sometimes that feeling is stirred within me by a homily on the Sunday Gospel, or when I read a few pages of the Bible before I go to bed. Just as the Gospels have the power to touch and renew people's lives, so movies have a power of their own. They reach the minds and hearts of millions of people at once. Cinematic art gives us a place to see how the worlds of spirituality and everyday life coexist. *Lights, Camera...Faith!* shows just how movies can launch us on an exciting spiritual journey.

—CHAZZ PALMINTERI
Actor, Writer, and Director

Introduction

Storytelling

No matter who we are or what we do, we are all people of "the story." We like to hear, see, and tell stories. The various cultures of the world communicate their stories, passing down shared beliefs and values from generation to generation.

Faith, too, is passed on through story. We know about the Incarnation and Jesus' life, death, and resurrection through stories found in the Gospels. Theologian Anthony Kelly, CSsR has noted that when the Son of God was made flesh, he did not first become a doctrine or a dogma. He became human and lived his story. Because we now share our life stories with Jesus, we become part of God's story—God's "autobiography."

Sunday after Sunday, feast day after feast day, we listen to chapters of Jesus' story. Often what we hear is familiar. But some of it seems a little strange at times, and so we need to break open the Scriptures to understand God's love more fully and thus deepen our faith. A movie lectionary is one way of breaking open the Sunday Scripture.

The Movie Lectionary approach

All volumes of *Lights, Camera...Faith! A Movie Lectionary* are designed to help us better appreciate the Sunday Gospel as well as the other readings for each week. These volumes take the story found in a popular movie and create a dialogue between the movie and the Gospel reading. The film and its themes can help illuminate the Gospel, sometimes paralleling it, at other times providing a contrast. Conversely, the Gospel story can help us to find deeper levels of meaning in the movie, thus enriching both our liturgical and everyday lives.

In Cycle A of the liturgical year, the principal Gospel is Matthew's. Many of the readings are from the sermons that form so much of this particular Gospel. The movies used in that volume often illustrate or contrast with Jesus' teaching, rather than events in his life.

In this volume, Cycle B, the Gospel readings are mainly from Mark, the most direct of the four Gospels. Its straight-forward, vivid, and detailed portrait of Jesus might also be called "tough." Mark's Gospel shows Jesus confronting devils. It recounts stories of demonic possession, hostile inter-changes between Jesus and some of the religious leaders, and Jesus' teaching about taking up the cross. Some of the movies chosen for this volume correspond to this "tough-ness." We could say that these Gospel stories and movies challenge us to develop a stronger and more resilient faith. Such "tough" movies may be too difficult for some groups to watch in their entirety. However, leaders could select se-quences which contain the essentials of the movie but which could be viewed by all.

Sr. Rose Pacatte and I have shared an ongoing journey through the preparation of these volumes of the *Movie Lectionary* series. Rose has collaborated in these volumes and has made invaluable suggestions regarding movies to be in-cluded. She also amplified synopses and clarified the commentary. Her special and particular contribution is the section "For Reflection and Conversation."

The Format

The format of *Lights, Camera…Faith!* is simple and acces-sible.

Synopsis: Not all readers may have seen every movie in-cluded in this book, though it is strongly recommended to see a movie before using it in a homily or with a group. The synopsis offers details that may be helpful in recalling movie characters, plot, and sequence.

SYNOPSIS

COMMENTARY

Commentary: Each movie commentary provides information about the movie itself: actors, directors, producers, related films, etc.

DIALOGUE WITH THE GOSPEL

Dialogue with the Gospel: This is the core of each chapter: how the movie and its themes relate to the liturgical readings. Some movies and Gospel passages harmonize quite well. Other pairs do not correspond as clearly—for the most part, movie makers probably did not intend a scriptural message! Therefore, each dialogue begins with a short *Focus* to point the reader in the right direction.

KEY SCENES AND THEMES

Key Scenes and Themes: To enrich the dialogue, I highlight several sections of the movie that would be worth discussing thematically, or showing as a clip during group discussions, liturgy preparation, or course presentation if the scenes are sequential.

FOR REFLECTION AND CONVERSATION

For Reflection and Conversation: These practical, thought provoking comments and questions provide a focus for living the Gospel message in daily life.

Prayer

Prayer: My editor had the rather beautiful idea of adding a short prayer to bring the reflections to a conclusion.

The subtitle *A Movie Lectionary*, rather than **The Movie Lectionary**, is intentional. It would be possible to match the same readings with seventy-five other movies. In that sense, this lectionary is a set of samples; you might like to start constructing your own version as well!

Most of the movies used here have been released during the last fifteen years and are available on video or DVD. However, some earlier movies have been chosen because of their relevance to the Gospel. They, too, should be available, at least on video.

How to Use Lights, Camera...Faith!

Individuals who appreciate deeper meanings in movies may want to watch the film, read the scriptures, and use both for personal reflection and prayer.

Homilists will find suggestions for sermon preparation.

Young Adult groups will discover new ways to bring the Gospel message to bear on contemporary culture.

Parish study and discussion groups might find that watching a movie or sections of it will lead to discussion, further reading and viewing, and a deeper entry into the Liturgy of the Word.

Professors and students of film and media criticism will find a useful text for discussing the phenomenon of faith in film.

Again, it is recommended that a movie be seen before using it. The nature of some movies may suggest working with a film clip, since not every movie is suitable for wide audiences. Some themes demand greater maturity than that of adolescents; there may be certain movie sequences that are too strong or explicit regarding language, sexuality, or violence for some audiences. *Lights, Camera...Faith!* is not meant to be a "viewing guide." Checking with a publication that provides this type of information will be useful, although such guidelines often differ in their opinions.*

Each of the movies represented in *Lights, Camera...Faith!* has been chosen because in some way the movie portrays the real-life struggles of people—human struggles that beg a human response—and connects these struggles to the Christian story found in the Sunday liturgy's scripture readings. While not every movie may work for you, I do hope that the majority will.

—PETER MALONE, MSC

---

*From an international point of view, such publications might seem arbitrary in their comments. While acknowledging objective norms of truth and morality, sometimes what is objectionable to one culture is not to another; "infrequent coarse language" in one culture seems "far too frequent" in another. Modesty and nudity norms differ from one country to another. One culture deplores violence; another has a greater tolerance for visual violence. (See *Movie Ratings Chart* at the end of this book.) These are the hazards when movies are shown internationally.

The Remains of the Day
U.K., 1993, 134 minutes
Cast: Anthony Hopkins, Emma Thompson, James Fox,
Christopher Reeve, Peter Vaughan, Hugh Grant,
Michael Lonsdale, Ben Chaplin
Writer: Ruth Prawer Jhabvala
Director: James Ivory

The Remains of the Day

Dutifully Waiting

SYNOPSIS

Lewis, an American diplomat, arrives in England in 1958 with the purpose of buying the country house of a former acquaintance, the late Lord Darlington. He once again meets Stevens, who was the Darlington's butler during the 1930s. Stevens has been working hard, preparing to reopen the house. Lewis suggests that he take a holiday. Stevens asks to borrow Lewis' car and travels to visit Darlington's former housekeeper, Miss Kenton. Stevens hopes to persuade her to return and join him in working for the new owner.

Stevens remembers the heyday of the 1930s when Darlington Hall was a meeting place for diplomatic conferences between Germans, the British, and Americans. Lord Darlington favored appeasing the Nazi government because of his sympathy with the country's treatment following World War I. On one occasion, the Prime Minister secretly meets the German ambassador at Darlington Hall.

Stevens runs the household with a refined air and martial precision, but seems oblivious to matters of greater importance because he is so focused on his duty. Miss Kenton is quietly attracted to Stevens and visits him in his room one evening. It is a moment of deep intimacy full of possibilities, but the repressed Stevens rebuffs Miss Kenton. Suspecting that Stevens will never be able to make a commitment beyond that of his duty as a servant, Miss Kenton leaves Darlington Hall. She marries and raises a daughter. Stevens remains loyal to the service of his master.

Years later, Stevens and Miss Kenton, now Mrs. Benn, reminisce about the days at Darlington Hall. Stevens wants Mrs. Benn to return, but she has just learned that her daughter is pregnant, and she wants to be near her grandchild. Regretfully, they go their separate ways.

COMMENTARY

The production company, Merchant Ivory (named for James Ivory and Ismail Merchant), has a reputation for making elegant period dramas based on the literary works of such authors as E. M. Forster (*A Room with a View, Howard's End*), and Henry James (*The Europeans, The Bostonians, The Golden Bowl*). Their source for *The Remains of the Day* is the Booker Award-winning novel by Kazuo Ishiguro. Merchant Ivory's Ruth Prawer Jhabvala wrote the screenplay.

With its beautifully designed sets and costumes, *The Remains of the Day* gives the viewer a sense of an accurate re-creation of a 1930s upper class life of the English countryside. Anthony Hopkins gives one of his most restrained performances as the meticulous, inversely snobbish Stevens. Emma Thompson (who won her first Oscar in another Merchant Ivory film, *Howard's End*), matches Hopkins with her controlled sensitivity. The sequence in which Miss Kenton visits Stevens in his room and tries to make him show her the novel he is reading, is one of the screen's great scenes of understated love, tenderness, and regret.

DIALOGUE WITH THE GOSPEL

Focus: The Remains of the Day *presents Stevens as a perfectly trained, dutiful servant who is driven by his own idea of what service to his master means. Jesus tells us in today's Gospel to be watchful servants as we wait for his coming in glory.*

The Church's liturgical year begins with a sense of waiting and anticipation for the coming of Jesus. The reading from Isaiah refers to the people of Israel as servants and to God as a loving father who will redeem the people. The prophet asks the Lord to rend the heavens and come down, to visit the people who have not been faithful servants, but rebels. The reading ends with the image of God as the potter, molding the clay of Israel into a faithful people.

Jesus uses an analogy to highlight this sense of waiting. He warns his listeners to be on guard, to stay awake, to be alert like servants who await their master's return. The example Jesus uses calls to mind a household run by many servants, each with their own tasks, who must be ready to serve the master whenever he comes home.

As we watch Stevens manage the Darlington household with an unquestioning sense of duty, we perceive something of what an unfruitful Advent waiting could be like. We see personal, political, and social worlds that need, and unknowingly await, the coming of Christ to redeem them. We see a world of servitude where Stevens drills those under him relentlessly. He is unfailingly loyal to his role and supervises the minutiae of estate life. But he resists the offer of love out of a mistaken, blind sense of duty. Stevens realizes too late that while he has become the perfectly dutiful servant, he has also lost his chance for Miss Kenton's love. Our Advent hopes and our waiting as watchful servants can end differently than Stevens' because Jesus will fulfill all our desires for love if we watch, wait, and use our gifts as grace-filled servants.

- Stevens and his meticulous work in the house: supervising the staff, training them in every detail of what is required; Stevens' expectations of his father, and the formality of their working relationship; the impact of Mr. Stevens' death.

KEY SCENES AND THEMES

- Stevens' absolute loyalty to Lord Darlington; his ability to follow discretely and without question all of Darlington's orders; his "perfect" service and complete sense of duty.

- Stevens' relationship with Miss Kenton: his inner turmoil and expressionless demeanor, his inability to express his feelings when she visits his room; Miss Kenton's departure from the manor, her marriage; Stevens' final visit and the realization of what he had lost because of his rigid sense of duty.

FOR REFLECTION AND CONVERSATION

1. In a way, *The Remains of the Day* is a road movie suspended in time. Stevens and the other "career" servants pound the hallways and stairways of the house over and again, going nowhere. Miss Kenton takes to her bicycle when she begins to search for a new direction for her life's journey. By the time Stevens gets in the car to pursue Miss Kenton twenty years after she has left Darlington Hall, it is only to try to bring her back into the safe course he has found for himself. How do we reconcile the "waiting" in life with being on a journey? How can waiting be a journey when life's circumstances force us "to wait"?

2. Toward the end of the film, Stevens goes into the wine cellar and selects a dusty old bottle from the rack. He contemplates it, and we get the sense that perhaps he sees himself as an old vintage as well. While he was waiting on his master, life passed him by and now he, too, is covered in dust. When he drops the bottle on the stairs and it breaks, he explodes, revealing his humanity at last. How does this film use the story of a professional butler as the symbol of an old world teetering on the brink of dramatic social changes where

old ways are no longer tolerated? How did the coming of Jesus change the world of his time? How can his coming change our times?

3. Though it may seem so at first, Stevens is not the kind of servant that today's Scripture readings describe. He does everything perfectly, yet he is a servant who needs the coming of the Lord. What choices might Stevens have made if he had heard these readings? How might his "waiting" have been different? How does Stevens' mode of waiting differ from that of a Christian who waits for Jesus' return in glory? What are the characteristics of your "waiting" for the Lord during Advent and throughout the year?

Prayer

Lord, we wait for your coming at Christmas. Help us to remain alert, to stay awake, and to be ready to serve you whenever you come. Amen.

Angela's Ashes

U.S.A./U.K., 1999, 145 minutes
Cast: Emily Watson, Robert Carlyle, Joe Breen, Ciaran Owens,
Michael Legge, Gerard McSorley, Ronnie Masterson
Writers: Laura Jones, Alan Parker
Director: Alan Parker

Angela's Ashes

Longing in an Advent World

SYNOPSIS

It is 1935 in Brooklyn, New York. Malachy and Angela McCourt and their four sons, including a set of twins, live in a tenement. When their newborn daughter dies, Angela's mother sends money for the family's fare back to Limerick, Ireland.

Limerick seems worse than Depression-era Brooklyn. Life in the wet and dirty slums of the city is one of grinding poverty. After the McCourts arrive, the twin boys die. Malachy begins to drink and waste his wages, forcing Angela to ask for charity both from her family and from the St. Vincent de Paul Society.

Meanwhile, two more sons are born. Frank goes to school, makes his first communion, and eventually gets a job as a coalman's assistant. The dusty work nearly blinds him with conjunctivitis and he has to spend time in the hospital, where he develops a love for reading and literature.

Malachy always makes great promises to his family, but then drinks away his good intentions. He is unable to hold a job but finally goes to England to work. He briefly visits the family, but then disappears, never to return.

Evicted from their flat, Angela and the children go to live with their cousin, Laman. He and Angela begin sleeping together. At the age of fifteen, Frank gets a job delivering telegrams. He begins saving money because he longs to go back to America. He meets Theresa, who is dying of consumption, and has a short affair with her before she dies.

A moneylender also hires Frank to write debt collection letters. When she dies, Frank finds her stash of money and takes most of it. With this and his savings, he buys a ticket for New York and sails two weeks later.

Frank McCourt won a Pulitzer Prize for *Angela's Ashes,* his memoir of growing up in Limerick in the 1930s and 1940s, which sold millions in the English-speaking world. In his second memoir, *'Tis,* he continues his story where the first left off.

The film opens with a voice-over commentary on the severe reality of an Irish childhood at the time. Along with the extreme poverty portrayed, much of the film's harshness comes from the particular brand of Catholicism that characterized McCourt's youth: excessive piety and misinterpretation of the laws of God and the Church, often expressed in glaring forms.

Australian Laura Jones adapted the screenplay from McCourt's book. She also wrote the screenplays for *High Tide, An Angel at My Table, Oscar and Lucinda,* and *The Well.* Alan Parker co-wrote the script for *Angela's Ashes* and directed the movie. His directorial work over more than two decades includes classics such as *Bugsy Malone, Fame, Midnight Express, The Commitments,* and *Evita.*

Emily Watson's sensitive portrayal of Angela, a good woman who survives against overwhelming odds, creates an anchor for the film. Robert Carlyle plays the irresponsible yet charming Malachy McCourt. The three young actors who portray Frank at various ages give remarkable performances.

DIALOGUE WITH THE GOSPEL

Focus: The Gospel of the second Sunday of the Church's year announces the coming of Jesus to those who live in Advent hope, especially those who maintain that hope in suffering. Conscious of our need for God's grace in our lives, we look forward to the coming of Jesus.

The world of *Angela's Ashes* is an Advent world, one of the harshest imaginable. In an environment of poverty and squalor, Angela struggles to hold her family together, but fails. On the surface, the Church appears severe and unwilling to assist this poor, ever-struggling family.

The reading from the beginning of Isaiah is a profound prayer of Advent hope. The prophet promises that the time of servitude is over. Whatever guilt there might be is expiated. Isaiah uses the image of a tender shepherd holding a lamb close to his heart to demonstrate God's desire to comfort the people.

This passage from the Old Testament is also the beginning of the New, for it opens Mark's Gospel, likely the first to have been written. We hear of the voice of the one crying in the wilderness that desert paths will be made straight and that God will come to his people. This Gospel puts these words into the mouth of John the Baptist, who announces that this is the advent time, for Jesus is coming.

The reading from the letter of Peter takes a more apocalyptic approach to God's coming than the other readings. It emphasizes the need for right living in a world that will end in flames and disaster. Angela and her family seemed to face the end more than once, but in Ireland's rain rather than flames. Advent words of hope are spoken to just such situations, which Jesus came to change and save.

KEY SCENES AND THEMES

• The McCourt family in Brooklyn: the tenement house, the poverty, the baby's death and its effect on Angela and Malachy; the family's return to Ireland; Limerick's grim environment that is as squalid as Brooklyn.

- Life in Limerick, the house and its poverty; Malachy cheerfully promising his family the world and then drinking the money away, charity from the St. Vincent de Paul Society, Malachy deserting his family; Angela surviving with her children; Angela and Laman.

- Frank at home and at school, his teachers, his jobs, his illness, and his hopes; Frank's attitude toward his father, his mother, his encounter with Theresa; Frank's prayer and his meeting with the Franciscan, the stolen money, and his escape to America—the land of hope.

1. In an almost visceral way, *Angela's Ashes* makes us feel the weight of water. It is always raining, or about to. Water runs down the streets and into the McCourt house. The damp is so oppressive that it seems to reach the viewers. The frequent glimpses of the River Shannon are a filmic device to represent an unchanging conduit through the years. What is the significance of the Shannon when Frank tosses in the book of debts? How does this scene and the symbol of water relate to today's readings in particular?

FOR REFLECTION AND CONVERSATION

2. Religious icons play a strong role in *Angela's Ashes* once the family has returned to Ireland—from the Sacred Heart of Jesus to the picture of Pope Leo XIII and the statue of St. Francis. There are also three enduring secular icons: the Statue of Liberty, American movies, and money. What role do all these icons play in the film? What do they mean? Above all, how do

they relate to the themes of comfort, expiation of guilt, kindness, justice, peace, and salvation of which the readings and the responsorial psalm speak?

3. "God forgives you and you must forgive yourself," the priest tells Frank in the final church scene. "God loves you and you must love yourself, for only when you love God and yourself can you love all God's creatures." What do these words mean to Frank? What can they mean for each of us on this Advent Sunday as we long for the coming of the Lord?

Prayer

At times, it may seem as if our world is coming to an end. But in Advent, we wait and hope. Come, Lord Jesus, and fulfill our longing for eternal life. Amen.

The Truman Show
U.S.A., 1998, 105 minutes
Cast: Jim Carrey, Ed Harris, Laura Linney,
Natascha McElhone
Writer: Andrew Niccol
Director: Peter Weir

The Truman Show

Advent Freedom

Seahaven Island seems like the perfect planned community. And nothing much happens to disturb the tranquility of Truman Burbank, one of its inhabitants, who sells insurance. He is happily married to Meryl, a nurse, and they have no children. He has never left Seahaven, and is haunted by the memory of Sylvia, a friend who supposedly moved to Fiji with her family.

SYNOPSIS

Truman is alarmed one morning when a studio light with "Sirius" (the name of a star) written on it suddenly drops from the sky. He begins to notice other things that make him suspect that something is not quite right at Seahaven. The fact is, as an orphaned child, Truman was adopted by Christof, a TV producer who turned Truman's life into a television program. All the other inhabitants of Seahaven are actors. "The Truman Show" is filmed by 5,000 cameras and runs twenty-four hours a day, seven days a week.

Truman begins to suspect that even Meryl is not what she seems. He slowly begins to notice the "routine" of daily life in Seahaven and when he begins to question it, Christof changes the "plot."

Truman decides to sail to Fiji to be with Sylvia, only to find that the horizon is actually painted studio scenery. Christof tries to persuade him to return to Seahaven, but Truman opens a door that is part of the scenery and walks through it toward freedom.

COMMENTARY

At first glance, it does not seem possible that combining Peter Weir's dramatic directorial genius with Jim Carrey's gift for physical comedy could actually work. Weir's reputation as a director lies in his powerful dramas: in Australia with *Picnic at Hanging Rock, Gallipoli,* and *The Year of Living Dangerously;* and in the United States with *Witness, Dead Poets Society,* and *Fearless.* On the other hand, Carrey's frenetic clowning in such films as *Ace Ventura, The Mask, Liar Liar,* and *Dr. Seuss' How the Grinch Stole Christmas,* is a box office magnet. In *The Truman Show,* however, the Weir and Carrey partnership succeeds perfectly, proving their talent. Carrey demonstrates his ability at serious acting that creates pathos. Ed Harris plays Christof, the obsessive director with a God complex. Laura Linney is cast in the role of Meryl and exudes the artificial sunshine of an actress specializing in daytime television commercials.

The Truman Show is the second screenplay of New Zealander Andrew Niccol. The film highlights the modern world's fascination with technology and its power to control individuals and manipulate society. In addition, Niccol effectively uses *The Truman Show* to portray a consumerist interpretation of human nature and the temptation to "play God" that can afflict media moguls. The film is geared toward a mass audience rather than an "art-house" style exploration of these themes.

Nominated for an Oscar for Best Original Screenplay, *The Truman Show* won three Golden Globe Awards.

Focus: John the Baptist was a witness to Jesus, the true light. Truman Burbank is an unwitting prophet pointing the way to our need for freedom and salvation.

Advent asks us to go beyond the comforts of everyday life. We can live our lives in terms of TV's version of happiness or in terms of the real world of our relationships, responsibility, and freedom. This Sunday's readings remind us to be discerning participants in our salvation and to create the just world promised by Advent. The first two readings reassure us that we can be people of hope, because God has given us reason to rejoice. Our world is one of beauty where God will guide us by the light of his glory with mercy and integrity. Yet, St. Paul also tells us to test everything, to retain what is good and refrain from every kind of evil. He prays that God's peace will make us complete and holy.

Truman Burbank is unknowingly trapped in a world that is a television producer's version of human happiness. This manufactured world is not as vastly good or beautiful as the one Isaiah speaks of in the first reading. To Christof, however, Seahaven represents suburban American contentment—even if it is not true happiness—and the safest place a person could live.

While it appears that there is no need for salvation in Seahaven, Truman discovers otherwise. Once he begins to question the world around him, Truman realizes that he is at the center of a giant hoax: more than a billion people watch his every move. Christof thinks he has saved Truman from the pitfalls of life, but Truman must seek true salvation and human freedom for himself. He must be a prophet to himself and to his viewers. He dares to sail on seas formerly feared and chooses to go through the studio door to freedom because he listens to the spirit within. He is a true man, a prophet, showing all his viewers the way to freedom.

- Seahaven, the nice and perfectly planned community where everyone is pleasant and everything runs smoothly; Truman Burbank as a nice man with a wife, home, neighbors, friends, and job; comfort—the image of a perfect world, Truman content with his surroundings; the avid viewers.

- Christof's appearance, his "home in the sky" and "playing God"; how Christof controls a life without the person's knowledge, his rewriting the lines of the script when it gets too difficult to maintain control.

- Truman's conversation with Sylvia, becoming suspicious; the reappearance of Truman's father and the memory of his drowning, Truman's decision to face the sea; the storm, the confrontation with Christof, Truman opening the door to the unknown and walking through.

1. Discernment is a recurring theme in today's readings. Paul's first letter to the Thessalonians says to "test everything." In the Gospel of John, the priests and Levites ask John the Baptizer who he is and what he has to say for himself. At the end of the film, Truman asks Christof, "Who are you?" and, "Who am I?" Why does Truman Burbank start to question what he has always taken for granted? Is it a good thing that he questions the "reality" around him? Why or why not?

2. *The Truman Show* is a perfect case study for anyone interested in media literacy education. Because Christof directs everything, the point of view, ideology, "world view," and value messages are uniquely his—a reminder that all media are created, constructed realities, which use specific techniques (camera angles,

sound effects, and music) to communicate. The continual use of "product placement" to promote merchandise shows that media are businesses with commercial interests. The movie introduces us to many different audiences who watch the show and we discover that audiences interpret meaning in their own ways. How can being aware of the ways that television works make us more thoughtful viewers? How important is the ability to "read" and create all forms of media and think critically about them in our faith life?

3. As Truman begins to walk out the stage door, Christof tells him, "There is no more truth out there than in the world I created for you…but in my world you have nothing to fear." Is this a true statement? Why or why not? During this Advent season, we can question the nature of our relationship with television: what is it like and why? What kind of truth and freedom do we seek in the stories or reality TV that we watch? Also, each one of us can ask: Am I more like the Truman at the beginning of the movie or at the end, or somewhere in between? How spiritually free am I?

Prayer

Lord, we realize that we are sometimes trapped in our everyday lives and need your light to guide us to freedom. May truth and freedom be your Advent gifts to us. Amen.

2 Samuel 7:1–5, 8–12, 14, 16;
Romans 16:25–27; Luke 1:26–38

Agnes of God
U.S.A., 1985, 98 minutes
Cast: Jane Fonda, Anne Bancroft, Meg Tilly
Writer: John Pielmeier
Director: Norman Jewison

Agnes of God

And She Conceived of the Holy Spirit

SYNOPSIS

In a cloistered convent near Montreal, a young novice named Sister Agnes gives birth to a child in her room; the child dies. The superior, Sister Miriam Ruth, finds the dead baby wrapped in a towel in a wastebasket. The authorities suspect that Sister Agnes has murdered the baby.

Sister Miriam Ruth, Sister Agnes' aunt, allowed the simple-minded and extremely naïve Agnes to enter the convent in order to protect her from life. Sister Miriam at first refuses to cooperate in the criminal investigation, but eventually is forced to disclose information to the police.

The court appoints a psychiatrist to assess Agnes' mental state, find out how she became pregnant, and what really happened to the child. The case is personally challenging for the psychiatrist, Martha Livingston, who has become an agnostic. She abandoned the practice of her faith because of the poor treatment she received from teaching nuns during her childhood. Sister Miriam, who must face the truth of what Agnes has done, also proves challenging for the psychiatrist.

There is no clear conclusion as to what actually happened to Agnes. Various hypotheses are examined: she may have been assaulted and raped by an intruder, she willingly had sex with an outsider, or her pregnancy was psychosomatic. Finally, a mysterious religious cause is proposed, an overshadowing by the Holy Spirit. In the courtroom, Sister Agnes manifests signs of hysteria, mystical experience, and the stigmata.

COMMENTARY

Agnes of God was originally a play written by John Pielmeier who then adapted it for the screen. Director Norman Jewison has had a long and successful career. His movies cover a variety of genres, which include the Oscar winners and nominees *In the Heat of the Night, Fiddler on the Roof, Moonstruck,* and *The Hurricane.* He also directed the movie version of *Jesus Christ, Superstar.*

This film is a psychological study of a disturbed young woman who seems to have a low I.Q. Neither the screenplay nor the sometimes graphic images in the film offer clear answers about what really happened to Agnes. Rather, the audience is allowed to speculate from their personal perspectives—whether rationalist or religious or a little of both.

Three talented stars give forceful performances that enhance the frequently sharp dialogue. Jane Fonda plays the psychiatrist, Anne Bancroft is the superior, and Meg Tilly is the young novice. Bancroft and Tilly received Oscar nominations for their roles in the film.

DIALOGUE WITH THE GOSPEL

Focus: The virginal conception of Jesus is difficult for anyone—believers, agnostics, or rationalists—to imagine. While Agnes of God is a fictional story, it attempts to explore the idea of mystery through a modern day event that has no explanation.

Luke's version of the Annunciation is presented as a biblical poem that is part of the wonderful narrative of the life of Jesus. The Annunciation poem describes Mary in the tradition of so many Old Testament mothers of heroes like the

Judges, Gideon, and Samson. She is the special mother of the Savior. Gabriel, characterized as the revealer of the fullness of time in the book of the prophet Daniel, chapter 9, greets Mary. Mary's response to the angel is very similar to the oracle found in Zephaniah, chapter 3, which tells us that God rejoices in the beloved daughter of Jerusalem.

The virginal conception of Jesus is one of the great and distinctive mysteries of the Christian faith. *Agnes of God* invites us to consider how we might begin to understand the mystery of Jesus' virginal conception. Certainly, Sister Agnes' story makes us ponder the situation of troubled souls, the people who seek to help them, and even religious fanaticism. However, her bewildering experiences and the mysterious conception and birth of her child offer contemporary images of an unusual, seemingly impossible event. They lead us to ponder God's action in the world today, the limits of human reason, and the response of faith to what we cannot understand.

KEY SCENES AND THEMES

- The crisis in the convent caused by the baby's death; the response of the superior and the nuns; Agnes and her claims.

- The psychiatrist examining Agnes; the discussions and revisiting the sites of the experience; the psychiatrist changing her mind, and the challenge to her own experience.

- Agnes in court, the stigmatic experience, and the blood on her habit; the flashbacks to her experience; Agnes being overshadowed by the dove.

FOR REFLECTION AND CONVERSATION

1. When first released, *Agnes of God* upset some people because they thought it was a film attacking a doctrine of faith: belief in the virginal conception of Jesus.

The film somewhat parallels the Annunciation, yet at the same time, is an expression of the exact opposite. We are never sure from the film what really happened to Agnes. Was her experience a religious phenomenon, a crime, or the act of a mentally impaired person? What do you think happened at the convent and, more importantly, why?

2. As the film begins, each of the three main characters, Sisters Agnes, Miriam, and Martha are in different places regarding their relationship to God. Contrast the lives of the three main characters and the events that eventually bring them together. Do they grow from their experiences? If so, how and why? All three characters have Biblical names. What do these mean and how does their use influence the meaning of the story? For example, how might Agnes be considered a "lamb of God" ("Agnus Dei")?

3. Compare and contrast the experience of the Virgin Mary and that of Agnes. Talk about Mary's relationship with God at the time of the Annunciation. Why was she prepared to respond affirmatively to God? Each of us is called to follow God in the overall plan God has for us and in the smaller events of everyday life. How do you personally live your life to be able to say "yes" to God through events and people, on a daily basis? How can you grow spiritually during these remaining days of Advent?

Prayer

Mary, you said "yes" to the messenger of God. You were willing to become the mother of Jesus and to do whatever God asked of you. Help us to say "yes" to God in our lives. Amen.

CHRISTMAS MASS
AT MIDNIGHT

Isaiah 9:1–6; Titus 2:11–14;
Luke 2:1–14

Harry Potter and the Sorcerer's Stone
(Harry Potter and the Philosopher's Stone)

U.S.A., 2001, 152 minutes
Cast: Daniel Radcliffe, Rupert Grint, Emma Watson, Richard Harris,
Maggie Smith, Robbie Coltrane, Alan Rickman, Ian Hart, Fiona Shaw,
Richard Griffith, John Hurt, John Cleese, Zoe Wanamaker
Writer: Steve Kloves
Director: Chris Columbus

Harry Potter and the Sorcerer's Stone
(Harry Potter and the Philosopher's Stone)

A Special Child

SYNOPSIS

With the help of the giant, Hagrid, Professors Dumbledore and McGonagall of the Hogwarts School of Witchcraft and Wizardry leave baby Harry Potter with his Uncle and Aunt Dursley after his parents' death. They and their selfish son, Dudley, are cruel to Harry. On Harry's eleventh birthday, Hagrid returns to announce that Harry is a wizard and will attend Hogwarts. Hagrid takes him shopping to obtain everything he needs for school.

Ron Weasley meets Harry on platform "9 ¾" at the train station and befriends him. During the journey to Hogwarts, Harry meets Hermione Granger. At Hogwarts the three new friends are all assigned to the same dormitory house, Gryffindor. Hogwarts is a magical building with shifting staircases and secret rooms, surrounded by a forbidding dark forest. Harry is surprised that his name is well known among the students and staff; they know more about his family than he does. With a scar on his forehead from the villainous Voldemort, Harry is the one marked to win the struggle between good and evil.

Harry likes his teachers, though he is suspicious of Snape, the professor of potions and head of the rival house of Slytherin. During the Quidditch match (a sport played while flying on broomsticks), Snape appears to be casting a spell on Harry so Hermione lights a fire under him. Harry is released from the spell and wins the game.

The children find a huge three-headed dog guarding a trapdoor leading to the Sorcerer's Stone, an object with alchemical powers that can renew the strength of those who possess it. The children believe that Voldemort, who trying to regain his evil powers, is using Snape to get the stone.

When a magic harp lulls the watchdog to sleep, the children sneak through the trapdoor. They have to overcome a number of obstacles, of which the most dangerous is a game of chess with giant, deadly pieces. Ron is prepared to die so that Harry can go on to save the stone from Voldemort. Rather than Snape, Harry finds the quiet and stammering Professor Quirrell working for Voldemort.

At graduation, it appears that Slytherin House has won the annual school competition, but Professor Dumbledore gives extra points to Harry, Ron, and Hermione for their courage and Gryffindor House wins. The students all leave for their summer vacation.

J. K. Rowling's *Harry Potter* novels have sold over 100 million copies worldwide. Rowling retained tight control over the making of the movie and acted as a consultant. Like other movies that have attempted to make a book into a film, however, this one is an interpretation of the novel and not the novel itself. Nevertheless, worldwide audiences have found it a very enjoyable and fundamentally faithful rendition, imaginatively designed with exciting special effects and fine performances.

The *Harry Potter* novels and the movie have been the center of an enormous amount of attention. A number of parents

COMMENTARY

and teachers worry over children reading books about magic, but often tales for children take us not so much into a literal world of magic, but rather into the world of the imagination. In their own way, these fantasy stories are about good versus evil. Fantasy tales, unlike science fiction stories and films, suspend the laws of nature and are full of all kinds of imaginative creatures that bear very little physical resemblance to the real world. The Office of Film and Broadcast of the United States Catholic Conference of Bishops described *Harry Potter* as "innocuous" because it is so obviously make-believe.

From the start, we are assured that *Harry Potter and the Sorcerer's Stone* (the original title in every other country is *Harry Potter and the Philosopher's Stone*), is a story about the struggle between good and evil. Harry is a gentlemanly hero, a well-spoken and well-mannered eleven-year-old boy—a role Daniel Radcliffe plays as though born to it. Rupert Grint as Ron Weasley is Harry's rather more ordinary, gawky, but also heroic classmate. Emma Watson is a very prim Hermione, also heroic and kind as she learns to take life more lightly.

An all-British cast portrays the staff and student body at Hogwarts School, which is very reminiscent of an old-fashioned, strict, boarding school. The school's curriculum centers on training in magic, from mixing potions under the instruction of sinister-sounding Alan Rickman as Professor Snape, to broom flying under Zoe Wanamaker. Richard Harris is the headmaster and Maggie Smith is second-in-command. Robbie Coltrane is hugely (literally!) entertaining as Hagrid. This film definitely belongs to its young actors; to their credit the adult cast did not allow their professional stature to overshadow the film.

The American director and writer both deserve praise for preserving the very British atmosphere that J. K. Rowling wanted. Chris Columbus, who wrote the screenplays for *Gremlins* and *The Goonies* and directed *Home Alone* and *Mrs. Doubtfire,* once again demonstrates his ability in working with make-believe and with children. Most fans of the book think that screenwriter Steve Kloves managed to get to the heart of the novel in his vivid adaptation of what promises to be the first of several *Harry Potter* films.

> *Focus: Midnight Mass is a celebration of the birth of Jesus. He is a longed-for child who will bring peace and joy to the world. Stories of special and heroic children like Harry Potter offer links to Gospel themes and help us to imagine and appreciate the Scripture narratives about Jesus.*

DIALOGUE WITH THE GOSPEL

This night, we celebrate the birth of Jesus into our world and the promise of the triumph of grace over sin, of life over death. Isaiah sees the Messiah as the One who comes to bring light to those in darkness, to remove the yoke that enslaved the people. He presents the Savior in language that describes a hero who wins the battles and is a liberator. This wonderful and miraculous child fulfills all human hopes. In the letter to Titus, Jesus is seen as God's grace and glory. He delivers us from lawlessness and cleanses a sinful people. Luke's Gospel presents Jesus in his simplicity and poverty, born of Mary in the stable, cared for by Joseph the carpenter, and looked on in wonder by local shepherds. Jesus is God's glory and peace.

Grace and glory, forgiveness and salvation are rich words that come easily to our lips in this season, though we don't always know exactly what they mean for us or for the world. Fortunately, as we continue to read the Gospels, we come to appreciate their meaning more deeply as we see Jesus in the act of saving and forgiving.

These theological concepts often remain abstract for children, and here lies the value of mythical and magical tales, which use metaphor to teach lessons about virtue, goodness, and evil. It is helpful to recall that Jesus' parables are not factually true stories, but stories that teach us truth. Thus, fictional stories are not always something we believe, but tales we can understand.

Harry Potter is a special child in the wizarding world. Though Harry suffers early in life, he comes to realize that he is special when he discovers that his parents—good wizards who were destroyed by the power of evil—died so that he might live. It is this great love that gives Harry's life its meaning and helps him discover his purpose. Yet, while he has a mission and a destiny, Harry must remain humble and recognize himself as an equal among the other students, learning from them as well as leading them.

Voldemort is the embodiment of what the letter to Titus calls "lawlessness." Harry is called to confront Voldemort, to proclaim goodness, and to destroy as much of the evil as possible.

Clearly, the parallels between Harry Potter and Jesus are not to be overstated or stretched; J. K. Rowling did not have these kinds of connections in mind. Insofar as she wrote stories about a heroic boy, it is possible to see some links and parallels that might help readers and viewers to appreciate and understand Gospel themes such as loyalty, friendship, and self-sacrificing love, found most profoundly in the Child whose birth we celebrate tonight.

KEY SCENES AND THEMES

- The Professors and Hagrid rescuing the baby and leaving him with his uncle and aunt, Harry's suffering at the Dursleys' hands; Hagrid's arrival and announcement that Harry has been selected for Hogwarts School; Hagrid taking him shopping, others remembering Harry's parents; the train to school and Harry making friends with Ron and Hermione.

- Hogwarts School, the selection for households, the staff, the curriculum; Harry learning his abilities, yet making mistakes; his intelligence and his gifts; Harry's skill at Quidditch, his being named as a Seeker.

- The mission of Harry, Ron, and Hermione; their suspicions of Professor Snape and the revelation of the truth about Professor Quirrel; the three-headed dog, the game of chess, and Ron's sacrifice; the confrontation between Harry and Voldemort; the victory over evil.

1. The moral imagination is that function of our intellect, emotions, and conscience where we can "go" to observe the lives and choices of others through the story forms of books, films, songs, television, and even video games. Just as children learn how to act appropriately and morally in an adult world through the development of thought, language, and play, so adults can continue their own moral growth through the exercise of the moral imagination. By engaging it, we can enter into the moral decisions of others, "try them on," and compare them to our basic values and beliefs. Thus, we can better articulate what we believe to be important and are strengthened to make choices that are consistent with our faith and values. How is this movie an exercise of your moral imagination? Has it challenged you to grow as a person in some area? Why or why not? What in this movie strikes you as metaphorical of life?

FOR REFLECTION AND CONVERSATION

2. Recall some of the fantasy films you have seen: for example, the very first silent films of Georges Méliès (*Le voyage dans la lune: A Trip to the Moon*, 1902), *The Wizard of Oz, The Fellowship of the Rings: Lord of the Rings,* or others. What makes them appealing to audiences? Were there morals to the stories, or more than one

lesson to be learned? When did you last spend time with a child reading a book they liked or watching one of their movies and then engaging in conversation about it, respecting their views and then expressing your own?

3. One religious educator observed that Harry is a child who goes to a special school to learn to become who and what he already is: a wizard who will do good and overcome evil. As believers, we can draw a parallel between Harry's situation and our own. As children, we attend religious education and catechetical classes; then as adults we participate in adult faith formation courses such as Bible study to become who we already are: followers of Jesus Christ by virtue of the sacrament of our Baptism. On this night of wonder and blessing, as we ponder the mystery of Christ's birth, what practical steps can each of us take to better become who we already are?

Prayer

Lord, your prophets offered us the image of a special child as a sign of victory over evil and your peace and glory. You sent Jesus, your Son, to earth as a child in order to fulfill your promises. Help us to celebrate his gift of peace to all people of good will. Amen.

CHRISTMAS DAWN

Isaiah 62:11–12; Titus 3:4–7;
Luke 2:15–20

Little Women

U.S.A., 1994, 118 minutes
Cast: Winona Ryder, Susan Sarandon, Gabriel Byrne,
Trini Alvarado, Clare Danes, Eric Stoltz, Christian Bale,
Kirsten Dunst, Samantha Mathis, John Neville, Mary Wickes
Writer: Robin Swicord
Director: Gillian Armstrong

Little Women

Families and Peace

SYNOPSIS

It is Christmas Eve, 1862. Mrs. March, affectionately known as Marmee, lives with her four daughters in Concord, Massachusetts during the Civil War. Marmee reads a letter from Mr. March, who is away fighting in the Civil War. The next morning, Meg, Jo, Beth, and Amy share their special breakfast with a poor family, even though the five struggle to make ends meet.

The four March girls befriend their neighbors, the wealthy and gruff Mr. Laurence and his nephew Laurie. Jo, the liveliest of the girls and an aspiring writer, becomes especially good friends with Laurie, while the quiet and delicate Beth becomes a favorite of Mr. Laurence. The oldest girl, Meg, is attracted to John Brooke, Laurie's tutor, and they eventually marry. The youngest March sister, Amy, is rather vain and dreams of becoming an artist.

Laurie falls in love with Jo, but she refuses his proposal of marriage. Jo moves to New York, where she pursues a writing career while working as a governess. There, she meets and befriends a German tutor named Friedrich Bhaer, who helps

27

her with her writing. They begin to have feelings for one another, but Jo returns home when Beth becomes dangerously ill and dies.

Meanwhile, Laurie, distressed at Jo's refusal to marry him, goes to Europe where he unexpectedly meets Amy, who is traveling with her crusty, but rich, Aunt March. The two young people fall in love and decide to marry. They return home to Concord, where Meg and John have had twins and Jo has written a book about her family. Friedrich arrives at the March home and proposes to Jo, who accepts. Aunt March has died and left her large house to Jo, and she decides to turn it into a school with the help of Friedrich.

COMMENTARY

This is the fourth screen adaptation of Louisa May Alcott's classic nineteenth century novel. Some interpret this 1994 Gillian Armstrong film as more reflective of the feminist movement of the late twentieth century because the female characters represent women's concerns and spirit of independence more than earlier versions of the story. All of Armstrong's films (including *My Brilliant Career, High Tide, Oscar & Lucinda,* and *Charlotte Grey*) have had strong central roles for women, with particular empathy for their problems growing up.

Susan Sarandon has been noted for her compelling performances as Louise *(Thelma & Louise),* Sister Helen Prejean *(Dead Man Walking),* and the forceful lawyer in *The Client.* Here she plays the absolutely devoted wife and mother, continually advising her daughters on the right thing to do.

The men have a minimal presence in the film and, unlike previous *Little Women* films, Mr. March scarcely appears at all. Gabriel Byrne, Eric Stoltz, and Christian Bale are versatile actors whose performances give the women greater prominence.

Focus: The readings of Christmas morning, especially the Gospel, invite us to contemplate the wonder of God's peace, glory, and grace. In Little Women, *the character of Marmee vividly shows us how to ponder, like Mary, what it means to be a wise mother and a woman of peace.*

DIALOGUE WITH THE GOSPEL

Today's first reading from Isaiah contains encouraging words addressed to the ancient Israelites who had gathered in Jerusalem, "daughter Zion," to await the return of their fellow Israelites who had been scattered because of the Babylonian exile. The city is forsaken and desolate but the Lord proclaims that the Savior comes and will restore the city and redeem the people. The U.S. Civil War (1860–1861) desolated the land, turning brother against brother. In *Little Women,* the March family knows of the destruction and together, hopes for peace and the return of their father so that they may be restored and not forsaken. The March family's generosity on Christmas morning in lavishing the kindness and love of God on their poor neighbors imitates the generosity of Christ, as the second reading from Paul's Letter to Titus describes.

The Gospel motif offered to us this morning is that of the mother and the newborn child lying peacefully in the manger. Mary, with Joseph nearby, contemplates all that is happening and "ponders these things in her heart." Several times in Luke's Gospel we see the image of Mary who questions and ponders the wonder of God's action in her life. In today's film, Marmee shares her wisdom, the fruit of her reflection and life experience, with her daughters. She is a kind of Mary-figure who is full of wisdom and integrity. Marmee has experienced life, contemplated and learned what it means to live in Christian peace and harmony. She teaches her daughters through example and words while she continues to contemplate the events of their everyday lives.

KEY SCENES AND THEMES

- Christmas Eve at the March home in Concord, reading Mr. March's letter from the warfront; the girls giving their breakfast to the Hummel family, meeting Laurie.

- The sisters at home, becoming friends with Laurie, his grandfather, and Mr. Brooke, enjoying the parties and the theater, caring for the poor; Beth's illness and its effect on them; Marmee's special love for each daughter, her advice and serenity; her visit to her husband in the hospital; the father's eventual return on another Christmas Day.

- Meg marrying John Brooke and having twins, Jo's restlessness and her move to New York, meeting Professor Bhaer, writing stories, her creativity; Beth's death; Amy and Laurie meeting in Europe, Bhaer's visit to Concord.

FOR REFLECTION AND CONVERSATION

1. Christmas marks the beginning, middle, and end of this version of *Little Women*. The story opens on Christmas Eve with Marmee reading a letter to the girls from their father. When Mr. March does return home from the hospital, it is again Christmas Day. At the end, what does Jo find in the trunk in the attic? How do these objects and other symbols in the film (candles, light, snow, seasons, flowers, oranges, and others) help create its ethos?

2. The March sisters demonstrate how to extend Christmas kindness and generosity to others when they sacrifice their own comforts to help a poor family. In a world where the celebration of Christmas is so commercial, what do this morning's readings and the film remind us about what people who lack the very ne-

cessities of life need? What might some of these gifts be and how can they be shared with dignity?

3. Amy, as the youngest, seems at first the least likely to be reflective. However, it is she who loves Laurie and admonishes him to grow up. Beth, the gentle invalid, has plenty of time to ponder and offer loving support to the others. Meg witnesses her mother's love and decides to marry and raise a family as well. When Jo writes the novel that tells the story of her family, she shares the fruit of her reflections with others. What role do reflection and contemplation play in your life? What are your feelings, thoughts, and prayers as you ponder the mystery of the Incarnation on this Christmas morning?

Prayer

Mary, on this morning you help us imagine how a mother loves and cares for her child. You pondered the wonderful experience of Jesus' birth in your heart. May we share in this love for your son who is our gift of peace. Amen.

The Lord of the Rings: The Fellowship of the Ring

New Zealand/U.S.A., 2001, 178 minutes
Cast: Elijah Wood, Ian McKellen, Viggo Mortensen,
Sean Bean, Cate Blanchett, Liv Tyler, Christopher Lee,
Sean Astin, Ian Holm, John Rhys-Davies, Hugo Weaving
Writers: Peter Jackson, Frances Walsh, Philippa Boyens
Director: Peter Jackson

The Lord of the Rings: The Fellowship of the Ring

Light Conquers Darkness

SYNOPSIS

In a mythical past, nineteen legendary rings are forged in the fires of the Crack of Doom. The evil Dark Lord of Mordor, Sauron, made and kept a twentieth ring, the most powerful of them, the Ruling Ring that holds sway over the others, and uses it to conquer the regions of Middle-earth. In battle, Isildur severs Sauron's arm and the ring falls into the grasp of human beings for a brief time. Finally, it is lost at the bottom of a river.

Hundreds of years later, the hobbit Bilbo Baggins discovers the ring. When he leaves the Shire, the land of the hobbits, he gives it to his nephew, Frodo Baggins. Frodo meets his old friend Gandalf the Grey, a wizard, who advises Frodo to take the ring to Elrond in Rivendell to protect it from Sauron. Gandalf visits another wizard, Saruman the White, only to find that he has joined forces with Sauron to create an army of enhanced orcs to conquer the people of Middle-earth. Saruman imprisons Gandalf atop a high tower.

Frodo journeys with three hobbits, his friends Sam, Merry, and Pippin. They are pursued by wraithlike creatures, but are helped by the warrior, Aragorn. When Frodo is later wounded, he is saved by the elf Arwen, who loves Aragorn, a mortal. Frodo and his band arrive in the land of the elves and are reunited with Gandalf, who has escaped. When Sauron threatens the elves, their king, Elrond, the father of Arwen, calls a meeting of the council of elves, dwarves, and humans to decide the fate of the ring.

In the meeting, Frodo volunteers to take the ring to the Crack of Doom to destroy it. Frodo is joined by his hobbit friends and Aragorn; the warrior Boromir; the dwarf Gimli; the young archer elf, Legolas; and Gandalf himself. They pledge fidelity to their mission and form the Fellowship of the Ring. Queen Galadriel, who already possesses one of the Great Rings, tests Frodo. Although she is tempted to take possession of the Ruling Ring, she decides to sacrifice her ambition and allows Frodo to continue on his quest.

Orcs pursue the Fellowship, and as they make their way through the dark Mines of Moria, Gandalf falls into a chasm while protecting his friends. After finding the way out of Moria, they battle Saruman's orcs, who kill Boromir and imprison Merry and Pippin. When Frodo sets out alone across the river to continue the journey, Sam joins him.

COMMENTARY

The Lord of the Rings: the Fellowship of the Ring is the first of a trilogy based on J. R. R. Tolkien's classic novel sequence *The Lord of the Rings.* The book, divided into three parts by the publisher, was voted "The Book of the Century." Made concurrently over an eighteen-month period in 2000–2001, the three movies were scheduled for release at Christmas 2001, Christmas 2002, and Christmas 2003.

In 1978, Ralph Bakshi directed an animated version covering about half of the trilogy. Though critically well received, it was not a major box office success; no sequels were produced. New Zealand director Peter Jackson took up the challenge in the 1990s and co-wrote a screenplay with long-time partner Frances Walsh, and dramatist Philippa Boyens. All the filming took place in New Zealand, a country rich in the varied landscapes and spectacular scenery needed to create the Middle-earth locations.

The scope of the movie is extraordinary, and Jackson's creative team matches Tolkien's vision. Alan Lee and John Howe, illustrators of the Harper Collins edition of the novel, were invited to make numerous sketches, which in turn were developed into sets, thus assuring that the production design, costumes, and makeup had the best chance to capture the Tolkien spirit.

The film features an international cast. American Elijah Wood plays Frodo with intensity and charm. Ian McKellen is an imposing Gandalf, and Christopher Lee is impressive as the evil Saruman. Peter Jackson skillfully drew fine performances from Viggo Mortensen, Sean Bean, and Sean Astin.

Tolkien drew on an English and literary heritage to create a fantasy universe, which he described in meticulous detail. Tolkien was a professor of linguistics and actually created "Elvish," a language for the creatures of Middle-earth. His story has theological foundations, a reflection of his deep Catholic faith, though this does not seem to have been his direct intention. Peter Jackson is a Catholic director in sympathy with Tolkien's implicitly religious mythmaking.

DIALOGUE WITH THE GOSPEL

Focus: The Lord of the Rings *is a profound mythical story of the mission of one person to destroy evil and save the world. We see traces of this theme in the mission that Jesus is born to accomplish. Today's movie can draw us into a deeper reflection on the reasons that "the Word became flesh."*

The Christmas liturgy offers us stories that draw on the very human stories of Jesus' birth in poverty at Bethlehem: the Savior of the world comes in lowly form. We are also invited to meditate on the theology of the Incarnation: the Word, who was with God, through whom all things are created, is made flesh.

As the letter to the Hebrews reminds us, in times past, God spoke "in partial and various ways to our ancestors through the prophets." In our times, God can speak to us in partial and various ways through myths of grace and sin and of the struggle between good and evil. Although *The Lord of the Rings* is not a Christian story as such and does not invite exact parallels, its themes can illuminate the Scriptures and help us appreciate what is revealed in the Gospels.

What we celebrate today is the fullness of the revelation which is Jesus. Frodo is an image of Jesus, a person born in lowly circumstances whose mission is mighty and universal in scope: in bringing good news and announcing salvation, suffering people are comforted and all the ends of the earth will behold God's power. Frodo, in his own way, struggles to achieve these goals for the salvation of Middle-earth.

St. John's prologue reminds us that the birth of Jesus is a significant cosmic event. In him, God loves the world, and offers us grace and truth. The ring Frodo must destroy might be seen as a symbol of our state of brokenness: there is a propensity for evil in all of us which breaks out in greed, ambition, and darkness. This ring, this "original sin," must be destroyed so that all will be graced.

And in destroying the power of darkness and its hold on our lives, Jesus shows himself to be the true light, coming into the world, which darkness can never overcome.

KEY SCENES AND THEMES

- The forging of the rings, Sauron and his bloodthirsty conquests, the severing of his arm and the loss of the Ruling Ring; the humans who refuse to give up the ring, those who are transformed into ugly images of evil when their desire for the ring is tested: Saruman,

Boromir, Bilbo, Galadriel; Saruman and his evil creation of monsters that battle for the ring.

- Frodo as a modest hobbit, his friendship with Gandalf, Bilbo's gift of the ring to Frodo; Frodo's gradual realization that he is on a quest to save his world from evil by destroying the ring, his being wounded and healed, his acceptance of the quest, his being tested by Galadriel and sent on his mission; the obstacles in Frodo's way through the mountains: the mines, the river, and the lake; his acceptance of the fact that he is the only who can destroy the ring.

- Gandalf's friendship with the hobbits and his wisdom, his confrontation with Saruman and the powers of good and evil, his support of Frodo; Aragorn as the noble knight and warrior who protects Frodo; Frodo journeying on alone to destroy the ring.

FOR REFLECTION AND CONVERSATION

1. Like the work of other writers in the post-war 1950s, such as George Orwell's *Animal Farm* and William Golding's *Lord of the Flies*, J. R. R. Tolkien's *The Lord of the Rings: The Fellowship of the Ring* attempted to explore and comment on such issues as human nature, death, evil, and even the environment. At first, Tolkien's work may seem pessimistic about the future of the earth and humanity. Tolkien never recovered from the death of most of his friends in World War I, and he mourned the industrialization that ate away at the beautiful English countryside. His way of dealing with these issues was to create a new world, another place and time in which to muse about such profound matters. What does *The Lord of the Rings: The Fellowship of the Ring* say about human nature? Do you think

Tolkien's worldview is pessimistic or optimistic, or is it too early in the story to tell? Is this view consistent with Christian teaching? Why or why not? How does Tolkien's story compare with those mentioned above and others that you may want to add to the list?

2. Today's readings have a cosmic tone because the Creator of the universe has entered into history. Hebrews, John, and the responsorial psalm speak of Christ as the beginning and end of history, and that "all the ends of the earth have seen the saving power of God." Though Tolkien never thought of his work as an allegory, how might *The Lord of the Rings: The Fellowship of the Ring* be interpreted in the light of the Incarnation? Talk about the storyline as well as the symbolism in the film. What does the symbol of the ring mean? How is the fellowship itself a ring and how is it broken? What do the characters stand for? What human values are evident in the film?

3. The fantasy genre is very popular with some, less so with others who prefer the "real world" of the here and now. Fantasy suspends the rules of nature and lets the reader or viewer enter with his or her imagination into secondary worlds like Middle-earth, to step through the looking glass or over the rainbow to explore ideas and issues that are not so easy to deal with directly. Some people accused Tolkien of writing a literature of escapism. But as Tolkein's son Christopher pointed out in a documentary film about his father, Tolkien felt offended by such accusations. He asked why they could not see this kind of story as the escape of a prisoner, a noble act, rather than the flight of a deserter. What do you think Tolkien meant by

this? What could this mean for you personally in your relationship with entertainment media and your approach to spirituality?

Prayer

Jesus, today we remember with joy your birth in Bethlehem. Bless us as we celebrate you, the Word of God made flesh, come to earth to destroy sin and darkness. Bring us into the light of your grace. Amen.

THE HOLY FAMILY

Genesis 15:1–6, 21:1–3;
Hebrews 11:8, 11–12, 17–19;
Luke 2:22–40

The Seventh Sign
U.S.A., 1988, 105 minutes
Cast: Demi Moore, Michael Biehn, Jurgen Prochnow
Writers: George Kaplan, Sandy Kroopf
Director: Carl Schultz

The Seventh Sign

A Suffering Mother

SYNOPSIS

All over the world, apocalyptic signs indicate the approach of the end of time. There are rivers of blood in Nicaragua and ice storms in Palestine. David, a mysterious figure from the East, arrives in Los Angeles and rents an apartment from Abby and her husband, lawyer Russell Quinn. Abby, having suffered a miscarriage, is pregnant again.

Abby is curious about their new boarder and searches the apartment when he is not there. She finds what looks like religious documents. She begins to believe that David is Jesus Christ returned. She takes some of his documents to a Jewish scholar who explains they are quotations from Revelation describing the coming apocalypse. One document concerns the "Guf," the place where souls live before they are born. It is now empty.

The final signs of the end, according to the documents, are the execution of the last martyr and the stillbirth of the first soulless baby. Abby intervenes at the execution of Russell's client, Jimmy, thinking he is the last martyr. She also thinks her unborn child will be the first baby born without a soul.

Abby seeks advice from Fr. Lucci, a Vatican official, and is shocked when he shoots Jimmy. Flashbacks reveal Lucci to be a centurion who struck Christ on the way to Calvary and has been condemned to live until the end of the world. He is trying to hasten the apocalypse so that he can die. Abby discovers in a vision that she, too, has lived before, and that she had refused to die in Christ's place. She now sacrifices herself so that her baby will be born with a soul, and David tells her that the Guf is full of souls again.

COMMENTARY

The Seventh Sign is a supernatural thriller made in 1988, a precursor to other apocalyptic films made in the 1990s with the approach of the twenty-first century. It is also reminiscent of movies about diabolical possession made during the 1970s under the influence of *The Exorcist.*

Australian Carl Schultz (*Careful, He Might Hear You, Traveling North, To Walk with Lions*) directed the film. Demi Moore gives a credible performance as a mother afraid of Satanic threats to her child, but who is, at the same time, prepared to confront and do battle against the mysterious messengers of evil. Michael Biehn is her lawyer husband. Jurgen Prochnow appears as the brooding prophetic figure that Abby believes is Jesus Christ in his second coming.

The film relies less on special effects than other movies of its kind. It creates an eerie atmosphere by drawing on quotations from the Book of Revelation with an increasing sense of impending doom. The screenplay incorporates myths from Jewish tradition, especially the Guf, the special location for pre-born souls.

DIALOGUE WITH THE GOSPEL

Focus: Although this feast is a day of blessing, the Gospel contains a promise that Mary will suffer on Jesus' account. The Seventh Sign, *with its biblical overtones, is a story of a mother who suffers for her son.*

The first two readings today contain words of promise to our "first family" in faith: Abraham, Sarah, and Isaac. The

Lord tells Abraham in Genesis that his reward for believing will be great and that he and his barren wife Sarah will have a son. The reading from Hebrews reflects on the fulfillment of this promise and the test of Abraham's faith when God asks him to sacrifice his son Isaac.

The Gospel focuses on the presentation of the child of the "first family" of the New Testament, the Holy Family. This ceremony consisted in prayer and rituals for the mother, according to the law.

The prophetess Anna prays in thanksgiving because she has lived her whole life for the moment when she would encounter Jesus, the fulfillment of the prophecy. Simeon, however, comes upon the family and introduces joyful and distressing tones in his prophecy. He is the servant who sees salvation for the human race. Simeon goes on to talk about the child as a sign of contradiction and of the sufferings that Mary will have to undergo.

The Seventh Sign is steeped in mythic and cultural Judaic traditions with New Testament overtones. Abby is the specially chosen mother. She experiences the joy of her pregnancy and shares that joy with her husband.

David, the mysterious stranger who comes into Abby's life, hints at the suffering that she must undergo. There are biblical overtones from the story of Abraham sacrificing Isaac, and of Mary giving up Jesus and grieving for him at his death. Ultimately, the main sacrifice demanded is from Abby herself. She is willing to die for the world so that her son can be born.

KEY SCENES AND THEMES

- The prologue showing scenes in Haiti, the dead fish, the heated sea, Israel and the iced village, Sodom, the Nicaraguan scenes; Abby and her pregnancy, inquiring about kindergarten, her love for her husband, her dreams.

• David's arrival, his stories about the Guf, discussions with him, the breaking of the seal; the visit to the rabbi for the translation of David's documents, the boy and his translation; Abby's depression, the signs of her attempted suicide; her belief that Jimmy and his death are a sign; her giving birth, her joy in her child, but her willingness to die for the world.

• David as the reappearance of Jesus Christ, his challenging Abby to hope, confronting the evil spirit in the priest; the sparrows, their singing and death, the seals and the Book of Revelation, the catastrophes, the empty Guf, the dreams, Abby's death.

FOR REFLECTION AND CONVERSATION

1. The end of the world has fascinated believers since the very beginning of Christianity. The Plymouth Brethren, a fundamentalist sect founded in England in the 1800s, espoused a belief based on interpretations of the Scriptures that focus on the end times, called the "rapture." This is an event when the Lord will come again, take the chosen few to heaven, and leave the rest behind. At the beginning of the twenty-first century, this belief is the theme of many books of popular fiction and of movies. What do Catholic and mainstream Protestant Christian churches teach about the end of the world? How do these teachings contrast with the "beliefs" expressed in the film?

2. Today's Gospel says that Jesus will be a "sign that will be contradicted" and to Mary, "you yourself a sword shall pierce." How are these scriptural utterances paralleled in *The Seventh Sign*? Indeed, what is the seventh sign in the film and how does it relate to Simeon's prophecy? Why doesn't the baby touch his mother's face at the end of the film?

3. Today's responsorial psalm says, "The Lord remembers his covenant forever" and "Rejoice O hearts that seek the Lord." In what ways can the Christian family depend on the promises of the Lord? Recall the Rite of Marriage and talk about the implications of the covenanted vows exchanged by Christian couples living in today's world. How is marriage enhanced by the grace this sacrament brings? How does the grace of this sacrament make a difference for couples facing suffering?

Prayer

Mary, Mother of Jesus, you loved your son and cared for him as a child. You also suffered for him. Pray for all mothers who suffer for their children. Amen.

A view of a one-man space pod leaving the deep space exploration ship *Discovery* for a reconnaissance in *2001: A Space Odessey*.

2001: A Space Odyssey

U.S.A./U.K., 1968, 150 minutes
Cast: Keir Dullea, Gary Lockwood, Douglas Rain,
Leonard Rossiter, William Sylvester, Robert Beatty,
Margaret Tyzack
Writers: Stanley Kubrick, Arthur C. Clarke
Director: Stanley Kubrick

2001: A Space Odyssey

The Divine in Our World

SYNOPSIS

Four million years ago the earth was a desert. Vegetarian apes and other animals roamed the world peacefully together until a mysterious, perfectly shaped monolith appears among them. The apes reverence it and when they touch it, they begin to fight and prey on the other animals. The apes discover tools of bone and use them to hunt and, eventually, to fight and kill one another. They also begin to become more human in appearance.

Space travel in the year 2001 is a sophisticated, computerized experience. Dr. Floyd briefs his staff at a space station before traveling to the moon. Rumors of an epidemic are a cover for the discovery of the monolith on the moon, which sends out a radio signal directed towards Jupiter.

Some eighteen months later, a Jupiter expedition is underway. Dave Bowman and Frank Poole are in command of the space probe traveling to Jupiter, but HAL, an infallible computer, controls the voyage. HAL has been programmed to think, speak, simulate feelings, and never lie, but the astronauts become suspicious of HAL's advice. HAL causes Frank to be cut loose into space and Dave terminates HAL's functions.

Following the indication of the monolith, Dave continues the journey. He travels beyond the galaxies through mazes of color until he arrives at a classical-style mansion. He watches himself, aged, eating a meal. He then watches himself on his deathbed. The monolith stands before the bed. Dave reaches out to touch it. Seen among the planets is a star child about to be born.

COMMENTARY

Since it premiered in April 1968, *2001: A Space Odyssey* has puzzled, dazzled, and intrigued audiences. It brought science fiction films into the realm of cinema art. The author of the book on which this film is based, Arthur C. Clarke, co-wrote the screenplay with Kubrick and their *2001: A Space Odyssey* was released a decade before George Lucas' *Star Wars* changed our conceptions of science fiction and science fantasy.

The film is a combination of cinema poem and cinema essay. The extraordinary visuals and special effects are enhanced by the music of Aram Khachaturyan and Gyorgy Ligeti. Richard Strauss's *Also sprach Zarathustra,* matched with the images of the murderous ape and the birth of the star child, is unforgettable. Johann Strauss's *Blue Danube* is the perfect music for Kubrick's stunning vistas of space and spaceships. There is some action and human drama, but these are the least gripping parts of the movie.

Dave Bowman, the "Everyman," goes on a mystical journey through space and time via Kubrick's meticulously presented cinematic collage of the psychedelic—to the appreciation of the hippy audiences of the 1960s. The final moments of the film may indicate that we humans live our lives in a quest for meaning. We die but, like the star child, humanity is continually reborn.

DIALOGUE WITH THE GOSPEL

Focus: 2001: A Space Odyssey *is a cinematic poem about the wonder of the universe and God's creation. The prologue of John's Gospel is a hymn to the transcendence of God and to the Incarnation.*

The reading from Sirach touches on the wisdom of a Mighty God, come to dwell among us. This becomes more explicit in the reading from Ephesians when Paul prays that the Spirit will give us the wisdom to recognize this mystery: the revelation of divine wisdom and glory in Jesus Christ. The prologue of John's Gospel says that God's light shines in the darkness of the world, and that all things that are came to be through God. Transcendent and omnipotent, God is revealed to us in the beauty of creation and most fully in the person of Jesus, the Word made flesh.

The "prologue" of *2001: A Space Odyssey* shows the primitive world of creation. Via the symbol of the monolith, Kubrick suggests that there is a power beyond the human, an intelligent and creative power that transforms the animals into human beings. Some have interpreted the monolith as a symbol of God's light and creative power. Others disagree. The film suggests that God's presence among us continues to challenge us in our sophisticated world and enfolds us in the transcendent beauty of the Creator who is with us at every stage of our history. The star child is a reminder of the continual rebirth of the human race.

- The presence of the monolith and its effect on the apes: the primitive apes and their "animal" way of life; their gradual change and the beginnings of intelligence, the discovery of tools that are used as weapons, the primitive creatures killing each other.

- HAL representing sophisticated human development and the pervasiveness of technology; HAL taking on a life of its own and turning against the astronauts; HAL's malevolence toward Dave and Frank.

- Frank's odyssey, the vastness of the universe, its beauty; the presence of the monolith in the human quest for meaning; Dave, as Everyman, reaching out

KEY SCENES AND THEMES

to touch the monolith; the star child and hope for the universe.

FOR REFLECTION
AND
CONVERSATION

1. To call a film science fiction *and* science fantasy is a bit of an oxymoron. This film could be termed "speculative fiction"—a combination of science fiction (storytelling that presents a futuristic scenario that is at least scientifically plausible) and science fantasy (requiring a suspension of reality). Critics and audiences have never agreed on what *2001: A Space Odyssey* is about or what it's trying to say—and Stanley Kubrick liked it that way. He wanted audiences to react to and talk about the film. For a person of religious faith with an interest in science or speculative fiction, the film lends itself to religious interpretation. Do you agree with the commentary as presented here, or do you have your own "reading" of the film? How do you interpret the symbolism in the film? How might this film compare with Kubrick's final film, *A.I.: Artificial Intelligence,* as realized by Steven Spielberg?

2. The readings for this Sunday speak of wisdom, grace, glory, and the Word dwelling among us in the person of God's Son, Jesus Christ. Where does the film's wisdom lie? What is its ideology or worldview? What is the role of technology in our lives, whether at work or leisure? What are our beliefs, priorities, and values regarding technology, the human person, and God's involvement in the world? How do we communicate these values?

3. If one could say Christmas is about hope for humanity, can the same be said about the image of the human person conveyed in *2001: A Space Odyssey?* What

questions does it ask about the nature of God, humanity, and transcendence? What answers does it offer, if any? When reflecting on a cinematic poem such as this, is it more helpful to search for an answer or to remain with the questions?

Prayer

God, you are the all-powerful Creator of the universe. We praise you for the wonder of all that you have made. And, at this Christmas time, we thank you for revealing your Son, Jesus. Amen.

EPIPHANY
Isaiah 60:1–6; Ephesians 3:2–3, 5–6;
Matthew 2:1–12

Kundun

U.S.A., 1997, 134 minutes
Cast: Tenzin Thuthob Tsarong, Gyurme Tethong, Robert Lin
Writer: Melissa Mathison
Director: Martin Scorsese

 *Kundun*

Seeking God

SYNOPSIS
With the passing of the Dalai Lama in 1933, the Buddhist monks of Tibet travel around the country in search of Kundun, their spiritual leader: the new incarnation of the Buddha. After some years, they find a two-year-old boy in whom they sense the presence of the Buddha.

The boy is taken to Lhassa to be trained in Buddhist spirituality and traditions as the fourteenth Dalai Lama. At the same time, he is also introduced to some of the technical advances of the twentieth century, including a movie projector that is sent from the West as a gift. When he becomes the Dalai Lama, he begins to bring technology to Tibet to benefit his people.

When World War II breaks out, Tibet is isolated, but the people know about the global conflict through movie newsreels. After the war, the Dalai Lama has to face social issues concerning Tibet's place in Asia. China looms as a threat and makes advances on the country. The Dalai Lama's advisers are divided about what course of action to take.

Mao Tse Tung had risen to power in China in 1949, and the Dalai Lama-to-be travels to Beijing to meet the Premier.

Mao smiles in public while being photographed with the young leader, however his intentions are less than friendly. China soon invades Tibet to destroy much of the culture and oppress the people. Buddhist nuns and monks are massacred. China annexes Tibet. The new Dalai Lama makes his escape to India and becomes a leader in exile.

COMMENTARY

Martin Scorsese is considered one of the great directors of American cinema. Many of his movies have received outstanding critical acclaim, including *Mean Streets, Taxi Driver, Raging Bull, Goodfellas,* and *The Gangs of New York.* He made *Kundun* for reasons of personal conviction rather than profit.

Kundun recreates the world of Tibetan Buddhism and its long isolation from the rest of the world. It also shows Tibet's entry into the modern twentieth-century world. The thoughtful script is written by Melissa Mathison, who also wrote *E. T.: The Extraterrestrial.* Scorsese avoided Hollywood glamour by casting unknown Tibetan and Chinese actors and filming in Morocco.

Scorsese offers his audience both a narrative about and contemplation of Buddhism. Some of the rituals are beautiful, others alien. *Kundun* requires the open heart and mind of the viewer in order to appreciate the cultural differences, ancient traditions, and history. The succession of actors playing the Dalai Lama are convincing, especially the young adult leader. Nurtured as the Buddha for his times, he moves from a self-centered child to a humble and non-violent leader. *Kundun* is a movie of beauty, insight, and wisdom.

DIALOGUE WITH THE GOSPEL

Focus: The Gospel of the Magi's pilgrimage "from the East" proclaims the mystery of the Incarnation, the Word made flesh and dwelling among us, to the entire world. Today's feast can be an occasion for interfaith dialogue on the meaning of the mystery of the Incarnation of Jesus Christ.

The feast of the Epiphany is a celebration of the manifestation of Jesus to the world. During the Christmas season, we have listened to the nativity stories. We are now invited to contemplate the wonder of God revealed to all humanity, the Word of God who is one with the Father presented to representatives of the nations.

While Epiphany is a time for contemplation of the Incarnation, it can also be a day of dialogue with the other great world religions. The Magi came from the east to seek the special king. Their initial "dialogue" with Herod was not a fruitful sharing of a quest for God, because Herod was deceitful. Each world religion in its own way honors the transcendence of God. *Kundun* offers us an opportunity to look at a religion in which God is considered to be beyond all human knowledge. In a very interesting way, this movie contains echoes of the Gospel infancy narratives. We see wise men searching for a special child: the fourteenth Dalai Lama. The child grows in stature and wisdom; as an adult he begins his religious mission and exercises his religious leadership.

As we honor the Epiphany of Jesus, we can take this occasion to dialogue with people who follow the major world religions, to learn about their traditions and teachings, and to deepen our understanding of our own Christian tradition.

KEY SCENES AND THEMES

- The search by the wise men for the specially chosen child, the sense of finding the right child, training him as he grows in age and wisdom; his boyish petulance and childishness; the young Dalai Lama and his leadership, his advisers, his family and their status, the traditions of Tibet.

- World War II and its intrusion on Tibet, the Chinese Revolution and the consequences and ambitions for Tibet; the invasion of Tibet by China, the dilemmas for the Dalai Lama; the visit to Mao Tse Tung, his polite yet ruthless behavior.

- The Dalai Lama's reluctance to leave his people; his escape from Tibet; the years of his exile; his long-standing status and influence in the world.

1. Because of the visit of the Magi to Jesus, we can now say that Jews and Gentiles can walk together, glorifying the one God. What is interreligious dialogue and how is it present in your parish, community, or city? What distinguishes it from ecumenism? What is your particular stance as a Christian toward such dialogue? In what ways can mutual understanding and respect help promote this journey of the human family toward truth?

FOR REFLECTION AND CONVERSATION

2. The title *Dalai Lama* means "Ocean of Wisdom." His followers believe the current Dalai Lama is the fourteenth human manifestation of Buddha. The Dalai Lama is committed to ruling compassionately and nonviolently, a very difficult task for a national leader whose country is being invaded by foreign armies. What does Christianity teach about nonviolence? How can nonviolence prevail in an increasingly violent world? What message of wisdom can Buddhism give to the world today as we journey together toward God?

3. Epiphany means manifestation, a term that has entered popular culture because it so aptly describes a moment of inspiration. When a thing or an idea has been manifested to someone or he or she is enlightened: this is an experience of an epiphany. This word maintains its sacred character especially when it de-

scribes a moment of inspiration that prompts us to grow as human beings and children of God. Have you ever experienced an epiphany? Recall the moment and the truth or lesson learned. In what ways was it a sign, a manifestation of Jesus, the Word made flesh?

Prayer

Lord, the Magi sought the child Jesus to pay homage and bring gifts. May all people of good will share in their search for the divine presence in our world. Amen.

Lilies of the Field
U.S.A., 1963, 94 minutes
Cast: Sidney Poitier, Lilia Skala, Ralph Nelson
Writer: James Poe
Director: Ralph Nelson

Lilies of the Field

Amen!

Homer Smith is an unemployed handyman traveling the southwestern United States during the 1960s, heading nowhere in particular. When his car overheats, he looks for water and comes across a group of nuns. They are refugees from East Germany who have escaped across the Berlin Wall. They are trying to develop the farm bequeathed to their order, but the terrain is dry and rugged.

Homer does a day's work for the sisters. The mother superior, the only nun who speaks sufficient English, is very demanding. She pressures Homer into staying on to do some of the much-needed work on the property. The nuns and townspeople attend Mass outdoors when a visiting priest comes to town. On Sunday, the nuns insist that Homer drive them to the community's gathering place. Homer drives them, but being a Baptist, rather than going to Mass with them as the nuns had hoped, he goes to the roadside diner. He becomes friends with Juan, the owner. Both Juan and the priest warn Homer not to become entangled with the nuns.

But then Homer agrees to build a chapel for both the nuns and the people and starts to clear away the existing ruins of a building. He also begins to teach the Sisters English and shares in some of their community activities.

When materials for the chapel run out, Homer leaves, but feels drawn to return to the nuns. He takes a local construction job to earn money for food and building materials and then, with the help of local workers, completes the job.

Homer says his good-byes and leaves the nuns, singing a Gospel spiritual. The superior realizes how she has taken Homer for granted, and never said "thank you."

COMMENTARY

Lilies of the Field, based on the novel by William E. Barrett, was released in 1963, a significant and a symbolic year for African-Americans. That year was marked by the march on Washington when Martin Luther King gave his memorable, "I have a dream..." speech, which quickly became the inspiration for the Civil Rights movement.

Sidney Poitier became the first African-American actor to win the Best Actor Oscar for his role as Homer. This recognition by the Academy of Motion Picture Arts and Sciences acknowledged the place of African-Americans in the movie industry at a crucial moment in the history of the United States. The first African-American woman to win an Academy Award (for Best Supporting Actress) was Hattie McDaniel for her 1939 role in *Gone With the Wind*. In 2002, Halle Barry became the first African-American woman to win the Best Actress Oscar for her role in *Monsters' Ball*.

Director Ralph Nelson went on to dramatize race issues in *Tick, Tick, Tick...* (1969), and in *Soldier Blue* (1970), the clash between Native-Americans and white settlers.

Lilies of the Field is a gentle parable filmed in black and white. Lilia Skala is the severe, imposing, and demanding Mother Superior. Their edgy friendship and collaboration to build the chapel provides some of the film's humor. More seriously, Homer's generosity contrasts with the authoritarian presumption of the superior. The film concludes with the still popular and upbeat Gospel song, *Amen*, rather than the usual "The End" credit. A made-for-television movie sequel, *Christmas Lilies of the Field* (1979), repeated the original plot. This time Billy Dee Williams plays the role of Homer, revisiting the Sisters, and Mother Maria, played by Maria Schell, persuades him to stay to build an orphanage.

Focus: John the Baptist's role was to introduce Jesus through his preaching and to bear witness by baptizing Jesus in the Jordan River. Homer Smith brings a new vision of God to the nuns who live in the desert and then he disappears from the limelight, as the Baptist did.

DIALOGUE WITH THE GOSPEL

Today's feast directs our attention to the person of Jesus at the moment when the heavens open, the Spirit descends upon him in the form of a dove and God speaks, saying: "You are my beloved Son; with you I am well pleased." Jesus is the fulfillment of the Baptist's preaching that challenges the people to repentance and a change of heart and life.

In *Lilies of the Field,* we see Homer Smith as a John the Baptist figure in relation to the displaced community of sisters in the Arizona desert. Their shared enterprise to build the chapel points toward the message in the first reading from Isaiah. The Sisters are poor, but their desire to live and to honor God is earnest. Homer is a good man who brings life to the Sisters and who illustrates Jesus' words about God's providence (Mt 6:28–29) and the lilies of the field.

This film points to a deeper reading of 1 John that asks us to reflect on the role of a profound Trinitarian faith consisting in the love of the Father and Jesus in the power of the Spirit, and includes keeping God's commandments that are described as "not burdensome." Indeed, through Homer Smith, the grace of God has appeared to the nuns, modeling the goodness and love lived by the baptized. Homer teaches Mother Maria that she, like he, must decrease and allow God to work through the Sisters and the local people. They have every reason to trust because the presence of Jesus will be with them and God will become a center for the local community when the new chapel is built.

That Mother Maria has learned something from Homer is beautifully shown in her dawning awareness that she never said "thank you" to Homer. Homer disappears, showing Mother Maria and the Sisters the way to witness to Jesus among the people: they, too, must lead the way to Jesus, in whom the Father is well pleased.

KEY SCENES AND THEMES

- Homer Smith as a congenial man and his encounter with the Sisters; their persuading him to build the chapel and his decision to build it.

- The displaced Sisters in Arizona; the response of the itinerant priest, the community, Juan and his offering of help to gain some kind of "insurance" with God.

- The cheerful Sisters, the dominating Mother Superior and the way she bosses Homer; Homer with the community, helping them to learn English; the superior thanking God and realizing that she never thanked Homer; singing of the Gospel spiritual *Amen* as Homer disappears.

FOR REFLECTION AND CONVERSATION

1. In film studies, the "world" in which a film is produced and to which it refers is called "diegesis." What elements of the film explicitly suggest the Civil Rights era in the United States? (Some examples: it is filmed in black and white; the nuns treat Homer as if he were a servant, yet struggle to also treat him with respect; Homer insists that he is worthy of thanks for the work he does, etc.) How could the "diegesis" of the film have enriched the audience's interpretation in the 1960s?

How can we interpret the film today? What other films since the 1960s remind us of *Lilies of the Field* and may influence our understanding of it?

2. The humility of John the Baptist is evident in today's Gospel, and yet we know from the entire portrait painted by the Gospels that John the Baptist was no "push over." He was comfortable in his own skin and won the respect of his listeners despite his strong message. How is Homer a John the Baptist figure for the nuns in the arid desert, so well described in today's first reading? What does Homer teach us about respect for self and others?

3. *Lilies of the Field,* a delightful film, echoes with Scripture. For example, Homer and Mother Maria both use Scripture quotations to convince the other of his or her opinion. (Luke 10:11: "The laborer deserves his wages"; Proverbs 1:14: "Throw in your lot among us, we will all have one purse"; Matthew 6:28–29: "Consider the lilies of the field, how they grow; they neither toil nor spin.") What story does the song, "Amen" tell? What are some of the many Gospel-based themes that can be derived from the film, such as tolerance, dignity, gratitude, honoring the God who dwells in our neighbor, not taking advantage of others, even for a good purpose? How are these themes criteria for Christian living?

Prayer

Jesus, help us to make you better known and loved. May our lives humbly reveal the presence of God in every person we meet and serve. Amen.

Joel 2:12–18; 2 Corinthians 5:20—6:12;
Matthew 6:1–6, 16–18

U.S.A., 2000, 121 minutes
Cast: Juliette Binoche, Alfred Molina, Judi Dench, Lena Olin,
Johnny Depp, Carrie-Anne Moss, John Wood, Leslie Caron,
Victoire Thivisol, Hugh O'Conor, Peter Stormare
Writer: Robert Nelson Jacobs
Director: Lasse Hallstrom

 *Chocolat*

Lenten Penance

SYNOPSIS

On Ash Wednesday 1959, in the tranquil French village of Lansquenet, the mayor, Comte de Reynaud, supervises as the villagers come to Church. Once inside, Reynaud diligently examines the homily the newly assigned and very young priest preaches. The inhabitants of this sedate village greatly value the virtue of tranquility.

At the same time, a mysterious north wind blows, signaling the arrival of an equally mysterious woman, Vianne, and her daughter, Anouk. Vianne is the daughter of a French father and a South American-Indian mother. She carries her mother's ashes with her wherever she and Anouk go; they seldom stay long in one place. Mother and daughter have come to Lansquenet to open a chocolaterie. This upsets Reynaud, who always promotes a strict observance of Lenten fasting in the village. He confronts Vianne's defiance and tries to turn the village against her.

Vianne makes exquisite chocolates, which tempt the villagers, who cautiously begin to come to her shop and, by doing so, find their lives changed. Armande, Vianne's landlady, is one of these people. Armande is a strong-

60

minded older woman whose straight-laced daughter forbids Armande access to her grandson. Another is Josephine, the battered wife of Serge, who takes refuge in the shop and works with Vianne.

One day a band of river people and their leader, Roux, arrive at Lansquenet. The village resents them and treats them as social and moral outcasts. The mayor instigates a campaign against them. However, Vianne and her daughter ignore the mayor by welcoming them and Roux is attracted to Vianne. Serge takes the mayor's condemnation literally and sets fire to the boats after a celebration, forcing the river people to leave.

Vianne throws a party for Armande's seventieth birthday. Afterward Armande returns to her home where she quietly dies. As Easter Sunday approaches, the mayor desperately breaks into the shop to destroy the chocolates. Instead, he gorges himself on them. Shamefaced, he recognizes and admits his narrow outlook on life. The priest preaches on the love of Jesus. The villagers are transformed into a more tolerant community and Vianne, too, learns that she needs to change. She decides to stay in Lansquenet. Roux returns to the village.

COMMENTARY

Chocolat is a fable that combines the whimsical elements of a fairy tale and adult themes. Unfortunately, a number of critics judged the film as if it were intended to be a form of realistic drama and so dismissed it as implausible and sentimental. However, *Chocolat* touched the hearts of popular audiences. The Academy for Motion Picture Arts and Sciences nominated the film for a Best Picture Oscar, the luminous Juliette Binoche for Best Actress, and Judi Dench for Best Supporting Actress. The rest of the cast includes Alfred Molina as the mayor, Johnny Depp as Roux, Lena Olin as Josephine, and Carrie-Anne Moss as the repressed daughter of Judi Dench.

Lasse Hallstrom, whose movies are marked by a strong sense of humanity and compassion, directed *Chocolat.* His films include *My Life as a Dog, What's Eating Gilbert Grape, The Cider House Rules,* and *The Shipping News.*

Whether British novelist Joanne Harris sees her story as implausible and sentimental is uncertain. However, the movie is enjoyable and offers a challenge to believers.

DIALOGUE WITH THE GOSPEL

Focus: Jesus urges his disciples to pray, to fast, and to give alms. He also warns against the hypocrisy of parading virtue for others to see. Chocolat *shows respectable but hypocritical villagers who are challenged to imitate the human and compassionate Jesus.*

Chocolat is a moral and religious fable, a dramatic commentary on today's Gospel from the Sermon on the Mount. This is a film about the meaning of Lent. In fact, the film begins on Ash Wednesday in 1959, the same year that John XXIII officially asked Christians to re-pray and re-think the Gospel message for the modern world as the Church prepared for the Second Vatican Council.

Chocolat pits an outward show of fasting and mortification for Lent against a kind of spiritual goodness, a piety of the heart, which is loving and wants to help transform other people. Vianne has inherited from her mother a tradition which considers chocolate a mysterious and sacred food that delights those who eat and drink it, enabling them to see their true selves and to change. After the traumatic fire, the villagers must question the meaning of their external acts of penance, realizing how little these have really helped them to experience conversion. Vianne has helped the villages open themselves to what we might call "grace," but she has needed transformation as well. The chocolate, certainly an image of the experience of Eucharist, has had its effect.

- The mayor supervising the villagers as they enter the church, checking the young priest's homily, the judgmental attitudes; the homily denouncing Vianne; the contrast with Easter Sunday and the homily about the humanity of Jesus and his compassion.

- Vianne and Anouk welcoming people into the shop; Vianne discerning people's favorite chocolates; Armande mellowing and meeting her grandson; Josephine taking refuge with Vianne; Guillaume courting the widow; Roux's arrival and fixing the shop window.

- The mayor's acts of penance and going to the shop to destroy the chocolate; the mayor tasting a piece of chocolate and his suppressed feelings erupting; the final sermon and the villagers transformed at the festival.

KEY SCENES AND THEMES

1. The mayor in *Chocolat* epitomizes religious hypocrisy. The young priest, who the villagers expect to be the most "observant," enjoys rock 'n roll. His role seems to suggest that he might have a better grip on an integrated Christian life than the other characters. Vianne flouts the penitential tradition of the village and promises to save people through the freedom chocolate offers. Yet, she is also a hypocrite in her own way. How does Vianne's personal story entwine with that of the villagers? How does she change and grow? Are there any characters in the film that are spiritually free? Who are they and how might their approach to faith and life differ from each other?

2. Chocolate is the core of this film, a kind of maypole around which the characters move, dance, and interact with one another and in relation to their religious

FOR REFLECTION AND CONVERSATION

practices. What does this analogy say about the villagers' relationship with the person of Jesus Christ? How is our Lenten observance personal (chocolate) and how does it also have a social dimension (thoughts, words, habits of intolerance)? What did the various characters in the film *Chocolat* learn? What is the moral of this tasty fable?

3. A Franciscan preacher once told a group of people during an Ash Wednesday retreat: "I hate Lent, but I figure if I have to do it, I might as well go first class." He went on to urge his listeners, as Jesus did in today's Gospel, to "Be on guard against performing religious acts for people to see." But is that all the movie *Chocolat* is about? If there are other themes, what are they and how might they help us question and transform the integrity of our own behavior so that our personal relationship with Jesus may grow?

Prayer

Lord, as we begin our Lenten journey toward the promise of Easter, help us to purify our hearts so that we may share your compassion for all people in freedom and joy. Amen.

FIRST SUNDAY OF LENT

Genesis 9:8–15; 1 Peter 3:18–22;
Mark 1:12–15

The Firm

U.S.A., 1993, 154 minutes
Cast: Tom Cruise, Gene Hackman, Jeanne Tripplehorn, Hal
Holbrook, Terry Kinney, Holly Hunter, Ed Harris, Wilford Brimley,
David Strathairn, Gary Busey
Writers: David Rabe, Robert Towne, David Rayfiel
Director: Sidney Pollack

The Firm

Urban Wilderness of Temptation

Despite his humble background, Mitch McDeere gradu-
ates from Harvard Law School near the top of his class. A
small but respectable Memphis law firm offers him a salary
twenty percent above the other offers he has received. His
wife Abby is anxious about the impact of the firm's excessive
generosity and the control it will have on their private life.
Mitch is soon a star lawyer working with his mentor, Avery
Tolar. An FBI agent approaches Mitch to inform him of the
firm's money laundering arrangement with the mob. They
want Mitch to turn informant for them on the firm's activities, but Mitch refuses to believe them.

SYNOPSIS

Mitch accompanies Tolar to the Cayman Islands for business where the firm has two condominiums. On the way back
to his room one night, Mitch defends a young woman who is
apparently being attacked, and he is then seduced by her.
The firm secretly photographs their encounter to keep for
blackmail purposes. Mitch becomes suspicious when several
of the firm's employees die in the Caymans.

Both the FBI and the firm begin to pursue and blackmail
Mitch. When Mitch and Abby discover their house and phone
are bugged, he is forced to reveal his one-night stand to Abby,

who is so angry she decides to leave him. Mitch hires Eddie Lomax, a private detective, to investigate the firm, but Lomax is soon murdered. Lomax's secretary, Tammy, witnesses the murder. Once more, the FBI approaches Mitch and offers him an immunity deal based on his testimony indicting the firm. Mitch's brother Ray is in prison and Mitch wants him released as part of the deal.

Just as Abby is about to leave town, Tolar invites her to accompany him to the Caymans. She decides to go in order to help Mitch. She slips sleeping pills into Tolar's drink and helps Tammy to steal documents that will incriminate the firm. Mitch finally helps destroy the firm by accusing them of mail fraud. He convinces the mob bosses to agree to press charges. Mitch, Abby, Tammy, and Ray set sail to start a new life.

COMMENTARY

The Firm is based on the 1991 bestseller by lawyer-turned-novelist John Grisham.

The movie focuses on a central character who exemplifies the American Dream: he begins life in poverty, works hard, and succeeds. In the movie, Mitch is allowed to escape, both physically and morally, whereas in the novel, his situation is more ambiguous and he has to live the rest of his life in danger from the FBI, the mob, and the remnants of the law firm.

The movie stars Tom Cruise and has an excellent supporting cast, especially Gene Hackman as the aging corrupt lawyer, Tolar; Hal Holbrook as the sinister head of the firm; Wilford Brimley as the enforcer William Devasher; Ed Harris as the FBI agent Wayne Tarrance; Jeanne Tripplehorn as Abby, Mitch's wife; and Gary Busey as Eddie Lomax, the private investigator. Holly Hunter provides a small element of humor as Lomax's street-smart assistant, Tammy Hemphill, who helps Mitch to escape the firm. Holly Hunter was nominated for a Best Supporting Actress Oscar for her role in the film.

Focus: At the beginning of Lent we listen to the story of Jesus tempted by Satan and to Jesus' warning to repent. Mitch McDeere discovers a world of temptation at the firm. He is also given the opportunity to choose good over evil and to repent of his sin.

The first two readings introduce us to Lent. They speak of guilt and corruption. In Noah's day, the human race had succumbed to sin and God destroyed it in the flood. The first letter of Peter takes up the theme of sin and guilt in Noah's time, but looks at water not as a means of destruction, but as a way to save those who were faithful. The letter then moves to the ritual of Baptism, the central theme of the Easter vigil liturgy, toward which Lent journeys.

The Gospel introduces us to Lent by means of the narrative of Jesus' temptations. This year's Gospel of Mark is a capsule of Jesus' experience, which is followed by Jesus' initial preaching of repentance.

Mitch McDeere, an intelligent, idealistic all-American hero, experiences the gamut of human temptation: easy money, fame, status, and power. Feted and flattered, he willingly joins the firm and becomes its most eager member.

The FBI agent, Tarrance, focused on government interests, is a guardian angel figure looking after Mitch while he is in the grasp of the wild beasts at the firm—as long as his own interests are served. Tarrance unwittingly enables Mitch to move out of the corrupt world of temptation and to "repent" of his choice to join the firm. It is this choice for good over evil that allows Mitch to find salvation—for himself and for others.

- Mitch, the all-American boy, a poor young man, intelligent, bright, and ready to fight for status and ultimately to save himself, his wife; his denial of his background, his parents, and his brother; his loving yet weak relationship with Abby; Mitch's idealism and pragmatism.

- The firm, Lambert and his assistants: upright members of society and perfect gentlemen; Avery Tolar's cynicism, bad habits, freedom from home and family; Mitch rescuing the woman on the beach, their sexual encounter; his loss of innocence.

- Mitch's growing suspicions, the encounters with the FBI; his tactics and the personal, moral, and professional dangers; his deal with the FBI and the destruction of the firm.

FOR REFLECTION AND CONVERSATION

1. The responsorial psalm today says, "Your ways, O Lord, are love and truth to those who keep your covenant." What is the value of God's covenant in the corporate world today? How can love and truth to be the criteria for good business practice, employer/employee relationships, and respect for human dignity? Did love and truth ultimately serve Mitch McDeere? If so, in what ways? What did Mitch lose by not believing in and trusting Abby? What was his fear? Who was the real "hero" in the film?

2. Water is a theme throughout today's Scripture readings and the film. As a biblical symbol, water is a source of life, a cleansing agent, and a cosmic force only God can control. In what ways might the use of water, especially at the film's end, point toward these biblical images?

3. The appeal of a film such as *The Firm* is that it could be true. Any one of us could become caught up in the moral and/or legal dilemmas of these characters, though perhaps not on such a grand scale. *The Firm* is

a dense landscape for the exercise of our moral imagination in time of temptation. Step into the shoes of one of the characters. What would you have done in his or her place? How does each of the characters deal with the temptation for money, sex, and power? How might you? What evangelical virtues or teachings of Jesus come to mind that can counter these temptations?

Prayer

Jesus, protect us when we confront temptation in our lives, and when we fall, give us the grace to repent and to begin again. Amen.

SECOND SUNDAY OF LENT

Genesis 22:1–2, 9, 10–13, 15–18;
Romans 8:31–34; Mark 9:2–10

Billy Elliot

U.K., 2000, 107 minutes
Cast: Jamie Bell, Julie Walters, Gary Lewis, Jamie Draven
Writer: Lee Hall
Director: Stephen Daldry

 *Billy Elliot*

Inner Light Shines Out

SYNOPSIS

It is 1984 and coal miners in the north of England are on strike. Eleven-year-old Billy Elliot lives near Durham with his recently widowed father and older brother, Tony, who are also miners on strike. They go to the picket lines every day to denounce and heckle scab laborers being bussed into the mines.

Billy takes boxing lessons at the local club but is not very good at it. One day, he watches a ballet class and is fascinated. Debbie Wilkinson, the dance teacher's daughter, challenges him to join the class. Though he finds the steps difficult to perform, Billy continues to go to Mrs. Wilkinson's lessons, but does not dare tell his family.

Billy practices and, despite his initial clumsiness, he improves. When his father finds out about the lessons he forbids Billy to continue because he thinks dancing is for sissies. Mrs. Wilkinson, however, has faith in Billy's ability and trains him privately for a regional audition. Tony is hurt during a scuffle with the police at the mine, and Billy misses his audition.

One day, Billy's father sees him dance and Billy's movements reveal the energy and anger boiling within him. His father finally acknowledges his son's talent. In order to pay for Billy's trip to London and an audition for the Royal Ballet, he decides to cross the picket line, but other miners stop him and agree to raise the money for Billy. Billy and his dad travel to London for the audition where Billy is rude and aggressive. The judges are not impressed with him until they see him dance. They offer him a position at the ballet school.

Years later, Billy's father and brother watch as he dances the lead role in *Swan Lake*.

The film, originally titled *Dancer*, was a great hit at the Cannes Film Festival. However, it was decided that the film would do much better at the box office if the title were changed to the name of the main character. It is a very entertaining movie and had audiences laughing and crying.

Lee Hall's screenplay includes all the expected battles between a father and son over "sissy dancing" as well as discussions on equating dance with sexual orientation, which gives the film a great deal of bite. The relationship between Billy and his father is well drawn and provides the viewer with insight into the hard reality of a blue-collar worker whose life is centered on the mine, his family, and his co-workers, and who is challenged to come to terms with his son's incredible talent as a dancer.

Though *Billy Elliot* is theatre director Stephen Daldry's first movie, it reveals great self-confidence. Particularly striking are the sequences when Billy dances exuberantly with Mrs. Wilkinson, a rather acerbic but generous teacher, played by Julie Walters.

Jamie Bell is completely convincing as Billy. When we first see him, he seems to have no physical aptitude, either at boxing or dancing. Perhaps only a truly skilled dancer could be so convincing as a poor one. And Bell's acting and dancing performance rings completely true.

DIALOGUE WITH THE GOSPEL

Focus: Today's Gospel of the transfiguration is a symbol of light in darkness. Jesus shines out momentarily to give his closest disciples a glimpse of his divine nature. Billy Elliot *is a movie about light in darkness, an inner glow shining out for all to see.*

In some ways, *Billy Elliot* reminds us of today's Genesis text, which shows Abraham following the Lord's commands, preparing to sacrifice his son Isaac. As Abraham loved Isaac, Billy's father truly loves him, but feels compelled to kill the boy's hopes and talent because of the economic hardship the family faces and to live up to the town's "macho culture." But when he watches Billy's powerful and assertive performance he "holds back his hand" from killing Billy's dream. As Abraham released Isaac, Billy's father allows his son to dance and, therefore, to live.

The most telling sequences for today's feast are those of Billy dancing joyfully with Mrs. Wilkinson and with forceful passion for his father and the judges. Billy explains to the judges that, for him, dancing is like electricity: it is the spark, the light, and the energy that overwhelms him, exploding from inside. At the transfiguration, Jesus' Father speaks from the cloud, telling the apostles to listen to his beloved Son. Billy's father feels proud of him when he watches his son dance, and he wants everyone to watch his son perform. Mark's Gospel tells us that the Apostles, too, are moved by the Transfiguration experience. The memory of this moment will encourage them in the troubled times ahead.

KEY SCENES AND THEMES

- Billy trying to box and failing; watching the dance class; his first clumsy attempts at ballet, his growing confidence, the exhilaration of dancing.

- The miners' strike, the harsh atmosphere at home, no income, the picket lines; smashing the piano for firewood; the masculine culture of the father and older brother; the contrast between Michael and Billy and their friendship.

- Billy's "transfiguration" in the dance sequences; dancing with Mrs. Wilkinson, for his father, for the judges and, finally, as a professional.

1. The relationship between fathers and sons is a recurring theme in Scripture and in film. Some fathers can have high expectations and hopes for their sons; some fathers want their sons to do better in life then they have. Others may struggle to survive against great odds and hope that their sons will follow in their footsteps, or at least not embarrass them. Contrast the father-son relationships in *Billy Elliot* with *Dead Poets Society* (or others), and with the stories of Abraham and Isaac and the Prodigal Son. What lesson is there for fathers, sons, other family members, and friends in today's film and Scriptures?

FOR REFLECTION AND CONVERSATION

2. One of the film's themes asks questions about sexual identity and the difficulty of children and young people who struggle alone as they mature. What issues does this film raise about the involvement of parents in guiding and nurturing their children and being involved in their children's lives? In what ways can parents help to resolve the tension existing between work, family, religious beliefs, and the social/cultural expectations in which they live?

3. On some levels, *Billy Elliot* is more a fable than a real story. Lee Ann Womack's contemporary song *I Hope You Dance*, and the saying, "Dance as if no one is looking," both express the conviction that dance is about interior freedom. In the Old Testament both Miriam

and King David dance freely before the Lord. What is Billy struggling to free himself of through his dancing? How, if at all, do the other characters grow in freedom in the film? What lessons regarding our own interior freedom are here for us in this enjoyable and inspiring film?

Prayer

Lord, you are a light shining in darkness. May the glorious light of your presence transfigure our lives. Amen.

Jesus of Montreal

Canada/France, 1989, 119 minutes
Cast: Lothaire Bluteau, Catherine Wilkening, Remy Girard,
Johanne-Marie Tremblay, Robert Lepage, Denys Arcand
Writer: Denys Arcand
Director: Denys Arcand

Jesus of Montreal

The Zeal of Jesus

SYNOPSIS

The traditional Passion Play, performed annually on the mountain overlooking Montreal for forty years, has become outdated. The priest in charge of the event hires Daniel Coulombe, a young man who has been out of the country for many years, to write and produce a new version of the play. Daniel recruits a new cast and sets to work writing and directing. The cast includes Constance, who works in a soup kitchen; Mireille, a model; and Martin and Rene, who dub pornographic movies.

The play dramatizes best known episodes of the Gospel: the healings, raising people from the dead, Peter's attempt to walk on water, the miracle of the loaves and fishes, Jesus before Pilate, and his crucifixion. But the new Passion Play renders a rather unorthodox interpretation of the Gospel and is a popular success. Local Church authorities want the play toned down, if not cancelled all together, because of its message, which threatens their ecclesiastical establishment.

Mireille is invited to an audition for a commercial and Daniel accompanies her. When she is asked to open her shirt, Daniel confronts the producers and overturns all the equipment, driving out the media people. Daniel is arrested during a performance of the play for damaging property and is later released. During the play's final performance, the police arrive again and, during the ensuing scuffle, Daniel is injured. Although he says he is all right, he becomes delirious and collapses. There is no room for him at the Catholic hospital, but he is welcomed at the Jewish hospital where he dies. Constance donates his organs to save someone's life.

COMMENTARY

Jesus of Montreal and *The Last Temptation of Christ* were the two major Jesus movies of the 1980s. Both were interpretations of the Gospels and Jesus' life rather than straightforward presentations of the familiar narratives. *Jesus of Montreal* won many awards including the Ecumenical and Special Jury Prizes at the Cannes festival in 1989.

The writer and director, Denys Arcand, is a trained historian who believes that one can know only a little about the actual events of Jesus life. His screenplay highlights discussions in recent centuries about "the Christ of history." Arcand had already made several movies in his native Canada, including *Decline of the American Empire,* when he began *Jesus of Montreal.*

The character Daniel Coulombe is a profound Christ-figure and the film draws a number of parallels to the life of Jesus. Daniel emerges from his hidden life at age thirty and clashes with religious authorities. Like Jesus, he "calls" his cast from those who work at less respected occupations, and "cleanses" the modern "temple." Daniel is arrested, dies, is buried, and his body given for the sake of others. Daniel also performs scenes from Jesus' life and passion during the play.

Lothaire Bluteau plays a serious, sometimes pallid and wan Christ-figure who suddenly comes to life to defend others in a vigorous, even violent manner. Bluteau also played a seventeenth-century Jesuit missionary in the 1991 film, *Black Robe.*

Focus: Daniel Coulombe is a Christ-figure both in his "real" life as well as when he portrays Jesus in the Passion play. One of the strongest scenes in the film is when Daniel causes an uproar in the television studio, providing a visual parallel to the cleansing of the Temple in today's Gospel.

The reading from Exodus is the primary, clear declaration of God's law in the Decalogue. The Ten Commandments focus on our basic human experiences of relationship with God and neighbor. The foundation for Daniel's behavior in *Jesus of Montreal* is the law of God interpreted in a just and humane manner. There is no place for hypocrisy, whether in one's personal life, the media universe, or the world of the Church.

Paul's statement about Christ crucified being a stumbling block for some and foolishness for others is for all times. This is because Christ's humble self-giving goes against conventional wisdom whether of the first-century Greeks or the twentieth-century media industry. Daniel's attempt to reinterpret and stage the Passion Play in a modern setting brings new meaning to this centuries-old tradition. This new version, based on Daniel's religious study and experience, explains the meaning of his own death as a Christ-figure. "Zeal for your house will devour me" is a quotation from the psalms that summarizes Daniel's mission.

Today's Gospel also recounts the discussion about Jesus' risen body as the new Temple, the substitute for the old one that had been under construction for forty-two years. Daniel Coulombe will have no theater to keep his memory alive. Like Jesus, he will live on in the memories of his disciples.

- Daniel portrayed like Jesus: his "hidden years," calling his cast from those who work at unlikely occupations, welding them into a company.

KEY SCENES AND THEMES

- The parallels with the Gospels, the sequence in the television studio, the "temptation" of the media entrepreneur offering "the world" from the heights of the modern skyscraper; Daniel's ability, like Jesus, to see beyond the surface into people's hearts.

- The Gospel re-enactments; their impact on Daniel and the woman who comes to the cross and prays until a policeman removes her, on the cast members who reflect on the meaning of their roles, and on the public through the distribution of the bread; Daniel as Jesus on the cross, arrested, wounded, then dying and "rising" in his disciples' memories.

FOR REFLECTION AND CONVERSATION

1. The new Passion Play that Daniel and the cast have written and produced is certainly good theater. Yet, their interpretation makes Church authorities nervous and they take steps to stop the production. Why did this happen? Is there a right way and a wrong way to tell the truth? If so, how might Daniel and his cast have achieved this and to what purpose? How have spindoctors and the public relations process/crisis management changed the way we perceive truth? What kind of questions can we ask to sort out the truth from falsehood or hypocrisy, whether presented by the media, government, or Church ministers?

2. *Jesus of Montreal* is the proverbial "play within the play," but it goes a step further because the first play melds into the second, to the extent that the audience feels they are seeing Jesus alive today. What parts of the film blend the two "plays"? Do you think this technique enriches the meaning of the film? What do you think director/writer Arcand was trying to say in *Jesus of Montreal?* Do you agree? Why or why not?

3. The media "market place," whether commercials promoting materialism or the dubbing of porn films, seems an excellent parallel to the marketplace of Jesus' day. The events in the film say much about the dignity of the human person, how we treat one another, and to what lengths people will go for the sake of profit. How well do we know human nature and to what extent do we respect others and ourselves? How tolerant are we of weakness, whether in others or ourselves? To what extent do we consider the value and dignity of each human person in our relationships?

Prayer

Jesus, give us the courage of your zeal when we encounter corruption and injustice. Help us to live the way we profess to believe. Amen.

FOURTH SUNDAY OF LENT
2 Chronicles 36:14–16, 19–23;
Ephesians 2:4–10; John 3:14–21

A.I.: Artificial Intelligence
U.S.A., 2001, 145 minutes
Cast: Haley Joel Osment, Jude Law, Frances O'Connor, Sam
Robards, Brendan Gleeson, William Hurt, voices of Jack Angel,
Robin Williams, Ben Kingsley, Meryl Streep, Chris Rock
Writer: Steven Spielberg
Director: Steven Spielberg

A.I.: Artificial Intelligence

To Be Real and Loving

SYNOPSIS

In the near future, global warming melts the polar ice caps; large cities are partially submerged. The number of children a family may have is limited, and robots, called "mechas," perform domestic tasks.

The Cybertronics Manufacturing Company "creates" David, a child "mecha" programmed with sophisticated intelligence and simulated emotions. He is "adopted" by Henry and Monica whose son, Martin, is sick and being cryogenically preserved until a cure for his illness is found. At first wary, Monica becomes attached to David as a substitute child and she programs or "imprints" him to "develop" so that he can express his feelings and call her "mommy."

When Martin unexpectedly recovers and returns home, a rivalry begins between the two boys. Henry persuades Monica to return David to the company and have him destroyed. Instead, Monica takes David into the woods and, with regret, leaves him there.

David's only companion is a "super toy," a teddy bear robot programmed to walk and talk. They come across a junkyard for used robots and are captured and taken to the Flesh

80

Fair, an arena where coliseum-like games take place, and robots are destroyed for human entertainment. A robot designed as a sex-machine named Gigolo Joe is imprisoned with David, who becomes attached to him. When the two are taken to the arena to be destroyed, the crowd has pity on the child robot and attack Lord Johnson Johnson, the organizer of the fair, instead. David and Joe escape and go to the decadent Rouge City where Dr. Know, a carnival fortune-teller, tells David where to find the Blue Fairy, who has the power to make robots human.

Joe and David travel to New York City, where they find Professor Hobby, David's creator, who has made a series of David robot children. David encounters one of his replicas and destroys him, then runs away and finds the Blue Fairy in a Pinocchio theme park on Coney Island. He stands in front of the Blue Fairy pleading with her to make him real, but she cannot.

David waits 2,000 years until aliens discover him and use his stored memories to reconstruct his home with Henry and Monica. When Teddy produces a lock of Monica's hair, she too comes alive again, but only for one day. David spends a wonderful day with Monica, and she loves him as her son. When she dies at the end of the day, a tear falls from David's eye.

COMMENTARY

Stanley Kubrick had been planning for this film about a robot that wants to be real for almost twenty years, but died in 1999 before completing it. The film is taken from an idea in Brian Aldiss' 1969 short story, *Supertoys Last All Summer Long*.

Steven Spielberg inherited Kubrick's project and tried to fulfill his vision. Spielberg wrote the screenplay himself. While there are echoes of Kubrick's themes—human freedom from *A Clockwork Orange* and the voyage into the future from *2001: A Space Odyssey*—the treatment is very much in the Spielberg vein. Children have always played important and significant roles in Spielberg movies, especially *Close Encounters* and *E.T.: The Extra-Terrestrial.* Spielberg traces the journey of a robot child from machine to human in this film in three parts. The academic ideas proposed by the movie are interesting, but Spielberg develops an emotional approach to the story.

Spielberg incorporates the tale of Pinocchio, the puppet who wanted to become a real boy, into the story, focusing on the character of the Blue Fairy. Here she is a kitschy carnival statue voiced over by Meryl Streep. The integration of the myth of the Blue Fairy into the story seems a stretch because her role is insufficient to sustain the deeper questions about being human for David or us, the viewers.

Haley Joel Osment demonstrates his talent as an actor through his convincing performance of David as both mechanical and human. The audience empathizes with David as he awakens to the reality of having a mother, played by Frances O'Connor, and what this means for him.

DIALOGUE WITH THE GOSPEL

Focus: A.I.: Artificial Intelligence, *the story of a robot child sent into the world to be a means for people to learn to love, serves as an image to appreciate how God so loved the world that he sent us his only Son.*

Chapter three of John's Gospel is principally a conversation between Jesus and Nicodemus. Jesus speaks of being born again, of God's love and healing, eternal life, the light of good, and the darkness of evil. When we look at this list of themes and those from *A.I.: Artificial Intelligence,* a correlation emerges which provides images and points for dialogue to help us appreciate the Gospel. David is a created being who wants to understand what it is to be human, to love, and to live forever. In a sense, both Nicodemus and David want to be born again—for David from machine to human, and for Nicodemus from "mere" human to one who walks with God in light, truth, and the fullness of eternal life.

In the Letter to the Ephesians, we find Pauline reflections on the love and the mercy of the Creator God. Paul describes us as God's handiwork, "created in Christ Jesus for the good works that God has prepared in advance, that we should live in them." This expresses a Creator whose vision is love.

In addition to giving David the capacity to love, Professor Hobby's gift of David relieves Henry and Monica of their grief over Martin's illness. David's presence enables them to love again. It's a human image, but Jesus tells Nicodemus that the Father so loved the world that he gave us Jesus, his Son, so that we might live forever in that love.

Another theme in today's readings is that of good and evil, light and darkness. The Book of Chronicles recounts a period of infidelity and sin on the part of Israel and the need for repentance. Jesus tells Nicodemus that light came into the world, but people preferred darkness to light. In the second part of *A.I.: Artificial Intelligence,* David becomes a sign of light and love. Driven from the light of his family into the darkness of a world of terrifying and cruel humans, David continues to search for his identity. He learns to hope that he will become capable of real love, and of living forever in love.

- Professor Hobby's lecture to his staff about his hopes to make a boy who can love and be loved; David programmed to be a loving boy and son; his sharing in the love of a family, in games, in mimicking eating; his learning to say, "Mommy," Monica wishing that he could be human; David's experience of being jealous of Martin.

- David abandoned in the woods, his trust in Teddy and Gigolo Joe; his capture, being put on the platform to die, people not wanting to hurt a child; his escape and the quest to find the Blue Fairy.

KEY SCENES AND THEMES

- David pleading with the Blue Fairy to make him human; her reply that it is not possible, his 2,000 year wait; the aliens, recovering his memories; Monica and her temporary resurrection, their joyful day together as a son with his mother, his final tear.

FOR REFLECTION AND CONVERSATION

1. We might ask, why does today's film suggest a need to manufacture substitutes for children? The film seems to answer that we have worn out the earth's gifts so that it can no longer sustain us, thus we cannot continue to bring real, earth-dependent beings to life. We must depend on machines for love, affection, and simulated familial relationships. A confusing, ambiguous, nightmarish situation results. If this is a picture of humanity's future, then what does Jesus' conversation with Nicodemus mean for us? How does *A.I.: Artificial Intelligence* suggest that we resolve the problem of our future? How does Jesus suggest we resolve it? Does the film even hint at the existence of a supreme being? If so, how?

2. The philosopher Descartes once wrote: "I think therefore I am," David thinks, but can he really say "I am"? In the film, Monica's feelings for David grow so strong that she finally "imprints" herself on him, making him particularly her own. Yet, just because she has feelings for David, does that make him human? Then, despite these feelings, she abandons David anyway. What *were* Monica's feelings for David? Was love really involved?

3. *A.I.: Artificial Intelligence* is one of many films in this year's movie lectionary that engages in a conversation about what it means to be truly human (e.g., *2001: A Space Odyssey, The Truman Show, Edward Scissorhands*).

We know that *A.I.: Artificial Intelligence* is a work of the imagination, so we can step back and ask: who is a human person and what does our recognition of our common humanity demand from us as members of the human family? What do modern philosophies declare about the nature and dignity of the person? How do these philosophies contrast with the Christian Personalism of John Paul II (cf. *Catechism of the Catholic Church*, n. 1730 ff., n. 1928 ff.)?

Prayer

Father, you sent Jesus, your Son, into our world to be our light, our truth, and our love. Transform our lives from darkness to light. Amen.

The Burning Season
U.S.A., 1994, 115 minutes
Cast: Raul Julia, Sonia Braga, Edward James Olmos,
Esai Morales, Tomas Milian, Nigel Havers, Tony Plana
Writers: Michael Tolkin, Ron Hutchinson, William Mastrosimone
Director: John Frankenheimer

The Burning Season

Witness of Martyrs

SYNOPSIS

It is 1951 and the impoverished people of a small Brazilian jungle town tap trees in the rain forest for rubber. The storekeepers and landowners exploit the people who desperately need to organize to protect themselves and their families. A union leader teaches the young Chico Mendes how to read.

Thirty years later, the situation has not improved, in fact, it has grown worse. The landowners are clearing more land to build a road from the north Amazon region to Lima, Peru, in order to run cattle for the world's growing beef markets. This threatens to destroy the country's forests, harm the environment, and further edge out the rubber tappers.

One Sunday, moved by the union leader's speech at Mass, Chico asks himself where Jesus would be in such a situation. Chico becomes more politically active and attempts to unionize his people. Politicians move against him. He decides to run for office, but he loses.

A visiting British documentary maker films many of the violent incidents and sends them for screening abroad. Mendes now finds himself invited to international conferences on the environment. At first, political figures scorn

Mendes, but as they get to know him and his cause, they treat him with esteem. The Brazilian government is forced to stop burning the forests and declare much of it public land. Vengeful landowners murder Mendes, whom the people of Brazil and beyond now venerate as a martyr and admire as a liberator.

Raul Julia was born in Puerto Rico, and in 1964 began his career in New York as a stage actor. He made his passage to film in 1971 and became very successful in *The Addams Family* and *Addams Family Values.* Admired for his portrayal of Archbishop Oscar Romero in John Duigan's *Romero* in 1989, here Julia portrays another Latin American hero and martyr: Chico Mendes. Mendes was a simple and devout man who, like Romero, felt circumstances closing in on him and realized the inevitability of a violent death.

Director John Frankenheimer began directing movies for the big screen in 1957 with *The Young Stranger.* He continued to make movies with a justice theme, including *All Fall Down, Birdman of Alcatraz, The Manchurian Candidate,* and *The Train. The Burning Season* demonstrates his skill in recreating a particular world and injecting it with social consciousness. The story is based in part on the novel of the same title by Andrew Revkin.

In this made-for-cable film, one of the last before his death on October 24, 1994, Raul Julia is joined by some of the better-known Latin American character actors including Sonia Braga (*The Milagro Beanfield War* and *Kiss of the Spider Woman*), and Edward James Olmos. Nigel Havers appears as the filmmaker who publicizes the drastic situation in Brazil.

Focus: The grain of wheat that dies in order to grow is an image of Jesus and, in the early Church, of the martyrs. Chico Mendes is a twentieth-century martyr whose death brought about a new and better life for his people.

From its earliest times, the Church used today's Gospel reading to celebrate the martyrs. St. Ignatius of Antioch wrote of himself as a grain of wheat that would become pure bread ground by the teeth of the lions in the coliseum. It is also appropriate to see the life and death of Chico Mendes illustrating this text. Mendes saw himself as a simple man, alone and seemingly insignificant. Yet his life and death, and the books and the films about him, have helped to produce a harvest of justice.

In the Gospel today the Greek visitors want to see Jesus. Jesus says he is troubled and refers to his death; he speaks of discipleship, of the servant found with the master. He also speaks of honoring the faithful servant. The people living with Chico Mendes recognized the presence of Jesus in him, as the scenes of Mendes at Mass with the people attests. Although Chico Mendes desperately wants to live, he foresees that he will die for the sake of justice.

Jesus also gives us the image of his overcoming evil and drawing all people to himself when he is lifted up in death. This is true of all martyrs and of witnesses to social justice such as Chico Mendes.

KEY SCENES AND THEMES

- Brazil in the 1950s, the shop owner overcharging the poor rubber tappers and their inability to do anything about it; the union leader offering to teach Chico to read, Chico at Mass and the leader giving a talk about justice; the question of where Jesus would be in a situation like the one facing the people of the rain forest.

- The portrait of the landowners, their wealth, arrogance, brutality, greed, and the politicians using them to get rid of the tappers; Chico and the confrontations with the heavy road-clearing equipment; the people standing in solidarity; the removal of the trees and the burning of the forest.

• Chico in the United States, shunned by business and political interests, then listened to and becoming a media hero; his bewilderment over this kind of campaigning; his knowledge that the landowners are planning to kill him, the boy's warning; Chico at home with his family, his brutal assassination, the aftermath.

FOR REFLECTION AND CONVERSATION

1. This is a film filled with religious imagery, Christian teaching, and witness. How does the image of St. Sebastian and other religious symbols contribute to our understanding of the film? What is St. Sebastian's story and why is his image especially meaningful for the story of Chico Mendes? What is the symbolic connection between the Easter fire in the film and the burning of the rain forest? What does it mean when the church bells ring?

2. In Exodus, God manifests himself to Moses in the burning bush, the beginning of the covenant with God's chosen people. In the reading from Jeremiah, God speaks again about the covenant. God says that he will write his law upon the hearts of his people, that they will belong to him and will teach their friends and relatives to know the Lord. How did Chico Mendes and his people manifest God's presence and law in their lives? When they tried to "teach" the politicians and businessmen, what was the result? Why can we consider Chico Mendes and others like him martyrs?

3. At one point in the film, Chico Mendes says: "I am not fighting progress. We need jobs and we need development…but we need it to happen in a way that

does not keep us poor.... Protect the trees that give my people their jobs. If you help us keep the trees then we have a good chance of making good lives for ourselves and for our children." Compare the social, economic, and political issues of *The Burning Season* with *Romero, Men with Guns, The Mission, At Play in the Fields of the Lord,* and even the more lightweight *Medicine Man.* How does each one present one or more issues that go to the heart of Jesus' saying in today's Gospel and the reasons for working for justice for the land and the people?

Prayer

Lord, we need people who will witness to justice in the face of oppression. Encourage those who imitate you as they struggle and work for justice through nonviolent means. Amen.

PALM SUNDAY

Edward Scissorhands

U.S.A., 1990, 100 minutes
Cast: Johnny Depp, Winona Ryder, Dianne Wiest, Alan Arkin,
Vincent Price, Anthony Michael Hall, Kathy Baker
Writers: Caroline Thompson and Tim Burton
Director: Tim Burton

Isaiah 50:4–7; Philippians 2:6–11;
Mark 14:1—15:47

Edward Scissorhands

A Savior in Our Midst

In a castle high above a town, a master inventor creates Edward who, he hopes, will be an exemplary young man. The inventor had to work long and hard to perfect the young man's hands; meanwhile, Edward has been using large scissor shears. When he is finally ready to fit on the hands, the inventor has a heart attack and dies. Edward laments the fact that he does not have real hands; he also lacks a heart.

SYNOPSIS

The inventor, however, has infused the wonders of poetry and science into Edward's mind. A sweet Avon lady named Peg Boggs visits the castle and invites Edward down into her world, a pastel American suburb of little box-shaped houses. Everything and everyone looks the same. Edward goes with Peg and lives with her family. Edward, with his pasty complexion, unruly black hair, and his eccentric matching black clothes, appears vastly different from ordinary people. He soon wins them over, however, by wielding his scissors on shaggy dogs, shrubs, and on the hair of bored housewives to create masterpieces.

Peg's daughter Kim dislikes Edward at first, but then befriends him. Her jealous macho boyfriend, Jim, blames

Edward for a crime that Jim actually committed. People turn against Edward, but Kim saves him and he returns to the safety of his castle. She tells the hostile crowd that Edward is dead.

Now elderly, Kim recounts the story to her granddaughter to keep Edward's memory and spirit alive. Edward continues to shape beautiful gardens and ice sculptures. Kim dances with her memories in the falling snow.

COMMENTARY

Edward Scissorhands is a contemporary fairy tale, a spoof on modern suburbia and consumerism with touches of Gothic horror.

The film is based on a story by Tim Burton, a former animator who went on to make the films *Pee-wee's Big Adventure, Beetlejuice, Batman, Batman Returns, Ed Wood, Mars Attacks!, Sleepy Hollow,* and *Planet of the Apes* (2001). The story was co-written with novelist Caroline Thompson. The movie is imaginatively designed, as is typical for Burton's pictures.

Johnny Depp communicates the personality (or lack thereof) of the innocent Edward. He is a composite young man put together by an eccentric inventor played with customary relish by Vincent Price. The actors are particularly well cast, especially Diane Wiest as the Avon Lady who brings Edward into her home. At the beginning of the movie, her cheery visit and kind personality set a tone, which makes the unusual characters and events more credible.

The movie echoes such mythic films as *E.T.: The Extra-Terrestrial* where a stranger enters into a community and becomes a catalyst for change. With its focus on good and evil, right and wrong, innocence and guilt, the movie reminds us of Gospel imagery and stories.

DIALOGUE WITH THE GOSPEL

Focus: Edward Scissorhands *tells the story of a significantly effective Christ-figure who suffers a passion which brings to mind that of Jesus.*

Many of the characters of movie fables come from "up or out there," such as E.T. or Superman. Just so, Edward Scissorhands comes down from his castle high above the suburbs to enter the rather superficial and mundane human world. Initially Edward puzzles people, but the marvels he performs with his special scissorhands soon win everyone's admiration. When Jesus came to earth his disciples and the people could not understand him, yet his personality, preaching, and works of healing attracted them.

As his public life drew to a close, Jesus found that many of his followers were fickle and had grown tired of him. Jesus experienced the acclaim of the people as he entered Jerusalem, an event we celebrate today on Palm Sunday. Only five days later, the same crowd shouted for Jesus' crucifixion. Mark's version of the passion brings to mind the main events of Jesus' arrest, trial, humiliation, condemnation, and crucifixion. Edward is in a similar situation when the town turns against him after a series of mishaps. The crowd pursues Edward with the intention of killing him, and thus Edward experiences his own passion.

Edward flees back to the castle and survives, and Kim keeps his memory alive when she tells the story to her granddaughter. On Easter Sunday, we will hear again the Gospel account of Jesus' resurrection from the dead and how he overcame suffering and death—and we will rejoice.

KEY SCENES AND THEMES

- The elderly inventor creating Edward and his hands; the inventor's death before he can give Edward his hands; Edward's appearance, his scissor hands and lack of personality; Edward programmed as a soft-spoken person with good manners.

- Peg's sympathy and wanting to help; Edward at her home and helping people; tricked by Jim; the women who turn hostile, ruining his designs, Jim's violence.

- Kim telling the people that Edward is dead; Kim telling Edward's story; Edward continuing to shape ice sculptures in the beautiful garden.

FOR REFLECTION AND CONVERSATION

1. The film says that a fable is something you don't believe but that you understand. How is *Edward Scissorhands* a fable? Some critics have called it a social satire with a touch of comedy. To which genre do you think *Edward Scissorhands* belongs? What does it ask us to understand? Some critics think that the most successful films are those that evoke empathy for the characters. How did *Edward Scissorhands* make you feel? Which characters, if any, did you care about and why? How do these characters contribute to understanding the film?

2. In literary theory, a symbol is a sign, something that directs attention to another reality. What do the symbols of color and shape in the film signify? What recurring patterns and shapes create the image of the film? What do Edward's hands and how he deals with his image mean? How is the theme of image—internal and external, human and scriptural—projected in the story of *Edward Scissorhands*? Kim says, "Before he came down here, it never snowed. And afterward, it did. I don't think it would be snowing now if he weren't still up there. Sometimes you can still catch me dancing in it." What is the meaning of the snow and the dance?

3. Natural justice, or ethics, requires that we consider certain aspects of human behavior as intrinsically right or wrong even without reference to revelation or Christian beliefs. At one point in the film, Bill Boggs talks

about ethics. The audience is asked to think about what is more important: to be nice or to choose between right and wrong. What are some of the ethical dilemmas in the film? Who acts justly and rightly? Who chooses intrinsically wrong behavior? How are ethics, cultural mores, and the issue of image bound together in the film and in the life and passion of Jesus?

Prayer

Jesus, in your life, and especially through your passion and death, you offered us a pattern for our lives. In this Holy Week, may your suffering inspire us to pray for all those who suffer. Amen.

HOLY THURSDAY
Exodus 12:1–8, 11–14;
1 Corinthians 11:23–26;
John 13:1–15

Rain Man
U.S.A., 1988, 133 minutes
Cast: Dustin Hoffman, Tom Cruise, Valeria Golino, Bonnie Hunt
Writer: Ronald Bass, Barry Morrow
Director: Barry Levinson

 *Rain Man*

Love One Another

SYNOPSIS

Charlie Babbitt is a selfish, fast-talking car dealer in California. He receives a call and learns that his father has died. Charlie returns home to Cincinnati to attend his father's funeral. Always short of cash, Charlie is disappointed when he discovers that his only inheritance is an old car and a rosebush; all of his father's money has been put into a trust. He is further shocked to learn that he has an older brother, Raymond, an autistic savant who has lived in an institution for years. Raymond is the main beneficiary in their father's will.

Charlie wants his half of the money, so he decides to take Raymond back to California to live with him. Raymond refuses to fly and enumerates the statistics of airline disasters to date. The two brothers drive across the country in the 1949 Buick Roadmaster Charlie inherited. The journey is not simply a return home for Charlie, who is anxious to get back to his business and girlfriend. It is a journey that opens his eyes to the possibilities of a deeper and more compassionate world.

Charlie discovers that Raymond is his childhood "rain man." As a child, Charlie's attempts at "Raymond" become "Rain Man," a companion and protector that Charlie thought he had invented.

As they travel and Charlie gets to know his brother's abilities and limitations, he mellows. Among other adventures, Raymond's skills with numeric figures help them win money in Las Vegas. Ultimately, Charlie realizes he cannot take proper care of Raymond. Suddenly his journey is no longer about money, but about ensuring that Raymond is cared for by good and competent people.

COMMENTARY

Rain Man was the major Oscar-winning movie of 1988. Barry Levinson, initially a successful screenwriter, became an even more successful director. His films include *Diner* (made for TV), *Tin Men, Good Morning Vietnam, Avalon, Bugsy, Sleepers, Wag the Dog, Liberty Heights, Sphere, The Perfect Storm,* and *Bandits.*

Dustin Hoffman and Tom Cruise play the two brothers. Hoffman won his second Oscar as the autistic Raymond. With *Rain Man,* Cruise, certainly the most popular young actor of the 1990s, consolidated his success, which had begun with *Risky Business* and *Top Gun.* His next movie, *Born on the 4th of July,* reinforced his stature as a versatile, all-American, top box-office actor.

Audiences found the film both entertaining and difficult. The interaction between the two men and their journey across America helped Charlie grow to accept his brother and love him, but Raymond never changes.

The film engages our attention on the level of values because it probes the deeper issues of what it is to live, to die, and to accept others and oneself. Questions about what it is to be a person are fundamental to us all and movies that examine this theme are usually the most engaging and profound.

DIALOGUE WITH THE GOSPEL

Focus: On Holy Thursday night, Jesus revealed how we are to be truly brothers and sisters. That is, we are to imitate him by serving others. Charlie discovers this teaching in his relationship with his brother, Raymond.

Holy Thursday is a celebration of Eucharist and of service. The reading from Exodus reminds us of the Passover memorial feast that the Israelites ate before they fled Egypt. The Letter to the Corinthians recalls the Last Supper for the early Christian community. The Gospel, however, is about Jesus who washes his disciples' feet the night before he dies. The washing of the feet is the model of Christian service. It is a new commandment: "so that as I have done for you, you also should do."

Rain Man is a film that calls to mind the importance of relationships and service. Charlie must learn what it is to serve and to love in a self-sacrificing way. His motives for taking Raymond from the institution were mean, vengeful, and greedy. However, Charlie soon realizes he must do nearly everything for Raymond—and precisely as Raymond is accustomed to. The handicapped Raymond transforms the self-sufficient Charlie and liberates him from his selfishness.

Peter, whose relationship with Jesus is about to change when he betrays him, shows the same self-sufficiency. At first, he refuses to be served and then he entreats Jesus to wash his feet, hands, and head as well. In the same way, Charlie needs to become more humble and accepting and his contact with Raymond helps him develop these virtues. Charlie will learn to lay down a part of his life in service to Raymond, as Jesus bent to wash his disciples' feet and then went to his death as the Suffering Servant.

KEY SCENES AND THEMES

- Charlie, the wheeler-dealer, making his car sales pitch, his frantic need to be successful; his anger over his inheritance and discovery that Raymond is the sole beneficiary; his motives for taking Raymond to California with him.

- Raymond as an autistic savant; his routines and skills, the characteristics of his autism; the challenge to Charlie's self-sufficiency and his care for the "rain man."

• The journey the brothers make and the effect on each other; Charlie's realistic decision about Raymond's future; the visual and emotional impact of the final credits with the montage of photos of the journey.

1. Today's feast, Scripture readings, and the film all converge in two inclusive themes: Eucharist and service. They are inseparable in the Christian life. While the film reveals nothing of the Babbitt family's religious beliefs, we are able to view the film through the lens that today's liturgy provides. In some ways, we can fill in the blanks so that we are able engage in the movie as believers. How is Raymond a means of salvation for Charlie?

2. The road movie is a common formula that Hollywood uses to tell stories. Road movies almost always involve men (the one noteable exception is *Thelma and Louise)*, who for some reason embark on a journey, overcome obstacles—at times through much violence—grow as persons, and arrive at their destination where all will be right again. Does Rain Man fit into this genre? Why or why not? Why is the change and growth of the characters so important to our enjoyment of the movie?

3. Consider the other themes that emerge in the film, including how the audience is educated about autism, what it means to be cared for and to be a caregiver, the issue of quality of life, and what it means to be a human being. Also present are aspects of human, moral, and ethical growth and maturity; insight into one's spiritual, inner reality, needs, and motivations; the ability to change from selfishness to generosity; loving and accepting people for who they are rather than who we wish them to be. How do the themes of

Eucharist, the gift of God's loving and enduring presence among us, and Christian service interface with these themes? What place does the Eucharist and service have in our journey?

Prayer

Lord, on this night you gave us the gift of yourself in the Eucharist. You also gave us the gift of your love as a model for our love and service to others. Help us to manifest your presence when we serve others. Amen.

GOOD FRIDAY

Isaiah 52:13—53:12; Hebrews 4:14–16;
5:7–9; John 18:1—19:42

Judas

U.S.A., 2001, 90 minutes
Cast: Johnathon Schaech, Jonathan Scarfe, Bub Gunton,
Tim Matheson, Diane Keane
Writer: Tom Fontana
Director: Charles Robert Carner

Judas

Betrayal and Death

SYNOPSIS

As a young boy, Judas sees his father crucified for his rebellion against the Roman occupation of Palestine. Judas
grows up in the care of his devoted mother. Caiaphas, the
high priest appointed by Rome, knows the family and keeps
his eye on Judas for signs of rebellion.

Judas grows up an angry young man. He is resentful of
the Roman presence and critical of how Caiaphas seems to
accommodate them. Judas works as a wine merchant and is
eager to find a revolutionary leader with whom he can join
forces. He hears about John the Baptist at the Jordan River
and goes to see him. Judas first glimpses Jesus at the Temple
when Jesus overturns the moneychangers' tables. Judas is
impressed and invites Jesus to his home for a meal.

Pontius Pilate lives in luxury as governor of Judea. He is
on friendly terms with the dilettante king, Herod, and deals
diplomatically with Caiaphas. He hears about John the Baptist and Jesus. Pilate relies on Flavius, his centurion, to keep
him informed and maintain order among the people.
Flavius hears Jesus speak and is impressed. He asks Jesus to
heal his servant.

In the meantime, Judas is involved in civil disturbances and flees to Galilee to find Jesus. He listens to Mary, the mother of Jesus, and is amazed at her story of Jesus' birth. Judas feels repelled by such teachings as turning the other cheek, yet he is moved when Jesus heals a paralytic. When Jesus sends the disciples out two by two, Judas seizes it as an opportunity to win people to his cause and raise a military force. Judas and Andrew go together. When Judas is unable to raise a woman from the dead, Andrew prays and works the miracle.

Judas realizes that he cannot understand Jesus. Caiaphas pressures Judas to betray Jesus and he agrees to lead the soldiers to him. He greets Jesus in the Garden of Gethsemane with a kiss. After seeing what happens to Jesus, he is distraught and he urges the other disciples to try to free Jesus. Jesus is tried and sent to Pilate. The crowd cheers for Barabbas to be set free, and Pilate washes his hands of the matter.

Jesus is crucified. Judas hangs himself. Jesus is taken down from the cross. Peter and the disciples find Judas' body and bury it, "because that is what Jesus would want."

COMMENTARY

Judas is dedicated to the late Reverend Ellwood "Bud" Kieser, the Paulist priest who produced the television *Insight* programs for many years as well as some made-for-television movies and feature films. *Judas,* a co-production with ABC-TV, was produced by Kieser's successor, Reverend Frank Desiderio, C.S.P.

Desiderio describes the movie as a twenty-first century midrash (a meditative story woven around a biblical character or event) about Judas and the friend he betrayed. Thus, it is not meant to be taken literally, but rather as an interpretation of the text.

The screenplay is by Tom Fontana who wrote *The Fourth Wise Man* (a made-for-television movie directed by Fr. Kieser) and who was the creator of the television series *Homicide:*

Life on the Streets and *Oz.* Johnathon Schaech gives an impressive performance as Judas, the angry zealot. So far, Schaech has appeared in the movies *That Thing You Do, Hush,* and *Welcome to Woop Woop.* Television actor Jonathan Scarfe brings an almost too cheerful blonde presence to the movie's Jesus, creating a strong contrast with the dark, brooding, and explosive Judas. Scarfe seems to struggle with the screenplay, which makes a sincere but less than convincing effort at integrating Jesus' humanity and divinity.

Bob Gunton is one of the best villains on the screen *(The Shawshank Redemption),* and he brings a cold intensity to Caiaphas. Tim Matheson seems an unusual choice for Pilate because of his more typically lighter, comedic roles, though his recurring role as the vice president on TV's *West Wing* shows versatility. These details may make *Judas* a little too contemporary for some viewers.

> *Focus: Judas does not understand Jesus' preaching of love and peace. He hopes that Jesus will become a national liberator, but is disillusioned. He betrays Jesus and then he despairs.*

DIALOGUE WITH THE GOSPEL

On Good Friday, we listen to John's passion account. In chapter 13, we read how, at the Last Supper, Judas asks Jesus whether he is the betrayer. This passage refers to John's theme of light and darkness as Judas leaves the upper room and "it is night." As the passion narrative opens, Judas gets "a band of soldiers and guards from the Pharisees." They take "lanterns, torches, and weapons," thus creating an artificial light in the darkness. Judas then disappears from John's Gospel. The information about his death comes from the Synoptic Gospels and the Acts of the Apostles.

The movie sees the arrest and the apostles' violent defense of Jesus from Judas' point of view. It also dramatizes such events as the appearance before Caiaphas, the torture by the guards, the confrontation with Pilate, and Pilate's offer to release either Jesus or Barabbas. The movie presents Jesus' crucifixion forcefully, but the climax of the film is Judas' suicide.

This contemporary version of midrash presents a challenge for today's Good Friday reflection because it evokes several questions. The movie opts to show some sympathy for Judas, symbolized by the apostles putting into practice Jesus' injunction to forgive, not just seven times but seventy times seven. Peter and the others bury the body of Judas because that is what Jesus would have wanted.

KEY SCENES AND THEMES

- The crucifixion of Judas' father and its lasting effect on Judas; his anger, his violence against Roman authorities, and Caiaphas and his accommodation to Roman rule; Judas beaten, spied and reported on; his mother's love and support.

- Judas seeing Jesus for the first time in his anger with the buyers and sellers in the temple; Judas urging Jesus to gather a military force and to develop a strategy; his shock at Jesus' preaching a more tolerant and loving way to confront enemies; his wanting to be a miracle worker; the effect of his disillusionment when unable to raise the woman from the dead.

- The reason Judas is disappointed in Jesus; his consent to betray Jesus; the Last Supper, the kiss in the garden; his cry for Jesus' freedom rather than Barabbas'; his growing despair and suicide; the apostles burying his body.

FOR REFLECTION AND CONVERSATION

1. Light is the first medium through which we see, and in the Bible, it is the beginning of creation. Biblical light is also demonstrated through the imagery of its conflict with darkness. Light symbolizes the sacred, goodness, and blessing. Darkness, as the absence of

light, is a physical and spiritual reality. How do today's Scripture readings and the movie set up light and dark as a metaphor for the passion and death of Jesus?

2. This made-for-television film seems to acknowledge contemporary psychological and theological considerations, because it invites us to ponder the questions of Judas' eternal damnation, his personification of evil, if it would have been better had he never been born, and how responsible he might have been for his actions. In the economy of salvation, did there not "have" to be a Judas? The question remains: was Judas intrinsically evil, did he choose evil or is it possible there were other reasons for his betrayal?

3. Because this movie ends with Judas' suicide, it can dominate the viewer's feelings as the credits roll. The Jason Foundation (www.JasonFoundation.com) reports that every hour and forty-five minutes another young person commits suicide in the United States alone. Recent statistics reported that suicide was the eleventh highest cause of death in the United States and the third leading cause of death for young people ages 15–24. Stories of suicide bombers who kill both themselves and others for a cause often headline the news. Read the references to suicide in the *Catechism of the Catholic Church.* Talk about numbers 2280–2283 and what this teaching means for our understanding of Judas and for us.

Prayer

Today, Jesus, we journey with you in your passion to your death. Judas betrayed you and despaired. We acknowledge that we betray you because of our sinfulness. Help us not to despair but to be confident in your loving forgiveness. Amen.

Daylight

U.S.A., 1996, 110 minutes
Cast: Sylvester Stallone, Amy Brenneman, Viggo Mortensen,
Dan Hedaya, Jay O. Sanders, Claire Bloom, Karen Young,
Barry Newman, Stan Shaw
Writer: Leslie Bohem
Director: Rob Cohen

 *Daylight*

Descending into a Hell

SYNOPSIS

Traffic moves steadily but slowly through the Holland Tunnel during afternoon rush hour in New York City. A convoy of trucks containing toxic material enters the tunnel, as does a vehicle carrying a gang that has just robbed a jeweler and stolen his car. When the traffic slows down, the driver of the getaway car begins to speed recklessly and crashes into one of the trucks, causing a fireball and explosion that seals both ends of the tunnel.

Kit Latura, a former emergency medical-service officer who was dismissed after being blamed for a fatal accident, volunteers to go into the tunnel. He enters through an airshaft, where he is almost killed, and meets a small group of survivors. He clashes with sports company executive, Roy Nord, who misjudges the way out and is killed. Kit begins to lead the group to safety.

The group includes a cross section of people: Madelyne, a playwright; an elderly couple and their dog; two quarreling parents and their daughter; and three petty criminals who were being escorted to jail in a police van.

The tunnel begins to flood. Parts of the roof collapse. A car crushes some of the survivors. Kit has to improvise. He builds a protective mud wall and then tries to find the abandoned living quarters of immigrant workers who built the tunnel in 1917. Everyone has to swim under water to reach an old chapel. They discover a tunnel behind a crucifix. The group climbs to the top. Kit and Madelyne, however, are trapped. Kit sets an explosive charge that releases a huge water jet and they ride the spout to safety.

This is not quite the slam-bang action movie of the 1990's that the name of Sylvester Stallone might lead us to expect. Rather, it seems more like a throwback to the 1970s, a disaster movie that frequently reminds us of *The Poseidon Adventure.*

The screenplay often makes use of the language of redemption and salvation. A crucifix figures prominently in the chapel sequence because it is the sign revealing the way to safety and survival. Rob Cohen *(Dragon: The Bruce Lee Story, Dragonheart, The Fast and the Furious)* knows how to direct action movies. The editing is paced for adrenaline and excitement. A supporting cast including Claire Bloom and Amy Brenneman gives the film a touch of star quality.

Focus: Jesus has died and been buried. An angel tells the women at the tomb that Jesus has been raised from the dead. Paul tells us that Baptism is our sacramental experience of dying and rising with Jesus. Daylight *offers images of death, burial, and rising to new life through waters of rebirth.*

The Gospel is reticent about the resurrection of Jesus. After the account of his passion and death, he is buried. The Apostles' Creed says that Jesus "descended to the dead," and other creedal statements say he descended into hell. Jesus went into "the depths" to announce salvation to those who had preceded him in death.

It is the reading from Romans that takes up the symbolism of this descent into death and ascent into rising from the dead. The symbol for this is the ritual of Baptism with its use of water. In Baptism, we join Jesus in death and in the tomb. Because we have done this, we can rise with him to new life. He has conquered death.

Though a predictable disaster movie, *Daylight* contains images that can evoke Paul's baptismal theology. Even the survivors of the terrible tunnel crash and fireball have had a "death experience." They are now below the surface of the river and the city, trapped in a dark underground where water threatens to drown them.

Into this situation comes Kit Latura, a literal savior-figure. He descends into a hell: the explosive tunnel inferno. He is a "wounded healer" because he has experienced failure in unintentionally causing another to die. Kit leads the group to safety through the darkness, even wading and swimming through water to show people the way. He leaves the survivors in order to find an exit route, but returns because he cannot abandon the people.

In the chapel behind the crucifix, the image of Jesus who suffered and died, the survivors begin their climb to safety and light. It is through the immense, energy-filled spout of water that Kit and Madelyne are saved. The *Daylight* of the title refers to the light of a new life at the end for those who have been freed from death.

KEY SCENES AND THEMES

- The explosion, the crash in the tunnel, the victims, the survivors; beginning a journey toward daylight, survival, and salvation; a cross section of people desperate to be saved.

- Kit volunteering to help, the danger of going down into the hellhole of the tunnel; his skills in reassuring people, in using his wits.

- The chapel, the crucifix; discovering the path to safety behind the crucifix; Kit's salvation via the explosion and the huge burst of water; the return to daylight.

1. There are many themes woven into this story. For example, the characters are all people who are either running away from something or on a journey and who become trapped in this "tomb-like" place, from which they will "rise." The writer in the story is leaving her life as it was behind, the young prisoners are on their way to jail, the mother is grieving the loss of her son, and Kit is fleeing his reputation as a coward. What are some of the others' journeys? How was this experience a cleansing time for the survivors? How were they changed? How is this a film about finding the light at the end of the tunnel on many levels?

2. This diverse group of people has to learn to communicate in order to survive. Indeed, the "communication" theme and symbols are strong throughout the film. As a social group, the interaction of the characters is reminiscent of *Lord of the Flies,* published in 1963, by William Golding (the first film version made in 1964 and the second in 1990), or more recently, *The Beach* (2000). How do these three films compare? What is the image of the human person that emerges from each film?

3. In the aftermath of the attacks on the World Trade Center on September 11, 2001, this kind of disaster movie may seem a bit too close to home. But this movie is like a microcosm of the heroic stories we have all heard since September 11, and reminds us that, as

one of the characters says in the film, "Together we can do anything." How is *Daylight* a film about hope in humanity and in God's help? What are the symbols in the film (such as water, fire, and light) that contribute to understanding the story as one that reaffirms human goodness and the benevolence of God?

Prayer

Tonight, Lord, our brothers and sisters share in your death and resurrection through the symbolic waters of baptism. Give them joy in their new, risen life. Amen.

EASTER SUNDAY

Acts 10:34, 37–43; Colossians 3:1–4;
John 20:1–9

The Matrix

U.S.A. 1999, 136 minutes
Cast: Keanu Reeves, Laurence Fishburne, Carrie-Anne Moss,
Hugo Weaving, Joe Pantoliano
Writers: Larry Wachowski and Andy Wachowski
Directors: Larry Wachowski and Andy Wachowski

 *The Matrix*

Loving into New Life

It is the eve of the millennium. Tom Anderson works for a software company, but by night he is a computer hacker whose screen name is Neo. Undercover agents pursue a mysterious woman named Trinity. She escapes and warns Neo that he is in danger as well, and must contact Morpheus. The agents capture, interrogate, and implant a tracking device in Neo. Morpheus and Trinity rescue him and take him to their hovercraft.

Neo learns about the Matrix: a computer, the result of artificial intelligence created by humans, that is taking over the world and programming unsuspecting humans to become slaves. Morpheus is the leader of a remnant group of humans who know what has happened. He has rescued a small team, led by Trinity, who manage to do their own programming from their hovercraft. They can travel into a digitalized world like the Matrix while their bodies remain dormant in their hovercraft.

Morpheus trains Neo in martial arts, because he thinks he is the One (the anagram of Neo) who will destroy the Matrix and restore the world. The enemy agents are trying

SYNOPSIS

to locate the underground city of Sion because it is the only one the Matrix has not yet conquered.

Neo is taken to an Oracle who makes ambiguous utterances about his and Morpheus's death. One of the members of their crew, Cypher, wants to return to the Matrix and betrays them. Morpheus is captured, interrogated, and tortured. Neo decides to return to the Matrix to rescue Morpheus, and Trinity goes with him. After deadly combat, good prevails and evil is destroyed. Neo offers the world new hope.

COMMENTARY

The plot of *The Matrix* dramatizes a world of computer programming and virtual reality. Its science fantasy or speculative fiction parallels such themes as waking and sleeping states and dreaming, illusion and truth. The movie proved extraordinarily popular with younger audiences and, surprisingly, academics, scientists, and philosophers.

The Matrix was filmed in Sydney with Australian technicians and supporting cast. The star is Keanu Reeves whose performance style tends toward "reacting" rather than acting. He played a similar role in Robert Longo's *Johnny Mnemonic,* written by cyber-author William Gibson. Two sequels to *The Matrix* were filmed in 2001.

The Matrix was written and directed by the Wachowski brothers who also wrote the screenplay for *Assassins* and wrote and directed *Bound. The Matrix* contains echoes of other science fiction or speculative fiction movies, especially *Blade Runner.* The Wachowskis are expert at creative cinematography and editing, as well as combat choreography, making the impact of image and sound particularly visceral.

The screenplay also draws on philosophical, mythical, literary, and biblical sources in order to give meaning to the events in the film that create the dramatic focus. Some of the biblical references include a Judas-like betrayal by Cypher, Neo's wound in his side, and his dramatic resurrection.

Focus: Science fantasy has become a way of imaginatively interpreting transcendent themes. The Matrix *imagines life and death, alternative worlds, other dimensions, and the possibility of love and resurrection as celebrated in today's Easter liturgy.*

DIALOGUE WITH THE GOSPEL

The Acts of the Apostles offers a résumé of the impact Jesus had as the Anointed One through his saving life, death, and resurrection. He is to judge everyone, living and dead, as the prophets had foretold. The Wachowski brothers drew on the Jesus story as a contribution to their own cyberspace, "otherworldly" myth-making in *The Matrix.*

Paul speaks about resurrection to new life in Christ. It is not too hard to compare Trinity and Neo with Mary Magdalene and Jesus. Trinity declares her love for the seemingly dead Neo. She kisses him, willing him back to life. Mary Magdalene's love and devotion compel her to seek Jesus who had disappeared from the tomb. It is she who is the first to see the risen Christ. While it is easy to understand why the Wachowski brothers chose Morpheus as the name for the leader who moves in and out of a waking and sleeping state, one can ponder why the leading lady is actually called Trinity.

Neo lives with the knowledge that all is not well with the world. Morpheus and his group recognize him as a chosen messiah-figure, but Neo does not become the superhero until Morpheus rescues him from certain death. Neo uses his wits and strength but, like true heroes, he is a "wounded healer." He dies, is raised to new life, and, with this new life, is able to save the world. No longer "Neo," he is the "One."

- Neo the hacker, the confrontation by Trinity, the agents searching his workplace, Morpheus trying to lead him; Neo's capture, interrogation, and the loss of his mouth; the explanation of the Matrix, human

KEY SCENES AND THEMES

beings as slaves to their own creation, Sion as the final refuge, and the technologically created world that is an illusion.

- Morpheus's hope that Neo is "The One," Neo's uncertainty; Cypher becoming Neo's "Judas"; Neo's visit to the Oracle and interpretation of her prophecies.

- The apocalyptic battle in the city streets, buildings, and underground railways, the shape-changing evil agents; Trinity loving Neo back into life; the resurrected Neo conquering the Matrix and giving life back to human beings.

FOR REFLECTION AND CONVERSATION

1. "Matrix" means "womb," an ambiance in which something is enclosed, the giver of life, the source that protects and nourishes humankind. The matrix of this film, however, is a human creation that has embraced and taken control of the world. Once again, a motion picture asks us to reflect on the role of technology in our lives, and what it means to be human. In what ways do these films compare? What do they say about human beings versus or vis-à-vis the computer?

2. No one remains neutral after experiencing *The Matrix;* people seem to either love or hate the film. Some see it as a search for faith; others see it as a vehicle for nihilism. It is interesting to note that the film itself is also a matrix. It is a kind of grid that holds intersecting ideas and themes that are expressed through the action, the decaying city, landscapes, and purposeful music. Across the top of the grid are the concept of the human person, human freedom, the meaning of a name, faith, reality, and how we "know." Down the side we have themes such as literature, Judeo-Chris-

tian religion, Eastern religion and thought, science and technology, and Western philosophy. How is each theme represented in the film? What is the function of each? What do you think the Wachowski brothers are trying to say via this speculative science fiction film? What is the film saying about our ability to question the consequences of our ability to "know" reality? How is the film a parallel to the Christian story?

3. There are several ways to approach *The Matrix*: as science fiction, science fantasy, or speculative fiction; as a martial arts flick; a comic book in live action; as the centuries-old question, "How do I know I know?" in twenty-first century terms; as a fresh interpretation of Christian biblical stories and tradition; as the universal need for salvation, an expression of spiritual searching in a high tech universe. How do these descriptions, or others you may think of, express your experience of *The Matrix*?

Prayer

Jesus, you are the risen Lord. Help us to grow in our appreciation for your love for us as we contemplate your death and the Father's love in raising you to new life. Amen.

SECOND SUNDAY OF EASTER

Acts 4:32–35; 1 John 5:1–6;
John 20:19–31

Cast Away

U.S.A., 2000, 145 minutes
Cast: Tom Hanks, Helen Hunt, Chris Noth, Nick Searcy
Writer: William Broyles, Jr.
Director: Robert Zemeckis

Cast Away

Alive Again

SYNOPSIS

Chuck Noland is a time and efficiency expert who works for FedEx. He works at the international level and helps to establish his company in Moscow.

He returns home to Memphis for Christmas intending to propose to his girlfriend, Kelly. He is called away suddenly to fill in for a training instructor in Asia and promises to be back for New Year's Eve.

On the flight out, his plane crashes in the Pacific, the crew dies, and Chuck is marooned on a tropical island. Tides prevent his sailing away. He has to cope with finding food and making shelter for survival. One of his greatest challenges is trying to light a fire.

He retrieves FedEx packages that wash to shore, and one of them contains a volleyball. Chuck paints a face on it and names it "Wilson," the name of the company that produced the ball. Over the years, Wilson becomes his companion and confidant. Chuck adapts to his timeless existence, although sometimes he is profoundly tempted to despair.

After four years of isolation, some corrugated plastic washes up on the beach and Chuck builds a raft. He sets off with enthusiasm, but soon drifts on the open sea, seeming to go nowhere. He is particularly distressed when he loses Wilson, who floats away.

Rescued by a freighter, he returns home to find that Kelly, presuming that he was dead, is now married and has a child. Chuck realizes that he must leave her to her new life. He goes to the Midwest to deliver a parcel that had washed ashore on the island with him and which he never opened. There is an angel design on its packaging. Shortly after, a woman in a pickup truck with angel wings on the tailgate sees Chuck stopped at a crossroads, checking his map. "Where are you headed?" she asks. And he answers, "I was just about to figure that out."

Cast Away is rather predictable—what else can one do to survive except collect rainwater, spear fish, try to get a fire going, and write "Help" in letters as large as possible in the sand? Yet, the predictable is enjoyable simply by seeing *how* the movie fulfills the expected. *Cast Away* asks not "what if?" but "how?"

COMMENTARY

Director Robert Zemeckis has had a successful career with his ability to tap into popular tastes. His films include *Romancing the Stone,* the *Back to the Future* series, *Who Framed Roger Rabbit, Contact, What Lies Beneath,* and *Forrest Gump,* for which he won an Academy Award. Tom Hanks, nominated for an Oscar for his role as Chuck, manages to infuse his role with humanity and credibility.

Cast Away begins on an isolated and deserted road in a rural section of the U.S.A. The camera pans to a crossroads. *Cast Away* ends at the same crossroads, but this time Chuck is there, studying a map. He has asked directions. He knows the options. He smiles gently to himself about the road he will choose.

Focus: It is a shock when someone who is believed to be dead reappears. Thomas found renewed faith in Jesus. Chuck Roland, the castaway, "comes to life again" and deals with a new lease on life.

Normal human experience is that the dead do not come back to life. Their memory can remain strong and their spirit can continue to inspire us, but they are gone from our midst.

Thomas could not imagine Jesus actually being alive after his crucifixion—no matter what the other apostles said. When Jesus invites him to touch his wounds, Thomas's self-assurance and doubt are shattered. He exclaims, "My Lord and my God."

Chuck Noland has a death experience. His plane crashes; he is washed ashore on an isolated island, a limbo where he might die. During the four years of being a physical, psychological, and emotional castaway, Chuck experiences a gradual "resurrection." He appreciates his life, adapts to a simpler existence, and sheds the compulsive drive that had once given meaning to his life. He is sustained by love and hope. Though tempted to give up, he never does.

When Chuck returns home, it is as if he has risen from the dead. He tries to reassure people that he is still the same person. Their response is a mixture of hesitancy and joy. Jesus inspires faith in his disciples, and they believe in his message and mission; they believe in him. Chuck has to make a new life for himself. He has to leave his past behind and believe in the values he learned on the island. Some of these values are praised in the first reading's description of the early Jerusalem communities. Chuck becomes a witness to more human and more spiritual values, reminding us of Jesus' witness to the ultimate power of life over death.

- Chuck giving pep talks, the efficiency exercise in Moscow; the contrast with the isolation on the island, a different pace of life, a different way of doing every-thing, a new appreciation of who he is.

- Chuck cutting his hand, smearing the blood on the ball and creating Wilson; his communication with Wilson; taking Wilson with him on the raft, losing the volleyball, swimming with the raft in tow, trying to retrieve Wilson; his grief when Wilson floats out of sight.

- Chuck's relationship with Kelly, his promise to return to her; Kelly's response to his "resurrection," his love for Kelly that enables him to leave her and let her live her new life; Chuck finally standing at the crossroads.

FOR REFLECTION AND CONVERSATION

1. At first glance *Cast Away* may not seem like a religious film per se. However, from the very beginning we are invited to consider the spiritual dimension of human life. Some images of the spiritual are light and dark-ness, water, eyes, time, crossroads, the whale, Christ-mas, Al giving his life for Chuck, the pilot's death, Chuck's climb to the top of the cliff, and his despair. What does the symbolism of the angel wings mean at the beginning, during, and at the end of the film? Why is the package with the wings on it the only one Chuck doesn't open? What other image of wings appears in the story? How are these symbols, and others you may notice, related to Chuck's resurrection? How do all these elements, including the music, work to-gether to create spiritual meaning? What do they mean to you?

2. Every element in a film has at least one purpose. Consider this film's title, for example. What is the difference between "cast away" and "castaway"? What does

the title indicate about the story? Who or what is cast away in the film? Is Chuck really a castaway in the dictionary sense of the word? What commentary does the film make on American culture and spirituality in the light of the term "cast away"?

3. Product placement, a mainstay of the principle of media literacy education, says that all forms of entertainment and information media are created realities with commercial interests. FedEx and its logo is a "star" in this film, and very prominent in *The Runaway Bride* as well. What other products and services seem to be promoted in this film and other movies and television shows you may have seen? What role does FedEx play in the film? Besides product placement, does it also have the opposite effect of moving us beyond the commercial and materialistic aspects of our life to consider the spiritual dimension of the human person and society? Why or why not?

Prayer

Jesus, you died and rose to new life. Help us to recognize when people have changed, and lovingly support them as they move into a new life. Amen.

The Legend of Bagger Vance

U.S.A., 2001, 135 minutes
Cast: Will Smith, Matt Damon, Charlize Theron,
J. Michael Moncrief, Bruce McGill, Joel Gretsch,
Lane Smith, Jack Lemmon
Writer: Jeremy Leven
Director: Robert Redford

The Legend of Bagger Vance

On the Emmaus Road

SYNOPSIS

Rannulph Junuh is the golden boy of golf who wins the Georgia Open at the age of sixteen. He is in love with Adele Invergordon, daughter of a Savannah businessman. When Junuh volunteers to fight in World War I, he leaves for Europe in a blaze of glory, but his combat experiences traumatize him so deeply that he loses all self-confidence and his golf swing. When he finally returns to Savannah after an absence of twelve years, he spends his time drinking and playing cards with his African-American friends.

John Invergordon has built the most luxurious golf course in Georgia. Following his suicide at the onset of the Great Depression, creditors demand compensation from his daughter, Adele. She impulsively promises to host a golf championship that will attract people to the golf club and make it a financial success. Using her considerable charm, she manipulates two champions into participating. When the townspeople complain that there is no Savannah contestant, young Hardy Greaves suggests that Junuh play and tries to persuade him to enter the competition. Junuh finally consents.

Bagger Vance, a vagabond, bets Junuh that he can win and offers to be his caddy for five dollars. He helps Junuh to train hard for the tournament, face his demons, and acknowledge his love for Adele.

Junuh plays erratically, but relies on Bagger's wisdom and Hardy's support. As victory seems a real possibility, Junuh regains his swing and his self-confidence. Bagger moves on, leaving Junuh to win on his own.

COMMENTARY

Golf is not a sport that readily lends itself to screen drama. While there have been biographies of champions like Ben Hogan (*Follow the Sun*, 1951), or comedies like *Caddyshack*, the major golf movie is Ron Shelton's *Tin Cup* (1995) with Kevin Costner.

Robert Redford's movie is based on the novel by Steven Pressfield and allows its audience to follow the golf tournament process closely and clearly. Redford, however, is more interested in golf as a metaphor for life. The movie is a "legend." As with fly-fishing in *A River Runs Through It*, golf is used as an analogy for the human struggle.

Rannulph Junuh, played by Matt Damon, is a hero, a young sports champion, and a decorated soldier. Disillusioned by the horrors of war, he has abandoned any effort to regain control of his life. Adele, played by Charlize Theron, still loves him, though she is desperately hurt by his neglect.

Will Smith gives a pleasingly restrained performance as the unexpected mentor that guides Junuh in his struggles and leads him to rehabilitation. Some viewers, however, may find Will Smith as Bagger Vance implausible because of the racism and bigotry toward African-Americans in the 1930s era South.

DIALOGUE WITH THE GOSPEL

Focus: Jesus' disciples experienced a profound disappointment and shock at his death. The disciples who walked to Emmaus with Jesus had their eyes opened, and they rediscovered Jesus as the risen Lord. Bagger Vance accompanies Rannulph Junuh during the championship golf tournament and helps open his eyes to new life as well.

The Easter season offers us a spirituality of hope. If Jesus can undergo such suffering and death and rise to new life, as his followers, we, too, can experience God's grace and support as we struggle with our own sufferings.

Today's Gospel describes the aftermath of one of the most celebrated walks of all time—when Jesus accompanied the disciples on the road to Emmaus. They had given up hope in him. It was only when Jesus joined them on the road and reminded them of what they had experienced while he was with them, that their courage returned. Back in Jerusalem, they found that Jesus had appeared to the other disciples who had also found new hope. Jesus then appears to all of them again to reinforce the lesson that it is through suffering that we come to a new life.

Peter's preaching in the reading from Acts powerfully demonstrates the result of the disciples learning what Jesus taught them. The reading from the first Letter of John describes how they will now keep God's word and live in God's love.

Rannulph Junuh is an "Everyman" figure. He is a young, heroic American, a golf champion—and a victim of the injustice of grim warfare in the trenches of World War I. Savannah is his old home, the Emmaus that he returns to. Shattered and unable to see any hopeful possibilities for his life after his battle experiences, he seems incapable of rising to new life.

The mysterious Bagger Vance joins him on what will be his journey to recovery: the golf tournament. Bagger Vance is a genial stranger, a modest caddy, and the catalyst for Junuh's eyes to be opened in self-awareness. Bagger reminds him of his talent and helps him to reawaken his love for Adele.

When Junuh recovers hope and embraces his life, Bagger Vance disappears to accompany others on their Emmaus walk, as Jesus must have done after the disciples recognized him.

KEY SCENES AND THEMES

- The successful Rannulph Junuh as golf champion, status in Savannah society and with Adele; going off to war in a blaze of glory; the bitterness of trench warfare and death; Junuh's loss of nerve, finally returning home, but avoiding any involvement with golf and old friends.

- The casual arrival of Bagger Vance, his genial company, his work as caddy and coach, his role as a catalyst for Junuh's recovery; Bagger's departure before the victory.

- The golf tournament and what it means to Junuh's self-respect, his game, and his swing; the support of Hardy, Bagger, and the people; the ups and downs of the game, the final victory.

FOR REFLECTION AND CONVERSATION

1. *The Legend of Bagger Vance* philosophizes about life and offers us religious imagery to ponder as we journey with the characters from sorrow and difficulty to triumph and new life. What other elements does *The Legend of Bagger Vance* provide that might evoke a spiritual response from the audience? How does this particular game of golf parallel the Emmaus walk?

2. The Scots devised golf more than five hundred years ago. Today, there are more than fourteen thousand golf courses in the United States and twenty-four million people play golf at least once a year. Jokes about "golf widows" abound. These statistics place the game of golf prominently in the national consciousness.

How is golf presented as a metaphor for life in *The Legend of Bagger Vance?* How does the advice of Bagger Vance help Junuh heal and grow as a person? Contrast the worldview of Walter, Junuh, and Bagger. Who grows and changes? What is your worldview and how does it affect the choices you make every day?

3. *The Legend of Bagger Vance* presents a black man as Junuh's guardian angel and the means of his salvation. It seems unlikely that an African-American would have done what Bagger did in the American South of the 1930s, as both the film and the novel on which it is based propose. Yet, Bagger is the hero of the story and the means of bringing peace and new life to Junuh. How are issues of race, social class, age, and the role of women represented in the film? Why might these issues be important to any conversation about justice in entertainment and information media? How do justice and peace work together to create a culture that is truly human and reflects the grace that the presence of the risen Christ gives?

Prayer

Jesus, we ask you to walk with us so that we can understand our struggles. Give us the confidence to hope in our rising to new life. Amen.

Jack Lemmon and Željko Ivanek in *Mass Appeal*.

Mass Appeal

U.S.A., 1984, 96 minutes
Cast: Jack Lemmon, Željko Ivanek,
Charles Durning, Louise Latham
Writer: Bill C. Davis
Director: Glenn Jordan

 *Mass Appeal*

Priestly Leadership

During a "dialogue sermon," a young jogger named Mark Dolson asks questions of the parish priest, Fr. Farley. It turns out that Mark is a transitional deacon, a seminarian just finishing his studies. The seminary staff finds him abrasive. When two seminarians are suddenly expelled, he angrily questions the seminary rector, Monsignor Burke.

SYNOPSIS

Fr. Farley pleads Mark's cause with Monsignor Burke who, in turn, asks him to train Mark in his own parish for a month to test his suitability for the priesthood. Though Fr. Farley coaches Mark for his first homily in the parish, Mark becomes aggressive and alienates the parishioners.

However, Fr. Farley appreciates Mark's passion and tries to help him reach a greater level of maturity. The sincere young man impresses Fr. Farley, who is dependent on the parishioners' good opinion of him, drinks too much, and tells white lies to get out of doing what he doesn't want to do. They talk frankly to each other about their lives and their families.

Fr. Farley gives Mark another chance at a sermon. Mark delivers it in a more heartfelt manner, and it is well received by the congregation. This annoys Monsignor Burke, who expels Mark from the seminary. A drunken Fr. Farley tells off

Monsignor Burke. He tries to get support for Mark from the parishioners but fails. Mark and Fr. Farley talk things through. Fr. Farley speaks with great feeling about his own priesthood at Mass, and Mark leaves.

COMMENTARY

Mass Appeal was a popular stage play produced in the 1980s. Written by Bill C. Davis, it echoed the changes in parishes, seminaries, and priestly life in the Church in the United States after the Second Vatican Council (1962–1965). The movie's dialogue, as well as the portrayal of a priest's life, is authentic. It represents the clashes between the sometimes more authoritarian, ecclesiastical clergy and the younger, sometimes brasher, seminarians and priests in those years.

During his long and impressive career, Jack Lemmon assumed a wide range of both comic and serious roles. His portrayal of Fr. Farley, who is a good man with painful memories of family problems, is realistic and credible. Lemmon's character is matched by the intensity and single-mindedness of Željko Ivanek's portrayal of Mark Dolson.

Charles Durning is the bullying seminary rector, and Louise Latham brings some light relief as everyone's idea of a pleasant, but anxious, rectory housekeeper.

DIALOGUE WITH THE GOSPEL

Focus: To be popular or to have mass appeal, no matter how attractive it is to preachers, is not the first quality for leadership in the Church. The pattern of Jesus, the Good Shepherd, is one of loving and protecting the sheep, and laying down his life for them.

The first reading continues the narrative of the Easter ministry of the Apostles. Mark Dolson imitates the forthrightness of Peter during Peter's confrontational sermon to the authorities. Peter points out that the stone rejected by the authorities has become the cornerstone. Perhaps this will be the image that Mark Dolson's spiritual journey will leave with viewers.

However, the focus of the Gospel is on Jesus as the Good Shepherd. This image of a loving shepherd challenges the Church to ask what kind of leadership is required for today's Church and what kind of priests are needed to minister to people in a changing world. The Gospel shows us a Jesus who knows each of the sheep by name. They listen to him because he is a genuine shepherd. Jesus gives his life to protect the sheep that God, his Father, has entrusted to him.

The issues about priesthood and Church leadership dramatized in *Mass Appeal* are still valid, though the film was made in 1984. Fr. Farley tries to live out the Gospel mandates and be a good priest, but his own neediness has prevented him from being as self-giving a pastor as he wants to be. Yet, he is a good man who, at his stage of life, needs to be challenged once again.

Mark Dolson suffered a difficult home life and has seen the world. His capacity for love has been tested in all kinds of ways, and he has responded to a vocation of celibacy and ministry. He is trapped by his own anger and idealism, and comes across as brazen and critical. He does not fit the "priestly mold."

The final truth-telling encounter between the two men, and their acknowledgment of past hurts, enables each to become a better person. They look to the model of the Good Shepherd as the ideal of self-giving ministry.

KEY SCENES AND THEMES

- The dialogue sermon, Fr. Farley's agreeable style, and Mark's questions; Mark's persistence and the effect on the people and Fr. Farley.

- The issue of the expulsion of the seminarians and the approach taken by Monsignor Burke; Fr. Farley questioning the students; Mark finding them gone and his outburst at the meeting; Monsignor Burke interviewing him about his sexuality.

• Mark's aggressive sermon, not following advice, the criticism of the people; Mark and Fr. Farley working together, their talk about their families and their past, the mutual confession; Mark being prepared for his second sermon, the delivery, and its effect; Fr. Farley's confrontation with Mark and punching him; Fr. Farley's final words and his honesty with his parishioners.

**FOR REFLECTION
AND
CONVERSATION**

1. Leadership is the ability to hold an office and/or to guide, direct, and influence people. In the Year A cycle of readings, *Erin Brockovich* is the film considered for this Good Shepherd Sunday, and we contemplate her ability to lead, guide, and influence the people of Hinkley, California, in their struggle against a giant utilities company. *Mass Appeal* is a film about leadership as well, though this year we move from the conflict in a small town to the world of the Church and dramatic conflicts in parish and seminary. Our focus is directed on the clergy. Who emerges as a leader in *Mass Appeal?* Why? How are the characteristics of a leader evident in the development of the characters and the action?

2. *Mass Appeal* takes place in a post-Vatican Council II environment that consisted in many changes in the way the Catholic Church viewed itself and the world. These changes touched every part of Church life and even today, forty years later, its teachings and effects can still cause controversy, misunderstanding, and lack of charity. On the other hand, the Council paved the way for growth in many areas, including a more meaningful life and ministry for both clergy and laity, together the People of God. Compare the personal,

seminary, and parish clashes in *Mass Appeal* with your own ecclesial experience. How real are they? Compare how these conflicts are resolved in the film. Are these resolutions still valid for situations that may occur today?

3. Mark Dolson is an intriguing character, because at the end of the film we don't know where he really came from or where he is going. Is he believable as a real person, or is he a dramatic device, a kind of mythic character who takes us through the story? Does he represent someone? If so, who? Why is Mark in danger of being rejected? How does his manner of telling the truth get in the way of the truth he wishes to tell? How is this a film about authenticity and authentic leadership?

Prayer

Lord, you knew your sheep by name and laid down your life to protect them. Give your Church leaders who will be good shepherds like you. Amen.

FIFTH SUNDAY OF EASTER

Acts 9:26–31; 1 John 3:18–24;
John 15:1–8

The Mighty

U.S.A., 1998, 92 minutes
Cast: Kieran Culkin, Elden Henson, Sharon Stone, Gena
Rowlands, Harry Dean Stanton, Gillian Anderson,
James Gandolfini, Meat Loaf
Writer: Charles Leavitt
Director: Peter Chelsom

 *The Mighty*

One in Friendship

SYNOPSIS

Max, who is a large and heavy boy, narrates the story in chapters, as if from a book. He is a slow learner who has flunked seventh grade twice, mostly because he cannot read. Max lives with his maternal grandparents. He is afraid he will grow up to be like his father, Kenny, who is in prison for killing Max's mother.

Kevin, who suffers from a birth defect, and his mother Gwen, move in next door. The boys go to the same school and Kevin the "Freak" is assigned to be Max's reading tutor. The boys soon become friends.

Kevin asks Max to take him to the River Fair to see the fireworks. Max lifts the fragile Kevin onto his shoulders so that he, too, can see the world. Together they consider themselves to be a single unit, combining brains and strength. Kevin loves the Arthurian legends and the boys carry out deeds of valor against the local gang.

Kenny gets out of jail, and he abducts Max on Christmas Eve. Kevin goes on a quest to rescue Max and saves the day. A week later the two families celebrate Christmas, and Kevin gives Max a blank book to write in. That night, Kevin dies in his sleep. Eventually, Max puts his grief aside and begins to write the story of "Freak, the Mighty."

The Mighty is a blend of "buddy" movie and fantasy story based on Rodman Philbrick's 1993 novel, *Freak, The Mighty*. The story is set in a working class neighborhood in Cincinnati and this environment gives the film its realism. On the other hand, King Arthur and the Knights of the Round Table appear every so often and this furnishes a mythic touch to this American urban story. *The Mighty* is a variation on stories like John Steinbeck's *Of Mice and Men* and John Irving's *A Prayer for Owen Meany* on which the film *Simon Birch* was based.

Kieran Culkin plays the deformed and very intelligent Freak in a forceful and imaginative way in this encouraging story. Elden Henson is very good as the awkward and self-consciously slow Max, and James Gandolfini, star of *The Sopranos*, is convincing as his criminal father.

Englishman Peter Chelsom is the film's director, and his previous movies include the Irish/Liverpool story *Hear My Song* and *Funnybones* starring Jerry Lewis. In *The Mighty* he brings a human touch to the story and to the fine, somewhat self-effacing performances of Sharon Stone as Kevin's mother and Gillian Anderson as the alcoholic Loretta.

Focus: The image of the vine and the branches is a reflection of our union with God and love for neighbor. The Mighty *is an analogy of these bonds and offers a story of unity and friendship.*

Today's Gospel presents the oneness of the vine and the branches as a way to understand the relationship between the Father and Son. This is a model for the disciples who are to be one with Jesus for the sake of the community of his followers.

The story of Max and Kevin is a Gospel parallel. In *The Mighty*, it is only when the boys combine brains and brawn to become a single unit that they can accomplish noble deeds during their quests. If our union with Jesus is real, mystical, and grace-filled, we can then "bear much fruit" through our love for God and neighbor. We can follow the example of Jesus who laid down his life in love for us in concrete ways if we listen to his teaching and follow his example. The film's story of friendship helps us understand today's Gospel, because it is as if the Gospel has come alive and we can hear and more fully appreciate what Jesus is saying.

When Kevin goes to rescue Max after his father abducts him, it seems implausible and impossible that he will be able to save him. But with the strength of the friendship and the bonds that have been forged between the boys, it happens. Even after Kevin is dead, his spirit lives on in Max so that he has the courage to write down his "good news" about Kevin and how much his friend meant to him. As Jesus promised, his Spirit continues to live on in us, his followers, so that we may bear much fruit in living out the Good News.

KEY SCENES AND THEMES

- The way the local gang treats Max on the street, in class, and in the gym; how they ridicule him and Kevin when he appears at the basketball court, rolling the ball to make him fall and blaming Max; Kevin teaching Max to read, opening up the Arthurian legends with noble deeds and quests; the appearance of the knights and the king.

- The two boys, one on the shoulders of the other, becoming a unit; how they walk the streets, delight in the fireworks, cheer people on, run from the gang into the water, and retrieve the stolen purse; Kevin showing off in the cafeteria and choking, Max anxious and saving him.

- Kevin's quest to save Max, going through the streets, the park, and the snow; Max's grief at Kevin's death; Max taking out the book and starting to write their story.

1. Kevin has a condition called Morquio's Syndrome. It is a very rare genetic disorder that hinders cartilage from becoming bone and results in skeletal deformities, dwarfism, and death when the body can no longer cope. The stories of Kevin, Max, and other characters (such as Helen Keller and Simon Birch) whose abilities are challenged or who are different from the norm society establishes, engage us through film, literature, and television. We see how they are truly human and how they live fruitful, meaningful lives despite being "pruned." Think of literary or film characters whose stories impressed you. How are they models for us in day-to-day living, along with Kevin and Max?

2. *The Mighty* is a strong, dark film with much religious symbolism. Kevin and Max are children who represent light in that darkness and hope for parents, grandparents, families, and communities. How are Max and Kevin the vine and the branches? How do they bear fruit? Is either of the boys a Christ-figure? If so, how? How is water a sacramental sign in the film? What are the sacramental signs and symbols that give meaning to my own life?

3. Hope is trust and a confident desire in a reality beyond ourselves. It is also a virtue, a habit of good that transcends the selfishness of living only for one's own interests. Hope is eager, bright, and buoyant. It is a break in the clouds of doubt and a promise of good things to come based on the very promises of God

who is loving, faithful, and infinite. How is *The Mighty*—already a story of relationships, friendships, and families—really about the virtue of hope in God and in humanity?

Prayer

Lord Jesus, you are the vine and we are your branches. Help us to share this unity with our friends and those we love. Amen.

The Third Miracle
U.S.A., 1999, 114 minutes
Cast: Ed Harris, Anne Heche, Armin Mueller-Stahl,
Barbara Sukowa, Charles Haid
Writers: John Romano, Richard Vetere
Director: Agnieszka Holland

The Third Miracle

Household Saint

SYNOPSIS

Bombs fall on a Slovakian village toward the end of World War II. A little girl prays that they will not hit the ground and destroy her village. It seems her prayer is heard. There is no explosion or sound, and a flock of birds mysteriously flies away. A young German soldier witnesses this "miracle."

Thirty-five years later in Chicago, Fr. Frank Shore, the archdiocesan postulator for causes of saints, is in crisis after proving that a venerated local priest was not a saint or a miracle worker. Shore thinks he is responsible for destroying the faith of an entire community, which calls him "the miracle killer." Bishop Cahill now asks Fr. Shore to examine the miracles attributed to a simple local laywoman, Helen.

Fr. Shore is skeptical, but soon begins to believe that the woman may prove to be a saint, restoring his own faith in God and in himself. Helen's daughter Roxane does not testify in her mother's favor; she feels Helen abandoned her as a teenager by going to live in a nearby convent. Things become complicated when Fr. Shore and Roxane become attracted to one another.

A group of ecclesiastics, headed by Archbishop Werner, comes from Rome to discuss whether the woman's cause for canonization should go ahead. Werner is particularly loath to promote "little housewife saints" instead of martyrs. Werner demands that Fr. Shore recite the creed and denounces him for his lack of faith when he will not do so. The story of the bombing raid on the Slovakian village emerges, along with Helen's possible miraculous involvement.

As the hearings continue, Fr. Shore confronts the archbishop for his illogical, arrogant manner. Shortly after, Werner summons Fr. Shore and reveals that he was the German soldier who witnessed the miracle of the unexploding bombs that fell on the Slovak village. The little girl who prayed was Helen.

COMMENTARY

Director Agnieszka Holland was born in Poland and began her filmmaking career working with Polish Catholic director Krzysztof Zanussi. Holland's background is Jewish, yet she has made two films about Catholic characters with great sensitivity, including *To Kill a Priest* (1988), a movie about the real-life Warsaw martyr, Jerzy Popieluszko, starring Christopher Lambert and Ed Harris. *The Third Miracle,* based on the novel by Richard Vetere, is a serious and thoughtful drama that asks: are miracles still possible in today's world?

In *The Third Miracle,* the focus is three-fold. First, it rests on the spiritual state of the priest who is asked to investigate the life of a possible saint; second, it looks at Helen's life that may have indeed been marked by heroic virtue; and finally, it reveals the inner workings of the hierarchical Church and its leaders.

Ed Harris gives a most credible performance as the priest who struggles with his faith and who needs a miracle as much as anyone else. The woman's daughter, played by Anne Heche, has no belief and still resents the memory of her mother.

There are various portrayals of clergy in the film: Charles Haid's golfing, money-dealing bishop; and curial officials, especially Armin Mueller-Stahl's aristocratic presence as the representative from Rome. There is an authentic feel about the way the Church is presented, warts and all, as well as sympathy for those who experience a crisis of faith, and tolerance for various expressions of piety.

Focus: Jesus' commandment is to love one another as he loved us, to keep his commandments and remain in his love. The *Third Miracle shows an ordinary woman who has tried to keep the commandment of love.*

DIALOGUE WITH THE GOSPEL

The first verses of the responsorial psalm remind us that God has shown his salvation for the nations and worked wonders for them. In the first reading, the pagan Cornelius receives the gift of the Spirit. In the reading from John's letter, we hear that Jesus is the revelation of God's love and that we will have life through him.

In looking at the character of Helen, we see today's Gospel "come alive"—her holiness is a practical illumination of the Gospel. Even as a child in war-torn Slovakia, she was concerned for others and prayed that the bombs would not destroy the people in her village. After moving to America, she quietly cared for her terminally ill husband for many years, raised her daughter, worked with the sisters, and brought laughter and ultimately healing to children. She is considered for canonization because she loved others as Jesus loved her. The miracles that are worked through her are the concrete revelations of God's power, mercy, and love for the world.

On her journey to canonization, Helen's example touches the lives of many people and personifies Jesus' words that everyone will know his disciples by the love they have for one another.

KEY SCENES AND THEMES

- Slovakia, the war, the refugees, the bombs, Helen's prayer; the German soldier and his identity later revealed; the bleeding statue and those who believe in Helen's holiness in Chicago, the healings.

- Fr. Shore's crisis of faith, his acceptance of the assignment, his great desire that Helen be proclaimed a saint; Roxanne's lack of faith, her anger at her mother.

- The ecclesiastical hearings, the truth about Slovakia, the confrontation between priest and archbishop, the nature of sanctity; the archbishop and his acknowledgement of the miracle in Slovakia.

FOR REFLECTION AND CONVERSATION

1. Miracles are events that contravene the laws of nature. Because there is no natural explanation for them, some people have difficulty believing even in the miracles of Jesus, let alone more recent ones attributed to modern saints. What are the miracles highlighted in this film? Are they true miracles? Why or why not? How many miracles are needed for a person to be canonized a saint? Why? What is the purpose of the canonization process? What are the criteria for canonization? (Cf. *Catechism of the Catholic Church*, n. 828.)

2. Some viewers think that *The Third Miracle* is a "small" and insignificant movie compared to the pseudo-religious, pop mega-hits, such as the *End of Days* or even *The Exorcist*. For others, the flirting that goes on between Fr. Shore and Roxanne is distracting. Some think that, in order for the film to be credible, Fr. Shore must explicitly declare his faith by kneeling in front of the German prelate and reciting the creed. What is the third miracle in this film? What is the most significant miracle in the film? How does the end of the film work for you? Besides love, do Fr. Shore and

the others find the joy that Jesus speaks of in the Gospel? As the film seems to ask, are miracles ever wasted?

3. Love for one another, rooted in faith and action, is the theme of today's Scripture readings. Jesus specifically asks that his disciples remain in his love, that they keep his commandments. Helen does a strange thing that the film never quite explains: she abandons her sixteen-year-old daughter, the fruit of the love she and her husband shared, to serve the Church for the love of God. Was Helen right to do this? Why might Helen have thought this was what God wanted her to do? Is Helen's holiness really the point of the story? If not, what do you think is the real point, and why might this be important in today's religious climate?

Prayer

Lord, we hear your command that we must love others as you love us, even to laying down our life for others. Help us remain in your love. Amen.

The Mission

U.K., 1986, 125 minutes
Cast: Robert De Niro, Jeremy Irons, Ray McAnally,
Aidan Quinn, Liam Neeson, Daniel Berrigan
Writer: Robert Bolt
Director: Roland Joffé

 *The Mission*

That They May Be One

SYNOPSIS

It is 1758 and the Vatican begins to take a highly critical view of the Jesuits. Among the complaints against them are the Jesuits' involvement in commerce, their influence on European rulers and politics, and their missionary work among the Indians in South America. Colonial Spain and Portugal are particularly hostile toward the Jesuits.

Fr. Gabriel travels above treacherous waterfalls to get to the highlands of Brazil to minister to the native Indians. He attracts them through music, and brings them together to form settlements. Many Indians begin to learn to read and write.

Rodrigo Mendoza, a slave trader who traps Indians and sells them to colonial families, kills his brother over a woman. He has a spiritual conversion and travels with Fr. Gabriel above the falls. In a journey rife with symbolism, he carries all his armor and weapons in a bundle on his back until an Indian boy cuts the ropes and he is freed of his burden. Eventually, Mendoza asks to join the Jesuits, although he finds obedience difficult—especially when the missionaries must defend the mission against military attacks by the Spanish and Portuguese, but are told not to use violence.

Meanwhile, a Vatican official is visiting the missions to investigate the complaints made by Spanish and Portuguese officials who believe the mission interferes with their slave trading. The official's report will have definitive consequences for the Jesuit missions.

Fr. Gabriel, obeying orders not to take up arms, is martyred, standing in solidarity with the non-violent Indians outside the church. Mendoza chooses to go with the Indians who wish to fight the European soldiers. Everyone is massacred.

The pope suppresses the Jesuit order in 1773.

COMMENTARY

The Mission is the work of distinguished playwright and screenwriter Robert Bolt, who also published an adapted version as a novel the year of the film's release. Bolt has received much deserved acclaim for his films *Lawrence of Arabia, Doctor Zhivago, Ryan's Daughter, Lady Caroline Lamb* and *The Bounty*—as well as for his best-known work, *A Man for All Seasons.* Here, he combines his love for sweeping sagas with his interest in religion, Church and State, and matters of conscience.

Filmed on location in South America and, with a now-famous score by Ennio Morricone, *The Mission* is an impressive visual and aural experience. The film is also notable for its portrait of eighteenth-century missionary work in South America.

Robert De Niro is the aggressive and fearsome slave-trader and Jeremy Irons convincingly portrays the gentle Fr. Gabriel. Aidan Quinn and Liam Neeson, then both at the beginning of their successful careers, also appear. Legendary anti-war activist Daniel Berrigan, S.J. plays one of the missionaries. Roland Joffé, who also has *The Killing Fields, City of Joy,* and *Vatel* to his credit, directed the film.

DIALOGUE WITH THE GOSPEL

Focus: In his "priestly prayer," Jesus prays that his disciples will remain faithful despite the world's hatred. They are to give their lives for the truth—and it is this which motivates the priests in The Mission *to suffer martyrdom.*

The Mission recalls the "priestly prayer" in today's Gospel, because it portrays priests in situations parallel to those of Jesus. The Jesuit missionaries are criticized for their ministry and face persecution. The central characters die for the people they love and serve.

The Jesuits in the film do not belong to the world, because they are consecrated in the truth of God's word. They refuse to buy and sell human beings and to enslave them for economic or political purposes. Instead, they educate and empower the people. Thus, the world turns against these men of God.

Jesus prays not only for his disciples and their missionary activity, but also for those who will hear his word through them. Jesus prays that the world will realize how much he loved his disciples and friends, especially by laying down his life for them. His love and his death are a means to unite them in their faith and commitment after he is no longer physically with them. Jesus assures them that, as God's love will then be in them, so will he.

In a particular way, *The Mission* portrays the gentle witness of faith through the symbolism of music. The film also shows the extremes to which those who believe were willing to go to in order to defend the faithful, in imitation of Jesus.

KEY SCENES AND THEMES

- The speeches of the papal nuncio and the image he presents of Church and ecclesiastical authority; the missions, the papacy and its temporal powers and their influence.

- The mission of Fr. Gabriel, the gentle priest, and his music; how he draws the people to the mission; his personal witness even to laying down his life with the people.

- The priests and martyrs; the opening scene with the Jesuit on the cross being thrown over the waterfalls by the Indians; the priests killed by the Spanish and Portuguese; Rodrigo's conversion and death with the Indians.

1. In film, the symbol of water often implicitly or explicitly signifies religious or transcendent meaning. Trace the use of water in *The Mission*. How is water a thematic and cinematic device that moves the story along? What other significance, besides religious, might water have?

FOR REFLECTION AND CONVERSATION

2. Liberation theology is the form of theological inquiry that takes as its first principle and ordering idea the emancipation of oppressed peoples from unjust political, economic, or social subjection" (*Encyclopedia of Catholicism,* Richard P. McBrien, 1995). Liberation theology arose in Latin America in the 1960s and 1970s as a socially conscious Catholic theological response that has since influenced feminist, black, Hispanic, and other theologies. Its primary themes are a preferential option for the poor, a unity of theory and practice, a critique of ideology, and a dependence on the Word of God as its theological center. *The Mission* has several elements in common with *At Play in the Fields of the Lord, The Burning Season, Men with Guns,* and *Romero.* How might the themes of these films be

understood through the lens of liberation theology today? Have the problems that began so many centuries ago been resolved? Why or why not?

3. It is often an interesting exercise to choose a character in a film and then watch the film from that character's perspective. This activity permits us to deepen the experience of the movie and contributes to a richer conversation afterward. There are several prominent characters in *The Mission:* Rodrigo, his brother, his girlfriend, Fr. Gabriel and the other missionaries, the Indians, the young Indian who cuts the ropes of Rodrigo's burden, the papal nuncio, the Portuguese and Spanish colonists, soldiers, and kings. Who are these characters and what do they bring to the story? What point of view or ideology do they offer so that we can create meaning from the movie?

Prayer

Lord Jesus, you prayed for your apostles and for your priests. Consecrate them in your truth so that they may serve all people in love. Amen.

Acts 2:1–11; 1 Corinthians 12:3–7, 12–13;
John 20:19–23

The End of the Affair

U.S.A./U.K., 1999, 102 minutes
Cast: Ralph Fiennes, Julianne Moore, Stephen Rea, Ian Hart,
Jason Isaacs, James Bolam
Writer: Neil Jordan
Director: Neil Jordan

The End of the Affair

Sin, Forgiveness, and Miracles

SYNOPSIS

Civil servant Henry Miles and novelist Maurice Bendrix meet in London in 1946. Maurice remembers his affair with Miles' wife, Sarah, that began before the outbreak of World War II. Back then, in 1944, Sarah suddenly broke off the affair without any explanation.

Henry never knew of the affair, but he did have suspicions that something was happening. Now, he is once again suspicious of Sarah. Maurice, ever jealous himself, becomes interested and encourages Henry to hire a private detective. Henry refuses, so Maurice does, without Henry's knowledge. The detective's name is Parkis. He has a son, Lance, who always accompanies him and works as his lookout. Lance has a very notable birthmark on his face.

Parkis manages to steal Sarah's diary and gives it to Maurice. The truth is revealed: in 1944, Sarah found Maurice unconscious after a bomb raid and in a rash moment promised that if God allowed Maurice to live, she would end the affair. Maurice miraculously revived.

Sarah is now secretly visiting Fr. Smythe, who is instructing her in the Catholic faith. When she and Maurice encounter each other again, she decides to go away to Brighton

147

with him, knowing that she is breaking her promise to God. When Henry confronts them, Maurice learns that Sarah is dying of cancer. Parkis and Maurice meet at her funeral. Parkis tells Maurice that Sarah had once kissed Lance and his birthmark disappeared.

COMMENTARY

Confession and guilt over sexual sins are key themes of many Graham Greene novels. He published *The End of the Affair* in 1951, and a rather restrained or sanitized film version of the book was released in 1955, starring Deborah Kerr and Van Johnson. Neil Jordan, who has an Irish Catholic background and directed the movies *Mona Lisa, Michael Collins, The Crying Game,* and *The Butcher Boy,* adapted this most recent version of Greene's novel to produce a mature, intelligent drama.

Ralph Fiennes brings his usual intensity to the role of the writer, Maurice. Julianne Moore was nominated for an Oscar for her deeply felt and believable performance as the conflicted Sarah. Although an American, Moore seems the perfect Englishwoman. Stephen Rea, a Neil Jordan favorite, is the prim-but-grieving husband and Ian Hart is excellent as Parkis.

Sarah is a baptized, but uninstructed, non-practicing Catholic who grows in holiness through her exploration of her relationship to God. The movie differs significantly from the novel; in the film, Sarah goes back on her word to God by returning to Maurice. Nevertheless, Sarah's love for God has a literally miraculous effect on the son of the private detective. Greene and Jordan challenge their audiences to ask questions about the nature of faith and holiness and the meaning of love and self-sacrifice.

DIALOGUE WITH THE GOSPEL

Focus: The Gospel celebrates Jesus' promise to send the Spirit for the forgiveness of sins. Sarah Miles is a repentant and struggling sinner who finds grace, even sanctity, in her struggle.

The Pentecost liturgy celebrates several gifts of the Spirit to the Church. The first of these gifts, narrated in the reading from Acts, is the Spirit's abundant courage given to Jesus' fearful disciples, so that they are able to proclaim his message in many languages. The people who gathered in Jerusalem shared in this gift, amazed that they understood what the apostles were saying in the hearers' own languages. Other gifts of the Spirit are the peace given by Jesus after the resurrection, and the spirit of forgiveness to those who repent. The effects of these gifts are summarized well in the responsorial psalm refrain that asks the Lord to send the Spirit to renew the face of the earth.

Sarah Miles sees herself as a sinner. In Neil Jordan's adaptation of Greene's novel, she has to face this reality twice. The first time is when she recognizes her affair as wrong and prays for Maurice Bendrix's life. Her diary reveals that she then embarks on a journey to God. The second time is during in the final stages of her cancer when she relapses into her sin. The story shows that she is forgiven: the first time in Maurice's life being saved in answer to her prayer, and then in Lance being healed through the kindness of her touch.

The reading from Paul throws light on Sarah's experience. Paul talks about the opposition between the flesh and the Spirit. Sarah might be judged not only as a sinner, but one who continues to struggle and who lapses. Author Graham Greene wants people to know that God works in quietly mysterious ways. Paul uses this truth as a starting point to contrast the works of the flesh with the fruits of the Spirit's action in our lives. Sarah's erratic, gradual spiritual healing under the influence of the Spirit is a symbolic reminder of God's graciousness in forgiving the repentant sinner no matter what his or her offense.

- Sarah seen through Henry and Maurice's eyes, and then seen in her own words; the impact of the affair on each of these characters.

KEY SCENES AND THEMES

- Parkis and his son following Sarah, the discovery that she is seeing a priest; Parkis stealing her diary and the revelation to Maurice of her search for God.

- The bomb and Sarah's prayer, Maurice's recovery and the end of their affair; the resumption of the affair and Sarah's need for God's forgiveness, as well as that of Henry and Maurice; the meaning of her kiss that heals Lance.

FOR REFLECTION AND CONVERSATION

1. In the film, after a bombing raid, Sarah thinks Maurice is dead and she promises God she will give him up if only he will be all right. Miraculously, he is. Sarah then tells Maurice, "Love doesn't end just because we don't see each other. People go on loving God all their lives without seeing him." He says, "That's not my kind of love." Sarah responds, "Maybe there's no other kind...." What kinds of love are found in this film? At the end of the film, which of the characters has the last word? How does the film show the difference between sex, love, intimacy, and commitment or their absence?

2. The novel and film version of *The End of the Affair* practically beg to be compared. There are some detail and character changes in the film, and certainly Sarah's relapse toward the end of the film is a significant difference between the film and the novel. As the film opens, Maurice types, "This is a diary of hate." How do both the film and the novel deal with issues of love, hate, intimacy, commitment, and God's pursuit of the human soul? The film ends with Maurice once again typing, "I hate you as though you existed. You use my hate to win my acknowledgment." What does he mean?

3. When Maurice goes back into the bedroom and finds Sarah on her knees, he asks her what she is doing. She replies that she is praying. He asks what for and she says, "A miracle," and, as if they had come to some previous agreement on the matter, he says, "And we don't believe in those." How is *The End of the Affair* about miracles and faith? Talk about other parts of the film that concern God's intervention in the lives of the characters. How did the film make you feel about God's presence in your own life today? Do you think this is an appropriate film for Pentecost? Why or why not?

Prayer

Lord, as you send your Spirit to the whole Church today, send the Spirit of forgiveness and healing into our own hearts. Amen.

Black Robe

Australia/Canada, 1991, 101 minutes
Cast: Lothaire Bluteau, Auguste Schellenberg, Aden Young,
Frank Wilson, Tantoo Cardinal
Writer: Brian Moore
Director: Bruce Beresford

Black Robe

Authority in Heaven and on Earth

SYNOPSIS

It is the winter of 1634 in French Canada. The Jesuits have begun missions in the territories of the Algonquin, Huron, and Iroquois tribes. The French assume that the Native people are pagan savages with little culture, intellectually and morally ignorant, and, unless they are baptized, destined for hell. Governor Champlain is the civil administrator at a fort near Quebec. Many greedy and unscrupulous trappers pay for the Natives' furs with guns and ammunition.

The Jesuit superior persuades Champlain to allow the young and newly arrived Fr. Laforgue to canoe upstream with a contingent of Algonquins and a young French carpenter, Daniel, who speaks the Algonquins' language. The Algonquins pledge to safeguard the two Frenchmen. Daniel says he wants to be a Jesuit, but he is attracted by the Algonquin chief's daughter. He realizes that his real desire is to escape life in the fort.

During the journey, Fr. Laforgue gains insight about himself as a human being and is introduced to the wisdom of the Indians. Gradually he adopts the Algonquins' methods for survival, even when they are alien and personally repugnant.

The journey to the mission is arduous. Several of the travelers are captured by another tribe and must run the gauntlet. Fr. Laforgue finally reaches the mission outpost, only to discover that other tribes have attacked it. He stays with the Huron survivors, and finally learns to love them as people. He is no longer a missionary out of a sense of duty, but of love.

COMMENTARY

Black Robe is based on a 1985 novel by Canadian author Brian Moore. Moore adapted his novel for the movie. Other Moore novels adapted for the screen have deeply Catholic themes, such as *The Lonely Passion of Judith Hearne, Catholics,* and *Cold Heaven.*

Bruce Beresford, who is known for his ability to examine the vulnerability of the human condition and what happens when diverse cultures clash, directed the film. Some of his other films include *Tender Mercies, Driving Miss Daisy, Breaker Morant,* and *Crimes of the Heart. Black Robe* examines a Jesuit mission and its relationship with indigenous people some 120 years before that of the one portrayed in *The Mission.*

Laforgue, played by Lothaire Bluteau (*Jesus of Montreal*), only recognizes the authentic humanity of the Huron Indians when he is captured and tortured by the Iroquois. The movie is an allegory of Laforgue's own spiritual journey from a faith only understood as an assent to truth to one also understood as love for his brothers and sisters. As with *The Mission,* the film ends on a pessimistic note as we are told that a mere fifteen years later, the persecution of the Huron Indians by the Iroquois resulted in their annihilation and the closure of the Jesuit mission.

DIALOGUE WITH THE GOSPEL

Focus: The end of Matthew's Gospel has always been heard as a command to the Church for mission, to make disciples of all nations and baptize in the name of the Trinity. Black Robe *shows us how Jesuit missionaries tried to fulfill this command in seventeenth-century North America.*

All the readings reinforce God's love for his people who must listen to the divine word and keep God's law. The Gospel has Jesus' version of this command, and Jesus pledges to be with his disciples for all time if they obey his word.

The Jesuits in the film believe that they have been called and commissioned by the risen Lord. *Black Robe* shows us how these missionaries interpreted Jesus' command in a particular time and place. They were completely self-sacrificing but exercised "colonial" religious attitudes in making disciples and baptizing the indigenous people. The missionaries had to learn that the authority Jesus had from the Father, and the commands that the apostles had been given, were about love, not intellectual force. The new commandment of Jesus was to love as he did and lay down his life for his friends. The disciples were commissioned to proclaim this revelation and to baptize in the name of the Father, Son, and Holy Spirit. How to bring these inclusive elements together in mission is what we celebrate on Trinity Sunday.

KEY SCENES AND THEMES

- The Jesuits and their black robes, their community, culture, spirituality, sense of mission; their almost fundamentalist understanding of proclaiming the truth of the Gospel, the necessity of baptism for salvation.

- Fr. Laforgue, a man of prayer; an earnest missionary with a strong theological background, his absolute belief in the truth, his philosophical training and religious formation as a Jesuit; his puritanical approach to joy and sexuality, his attitude toward the Native Americans as savages; Laforgue offering hope and baptism.

- The Hurons asking how long Laforgue will stay and if he loves them, the pause as he gazes at them, remembering the Native Americans he had encountered, his declaration that he does love them; baptizing the Hurons out of love and respect rather than blind obligation.

1. *Black Robe* is a rather bleak film that contrasts the light and dark in both the lives and beliefs of the missionaries and the North American Indians. We are faced with Laforgue's philosophy, theology, determination, and personal austerity, as well as the culture, beliefs, and wisdom of the Native Americans. How and why does he grow as a person and a missionary? What challenges face contemporary missionaries today, whether at home or abroad?

2. The *Catechism of the Catholic Church,* based on the documents and decrees of the Second Vatican Council (1962–1965), addresses the mission of the Church extensively. For example, number 856 of the Catechism states, "The missionary task implies a *respectful dialogue* with those who do not yet accept the Gospel." Why is this concept not expressed in the film? How can the explicit mandate of Christ about the necessity of baptism be reconciled with the precept of respectful dialogue? What does missionary activity mean in a culture of religious dialogue?

3. *Black Robe* is sometimes described as a cross between *The Mission* and the politically correct *Dances With Wolves.* We see Jesuit missionary activity in both *The Mission* and *Shogun,* as the Jesuits seek to proclaim the Gospel to cultures different from their own. As a film representing Native Americans and Europeans, how does *Black Robe* compare to the representation of non-Europeans or Westerners in similar films? How

evenhanded are the different worldviews and cultures expressed in the film? Where does the truth about the human person emerge, if at all, in these films?

Prayer

We pray in the name of the Father, and of the Son, and of the Holy Spirit that our Christian witness will always conform to Jesus' commandment of love. Amen.

Cher in *Moonstruck.*

BODY AND BLOOD OF CHRIST

Exodus 24:3–8; Hebrews 9:11–15;
Mark 14:12–16, 22–26

Moonstruck

U.S.A., 1987, 102 minutes
Cast: Cher, Nicolas Cage, Olympia Dukakis, Danny Aiello,
Vincent Gardenia, John Mahoney, Julie Bovasso,
Feordor Chaliapin
Writer: John Patrick Shanley
Director: Norman Jewison

Moonstruck

Much Deeper Than *Amore*

SYNOPSIS

Loretta Castorini is a widow living in New York City. Johnny Cammareri is a successful businessman who proposes to her. She accepts without investing too much into the relationship, and Johnny leaves immediately to be at the bedside of his dying mother in Sicily.

As he is leaving, Johnny tells Loretta to invite his brother, Ronny, to the wedding. The two brothers have not spoken since Johnny caused Ronny, a baker, to accidentally lose his hand in a bread-cutting machine. Loretta and Ronny are instantly attracted to each other and she spends the night with him. Afterward, Loretta just wants to forget the incident and she goes to confession.

Loretta's mother, Rose, suspects that her husband, Cosmo, is having an affair with a woman named Mona. Rose, out to dinner by herself, finds a middle-aged professor inviting himself to sit at her table and attempting to seduce her, but she resists him.

Loretta and Ronny go to the opera together. They meet Loretta's father Cosmo with his mistress. Rose discovers that Loretta doesn't really love Johnny, but Ronny.

Johnny suddenly returns from Sicily because his mother's health has improved. The next morning Ronny shows up at the Castorini home looking for Loretta. Over breakfast, Rose confronts Cosmo about his infidelity and he declares his love for her. Loretta's aunt and uncle arrive looking for some money Loretta forgot to deposit for them. Finally, Johnny comes and tells Loretta that his mother got better when he told her he was going to get married, so now he doesn't need to get married anymore. Ronny immediately proposes to Loretta and she accepts.

COMMENTARY

When *Moonstruck* was released it received rather indifferent reviews, especially from critics outside the United States. Nevertheless, it proved popular and a box-office success. It was then nominated for six Oscars, winning three. Cher won for Best Actress, Olympia Dukakis for Best Supporting Actress, and John Patrick Shanley for Best Screenplay.

Cher is completely believable as the down-to-earth Loretta. She is matched by the attractive and sensible Olympia Dukakis as her mother. Nicolas Cage, then at the beginning of his career, plays his role in this domestic comedy with just the right tension. John Patrick Shanley is a playwright and screenwriter with a fondness for comedy and romance. His other films include *Congo, Alive,* and *Five Corners.*

The setting is an ethnic Italian part of Brooklyn and the presentation, characters, and situations are more-or-less stereotypical, all pepped up by Dean Martin's singing "That's Amore." Veteran director Norman Jewison *(In the Heat of the Night, Fiddler on the Roof, Jesus Christ Superstar, The Hurricane)* gives the film a pleasing, glossy tone. Ronny's moonlight speech to persuade Loretta that life is not like romantic stories is a thoughtful sequence complemented by his proposal and declaration of true love around the kitchen table in the breakfast finale.

Focus: The Last Supper is a meal of the covenant of love where Jesus gives himself to his friends in the gifts of bread and wine. In Moonstruck, *meals are the occasions for giving and renewing covenants.*

Beginning with Exodus, covenant is the theme of all three readings today. God's choice to enter into a covenant of love with his people is ratified by the sacrifice of animals and the sprinkling of the life-blood of the victims. In the Old Testament, blood was the symbol of life. After the animals had been killed and offered to God, the people ate of the sacrifice as part of the covenant ritual. The Letter to the Hebrews takes us beyond the literal meaning of ritual sacrifices to the loving covenant of Jesus, which is his pledge of forgiveness and blessing. Jesus gives his body and blood to be shared and eaten in the "new covenant."

Mark's Gospel recounts how the disciples prepared for the Passover meal that was to be the Last Supper. It is the moment of the institution of the Eucharist and the repast that gives meaning to all meals where people gather together in love in Jesus' name. The feast of the Body and Blood of Christ takes us back to the Last Supper as the image of the banquet where we will sit at God's table, joined together in the Covenant of God's love.

All the important conversations take place over meals in *Moonstruck,* except Ronny and Loretta's discussion about love, choice, and commitment that takes place outdoors on a snowy sidewalk. The focus on meals in the film indicates why it might be a useful movie for dialogue on this feast.

In *Moonstruck,* covenant and meal seem meaningfully joined: Cosmo and Mona break a marriage covenant, a man tries to tempt Rose to break her covenant, Johnny proposes the marriage covenant, Loretta's parents ask her not to enter the covenant, and Loretta cooks a meal for Ronny, a sign of the covenant to come. The resolution of the confusion and hurts takes place at a family breakfast, which becomes a meal of love.

KEY SCENES AND THEMES

- Johnny's proposal and Loretta's acceptance; her parents' warning her against the marriage; Ronny's arguments against it; Johnny, under his mother's influence, finding it impossible to commit himself to Loretta.

- Ronny's relationship with Johnny; his infatuation with Loretta, his speech about romantic stories, his relationship with her and her resistance; the proposal in front of everyone; Loretta agreeing to marry him.

- The range of meals throughout the movie as scenes for commitment, betrayal, seduction, reconciliation, community, and covenants of love.

FOR REFLECTION AND CONVERSATION

1. Ronny's speech about love is memorable. He says, "Loretta, I love you. Not like they told you love is, and I didn't know this either, but love don't make things nice—it ruins everything. It breaks your heart. It makes things a mess. We aren't here to make things perfect. The snowflakes are perfect. The stars are perfect. Not us. Not us! We are here to ruin ourselves and to break our hearts and love the wrong people and die...." He goes on to say that what the storybooks tell us about love is worthless. In how many ways does *Moonstruck* demonstrate or define love? Is romantic love enough to sustain a lifetime commitment in marriage? Why or why not? What else is needed?

2. Rose, who knows her husband is cheating on her, asks the professor why men have affairs. He replies that maybe it is because they are afraid of dying. What does

this mean in the context of the film, life, maturity, and faith? What does it take for Cosmo to realize the value of the covenant of love between Rose and himself? How essential is love to all the relationships we see in *Moonstruck?* How might this film be about hope for the future of the family in society, despite personal sins and failings?

3. If the meal scenes in the film are indeed symbolically Eucharistic, what makes them so? Why does the film end at breakfast rather than at dinner? How important are family meals in our lives? What characteristics might make them covenant events, reminiscent of Eucharist? Compare this film with the closing scenes of *Places in the Heart.* How does the breaking of bread in the name of Jesus extend beyond individuals to families and communities?

Prayer

Lord, we celebrate in thanksgiving the fullness of your love that we remember in the Eucharist and in the meals, which bind us together as family and friends. Amen.

1 Samuel 3:3–10, 19;
1 Corinthians 6:13–15, 17–20;
John 1:35–42

Dead Poets Society

U.S.A., 1989, 128 minutes
Cast: Robin Williams, Robert Sean Leonard, Ethan Hawke,
Kurtwood Smith, Josh Charles, Lara Flynn Boyle
Writer: Tom Schulman
Director: Peter Weir

Dead Poets Society

Seize the Day

SYNOPSIS

John Keating, a former pupil of the prestigious preparatory school, Welton Academy, returns there in 1959 to teach English. He has a great love for poetry and teaches it with originality and creativity. He invites his students to tear out the staid introductions in their textbooks and then to stand on their desks to gain a new perspective on the world. Keating's motto is "Carpe diem," or "Seize the day." He urges the students to make their lives extraordinary. The headmaster and some of the other teachers take a dim view of Keating's methods.

Some of the boys respond well to his methods and reinstitute an organization, the Dead Poets Society, which flourished in Mr. Keating's day. The boys begin meeting secretly in the woods at night. Some of the boys are cautious, others enthusiastic. During class, Keating compels the shy Todd Anderson to compose an original poem on the spot, which he does to the admiration of his fellow students. One student in particular, Neil Perry, becomes so exhilarated by this new approach to poetry and English that he dreams of becoming an actor. His strict businessman father, however, disapproves. He wants his son to become a doctor. Mr. Perry forbids Neil to act in the school play.

Against his father's orders, Neil plays the role of Puck in the school's production of *A Midsummer Night's Dream.* His father reiterates his stand and threatens to send Neil to a military academy if he insists on acting in the play. Neil does anyway and then, depressed and hopeless, he commits suicide. The headmaster and the parents make John Keating the scapegoat. Keating loses his job and the boys salute him as he leaves the school.

COMMENTARY

Dead Poets Society is a Peter Weir film that takes place in an educational setting similar to that of his 1975 movie *Picnic At Hanging Rock.* Like *Picnic at Hanging Rock,* which portrays the reality of a girls' private school in 1900 Australia, *Dead Poets Society* explores the mystique of private education and problems of growing up.

Robin Williams is both exuberant and subdued as the creative English teacher, John Keating, and his performance shows a depth of understanding and compassion. The young actors are very good in their roles as adolescent students, especially Robert Sean Leonard who sustains the tragic aspects of the movie with self-confidence and conviction as Neil. Ethan Hawke excels in a key sequence as shy Todd whom the persistent Keating forces to create a poem.

Dead Poets Society is a film with a two-pronged message. First, it offers a critique of the pressures and expectations that parents and teachers can impose on students, and, secondly, it advocates thinking for oneself so as to creatively break free of molds and patterns set by previous generations. This is an emotional and exhilarating movie about the possibilities of imagination and education. The Oscar-winning screenplay is by Tom Schulman.

DIALOGUE WITH THE GOSPEL

Focus: Jesus made a vivid initial impression on John the Baptist's disciples who wanted to follow Jesus and listen to his teaching. John Keating, the teacher, shows a similar magnetism in Dead Poets Society.

The Old Testament reading focuses on the young Samuel, destined to be a prophet. He is mystified by the voice he hears calling his name. In the Gospel, John the Baptist points out the Lamb of God to his disciples who want to follow and stay with Jesus.

Jesus' first words characterize him as a leader and teacher. He asks his followers what they want, rather than telling them what they need. They see Jesus as a leader, indeed a rabbi, a teacher who can educate them, broaden their horizons, and give meaning to their lives. Jesus draws them to himself and they spend the whole day with him.

John Keating, the creative educator, parallels Jesus the teacher. Keating is not what people expect from a prep school teacher; he is original and his methods challenge the status quo. He inspires his students to use their imaginations rather than accept what they are taught without question. Just as the Baptist's followers become Jesus disciples, so the boys become John Keating's disciples, imitating him and leaving behind former ways of living. Neil becomes Keating's main protégé, just as Jesus especially chose Peter.

KEY SCENES AND THEMES

- The four pillars of the school: tradition, discipline, honor, excellence; the opening ceremony, the staff and faculty, the all male atmosphere, the regime and formalities, the elite status of the staff.

- Keating's first class, his introduction to the students and his philosophy of "Carpe diem," "Seize the day"; the students standing on their desks and looking at the world from a different perspective; Keating getting the boys to write poetry; Todd and his creative

efforts, Keating drawing him out so he can be sponta-
neously creative.

- The Dead Poets Society, Thoreau and "sucking the
  marrow of life"; the discussion with Neil about the
  theater; Keating urging him to tell his father the truth;
  going to the play, Neil's death; Keating and his farewell to the class, the boys standing on their desks as a
  salute to Keating.

1. The role of all educators is to draw out from students
   their physical, cognitive, affective, and volitional gifts
   and potential so that they may mature into adults who
   can think for themselves and make choices consistent
   with their beliefs and values. The parents' role as the
   primary educators of children is sacrosanct in Christian tradition. How are these elements present in *Dead
   Poets Society*? What forms of education are presented,
   and how are they explored in the film? What is education really for? How do Keating's methods differ
   from those of other teachers at the school? Does Neil's
   suicide invalidate Keating's methods? Why? What
   other options did Neil have?

**FOR REFLECTION
AND
CONVERSATION**

2. Numerous films about teaching have been made
   through the years, making it almost a subgenre, from
   the traditional *Goodbye Mr. Chips,* to the hard-hitting
   Blackboard Jungle, the inner-city challenges of *Dangerous Minds,* to the non-traditional teacher/student
   movies such as *The Karate Kid.* In what ways might these
   films (and others you may think of) reflect the relationship between Jesus and the disciples? How were
   the struggles between teacher and pupil similar or
   different? How do both teacher and student change
   and grow?

3. In Shakespeare's comedy, *A Midsummer's Night Dream*, Puck and the other fairies live in the woods where reality is suspended and the imagination runs free. Bottom and his companions are the realists and this provides the play's comedy. How might the elements of this play and *Dead Poets Society* be compared? Why do you think the screenwriter chose *A Midsummer's Night Dream* for the "play within the play"?

Prayer

Jesus, your first disciples were overjoyed to follow you and to be in your presence. Draw us closer to you as we seek to follow you in our daily lives. Amen.

Brother Sun, Sister Moon

U.K., 1972, 122 minutes
Cast: Graham Faulkner, Judy Bowker, Alec Guinness,
Leigh Lawson, Lee Montague, Kenneth Cranham,
Valentina Cortese, Peter Firth
Writers: Suso Cecchi d'Amico, Kenneth Ross, Lina Wertmuller,
Franco Zeffirelli
Director: Franco Zeffirelli

Brother Sun, Sister Moon

To Leave All

SYNOPSIS

In the early thirteenth-century Umbrian town of Assisi, Italy, Francesco Bernadone returns home very ill from fighting in a war and serving a year in prison. In his feverous state, he remembers celebrating the night before he and his friends left for the war, and meeting his friend, Clare Offreduccio.

As Francesco recovers from his illness, he begins to act strangely. He retreats from society, wanders the flower-filled fields, and grows in his appreciation of the beauty of nature and creation. He is distressed because he and his family are richly dressed and sit in places of honor in the church while the poor kneel at the back. When he visits the ruins of the church of San Damiano, he experiences a call to rebuild it and to help the poor.

He visits the workers in his father's dye factory and, realizing the oppressive working conditions, urges them to go outside and enjoy the fresh air. Worse still, Francesco decides he wants to free himself from all possessions and throws his and his father's belongings out of a window. Francesco's father is outraged, but Francesco declares publicly that he wants to be a beggar and to live the spirit of the Gospels. In the main square of Assisi, he takes off all his clothes and hands them to his mother. He is now free to follow his vocation.

When Francesco's friend Bernardo, realizing that he cannot fit into society either, joins him, other companions soon "drop out" of society and embrace Francesco's lifestyle. Clare joins the group a short while later.

Francesco decides to go to Rome with his brothers to appeal to the pope for confirmation of his way of living like Christ. Francesco speaks passionately about poverty to the pope and papal court. Pope Innocent III listens to his words and kisses his feet, encouraging him to continue his spiritual movement.

COMMENTARY

Franco Zeffirelli broke into cinema in the late 1950s and early 1960s with a strong reputation as a theater and opera director in Italy and London. His first English-language movies included versions of the Shakespearean plays *The Taming of the Shrew* and *Romeo and Juliet,* both produced in the 1960s. In 1972 he made *Brother Sun, Sister Moon* and then directed the epic made-for-television film *Jesus of Nazareth* in 1978. His later career has been a mixture of directing theater and movies including *Hamlet, Tea with Mussolini,* and *Callas Forever.*

Francis of Assisi is probably the saint most frequently featured in movies with Joan of Arc a close second. Both Bradford Dillman and Mickey Rourke portrayed Francis in other film versions of his story. In 1950, Roberto Rossellini made a film entitled *Franceso, givllare di Dio* from the songs and legends about St. Francis and his followers as recorded in *The Little Flowers of St. Francis* (*I Fioretti di San Francesco,* c. 1350).

Zeffirelli's interpretation integrates the story of Francis and the anti-war and pro-poor social upheaval of the late 1960s and early 1970s.

The acting, singing, preaching, and some solemn pious tableaux in *Brother Sun, Sister Moon* certainly seem dated and unsophisticated by today's standards. Although a box-office disappointment, Zeffirelli's sincere effort to combine the legends of Francis, his love for nature, and his spirituality of poverty can still inspire audiences willing to enter into the heart of the film. While this movie may be very much of its time, the story of Francis is for all seasons.

> *Focus: Jesus' call disrupts the daily lives of the fishermen Peter, Andrew, James, and John, but they stop everything and follow him. St. Francis of Assisi also hears the call of Jesus and leaves everything to follow him.*

DIALOGUE WITH THE GOSPEL

Today's readings are all about the divine "call." Like Jonah in the first reading, and in the spirit of Paul's Letter to the Corinthians in the second, Francis calls people to a change of heart. From the very beginning, the Franciscan movement has had enormous influence both in and outside the Church, because it continues to call individuals to conversion of heart, peace among nations, and a preferential option for the poor.

Above all, today's Gospel can be envisioned as the archetypal account of call and conversion. Jesus first proclaims repentance for the sake of the Gospel, and then he calls his first disciples, "Come after me and I will make you fishers of men." To onlookers, it must have seemed mad. Why would four fishermen drop everything and abandon their families and means of livelihood to follow this stranger from Galilee?

Brother Sun, Sister Moon shows a thirteenth-century version of that call. How could a young man from a merchant class family in the small city of Assisi start a movement that still inspires followers today? Like the sons of Zebedee, Francis left his father and home. There is a hint of madness about Francis in the movie. His behavior appears reckless and against all common sense, but it is the sign of his absolute commitment—later ratified when the pope kisses Francis' feet—to the person of Jesus and his teachings. The ideals

Francis proposed, to follow the Christ of the Gospels more closely, can utterly change people, setting them on paths toward an evangelical heroism they never dreamed possible.

KEY SCENES AND THEMES

- Francesco's delirium, remembering his life, the encounter with Clare, the war; his recovery and transformation; finding himself on the roof with the birds, discovering the dye-workers and inviting them outdoors, roaming in the fields, finding San Damiano; the continued images of the crucifix and their effect on him.

- His discomfort in the church with the poor at the back; stripping himself publicly and leaving Assisi to work with the poor and to rebuild San Damiano; Bernardo and Francesco's other friends and Clare joining him; their work in the fields, begging, and preaching.

- Francesco speaking passionately at the papal court and his forced removal; the pope calling him back, listening to him, remembering his own early enthusiasm, and kissing Francesco's feet.

FOR REFLECTION AND CONVERSATION

1. Francis journeyed from being a carefree, purposeless youth to finding his call through the contemplation of nature's beauty and the plight of the poor. He realized that only by following Christ in poverty, chastity, and obedience would he find meaning, joy, and purpose in life. How do you respond to the call of Christ in your life? What do you do when you feel that your life seems without purpose or meaning? Have you ever explored the possibility that Christ may be using these feelings to call you to follow him more closely in religious life, priesthood, or another form of religious commitment?

2. The symbol of hands is used repeatedly throughout the film, as are images of Christ and the cross, flowers, birds, and nature. There is also a texture to the way many of the scenes are prepared and shot (e.g., the fabric patterns and colors, the bricks), which may also be considered symbols of the rise of the merchant class, greed, and the materialism of that time. What do these symbols mean to you on a personal, religious, and social level? How do you think the director intended these symbols to help create meaning and engage our emotions? What other symbols can you identify in the film and what do you think they mean? What is the significance of the film's title, *Brother Sun, Sister Moon*?

3. The dialogue in *Brother Sun, Sister Moon* consists almost entirely of quotes from the Bible or writings and prayers attributed to St. Francis. The sayings and teachings of Christ were essential to Francis' life and mission because they continually called him to respond through repentance, prayer, and good works. Through Francis, his own parents and the religious and civil authorities were reminded of their Gospel responsibilities before God. How does the Word of God influence your attitude toward action with regard to reconciliation, dialogue, peace, and justice? The yearly meetings of world religious leaders in Assisi call each of us to be instruments of peace. How can we make this a reality to help change the world?

Prayer

Lord, make us instruments of your peace by imitating the life of St. Francis. Give us the strength to follow wherever you call us. Amen.

FOURTH SUNDAY OF THE YEAR

Deuteronomy 18:15–20;
1 Corinthians 7:32–35; Mark 1:21–28

The Exorcist

U.S.A., 1973, 121 minutes
Cast: Ellen Burstyn, Max Von Sydow, Linda Blair, Jason Miller,
Lee J. Cobb, Kitty Wynn, Jack McGowran,
Mercedes McCambridge, Fr. William O'Malley
Writer: William Peter Blatty
Director: William Friedkin

 *The Exorcist*

Confronting Unclean Spirits

SYNOPSIS

Chris MacNeil is making a film at a Jesuit college in Washington, D.C. She and her twelve-year-old daughter, Regan, live in a rented house in Georgetown. Regan begins to behave strangely and Chris takes her to doctors who initially suspect brain damage. However, they find nothing physically wrong with her. She is then taken to psychiatrists who, again, can do nothing for her.

Finally, it is suspected and then determined that diabolical forces have taken possession of Regan. She utters foul and blasphemous curses, levitates, experiences facial distortions, and her head rotates. One night after a party, the movie director is found dead outside Regan's window and no one knows what happened. Chris asks a priest-psychiatrist at the college, Jesuit Fr. Damien Karras, to pray for her—and, after consultation with Church authorities, he decides to perform an exorcism. Meanwhile, the police investigate the murder of the director.

Fr. Karras has been experiencing doubts about his faith. He soon realizes he is out of his depth with regard to Regan and decides to enlist the help of fellow Jesuit Fr. Merrin. An archaeological expert, Fr. Merrin has had experience with exorcisms; and while on a recent dig in Iran, he discovered certain objects that gave him premonitions of evil.

Fr. Merrin struggles with the ever more violent and deformed Regan. The devil shouts out from her and resists the prayers and rituals. During the exorcism, Fr. Merrin has a heart attack and dies. Almost simultaneously, the desperate Fr. Karras begs God to let the devil enter him so as to save Regan. When the demon accepts his offer, Fr. Karras throws himself out of the window to his death. Regan is healed.

COMMENTARY

From the beginning, *The Exorcist* had a more favorable response from the more mainstream churches than might have been expected. Noted critic Pauline Kael of *The New Yorker* wrote that the movie was the biggest pro-Catholic advertisement since *The Bells of St. Mary's,* but at the same time castigated Catholics for applauding a film that let "their faith be turned into a horror show."

It is a pity that *The Exorcist* is often remembered more for its special effects than for the serious theological issues regarding the presence of evil in the world, the struggle between good and evil, and, as Michael W. Cuneo expressed in his 2001 book, American Exorcism, "the power of supernatural faith, priestly virtue, and the transcendent authority of [the] Church." For secular audiences, *The Exorcist* seemed like a variation on horror themes. For Christians, it was the dramatization of an unfamiliar and uncomfortable reality.

The Exorcist was a superior production for its time, with a top Hollywood cast and an Oscar-winning director, William Friedkin *(The French Connection). The Exorcist* received several Oscar nominations, including one for Best Film. The screenplay by William Peter Blatty was based on his own 1971 novel about a 1949 incident in Mount Rainer, Maryland. Jesuit William O'Malley was a consultant for the film and appeared in it as the Jesuit friend of Fr. Karras. Two sequels followed: *The Exorcist II* in 1977, and *The Exorcist III* in 1990. A longer director's cut of *The Exorcist* was released in 2001.

DIALOGUE WITH THE GOSPEL

Focus: Today's Gospel reading portrays Jesus confronting the unclean spirit that has possessed an innocent man. Demonic possession is an experience of profound and disgusting evil, which requires prayer and sacrifice to overcome. The Exorcist *imagines and dramatizes this in a contemporary setting.*

The reading from Deuteronomy is part of the classic description of an authentic prophet, one who is called by God to mediate the divine presence through oracles and commands. Rather than hearing the voice of God and seeing the fire of God's presence directly, the prophet became the go-between for God and the chosen people.

In *The Exorcist*, Fr. Merrin and Fr. Karras are presented as contemporary prophetic intermediaries between God and the people. Their role goes a step further, however, when they act as consecrated "mediators" between people and the devil. Jesus is presented in the same way in today's Gospel, and we are introduced to evil's ugly manifestations as the legion of devils comes out of the man in the caves and enters the swine. When the possessed man cries out in hostility to Jesus, Jesus rebukes the unclean spirit, and the man convulses and screams as the devil departs.

Reading this Gospel episode may not be as visually impressive as the film's special effects. The Gospel challenges us to face the ugly reality of evil's influence and power in our lives. *The Exorcist* offers us some disturbing images of this, in the repugnant actions and language of the possessed Regan, but above all it shows us the generous self-sacrifice, faith, and prayer necessary to free those who are possessed.

KEY SCENES AND THEMES

- Regan, an ordinary young girl at home with her mother; her mother's religious background, but non-pratice of faith; the initial phenomena and the gradual possession of Regan; her mother's desperation, the response of family, police, the Church.

- Fr. Karras and his attempts to exorcise Regan; calling in Fr. Merrin with his background and expertise; the rituals and prayers of exorcism, the ritual confrontation between the divine and the demonic; the powerlessness of science, medicine, and human experience in the face of the devil.

- Regan's suffering, her transformation from normalcy to possession, the crudity of her language and behavior; the desperate prayer of the priests, their suffering; Fr. Merrin's death, Fr. Karras offering his life for Regan, the power of faith and prayer over the devil.

FOR REFLECTION AND CONVERSATION

1. The title of this film is *The Exorcist*, but who is it really about? Who is the main protagonist or is there more than one? What, if any, is the central conflict to be resolved? What are the main theological tenets of the film and how are these associated with the principle characters? What is the viewer left with spiritually by the end of this film? How true do you think Fr. Merrin's advice is to Fr. Karras about relating to the devil during the exorcism? Why?

2. *The Exorcist* was released during the academic debate initiated in the 1960s which claimed that God is dead. If God is dead, how is the problem of the origin and nature of evil, as personified by the devil, explained? Why do you think *The Exorcist* was so successful, and the argument about the death of God seemingly so ineffectual in 1973 when the film was released? What conclusions and consequences stem from arguments for and against the existence of God and the devil, and why might these be important to people today?

3. Exorcisms are rarely performed in our day and age. Only a few dioceses around the world have actually

named priests as official "exorcists," though the Archdiocese of Chicago has done so as recently as 2001. Several books have appeared in the last few years about this subject, and the Vatican published a new ritual in Latin, reserved to bishops and exorcists, in 1999. Popular news magazine programs, *Dateline* and *60 Minutes,* have aired investigative pieces about exorcism since 2001. Why do you think exorcism seems to fascinate believers and skeptics alike? What does the *Catechism of the Catholic Church* say about the existence and presence of the devil and the purpose of exorcism?

Prayer

Lord, when evil comes into our hearts, or when we find it present in others or the situations of life, in your mercy drive it out and give us peace. Amen.

Patch Adams

U.S.A., 1998, 112 minutes
Cast: Robin Williams, Monica Potter, Bob Gunton,
Philip Seymour Hoffman, Daniel London
Writer: Steve Oedekerk
Director: Tom Shadyac

Patch Adams

A Healer of People

In 1969, Hunter "Patch" Adams commits himself to a mental institution in Virginia because he suffers from depression. He attempts to commit suicide and fails. During his time at the hospital, he is able to make the other patients laugh and realizes that he has a gift for connecting with the sick. Adams decides to become a doctor and in 1971, at the age of forty-one, begins medical school.

SYNOPSIS

Adams is successful in his studies, but is unhappy with the lack of contact the students have with patients. The philosophy of the medical school is that doctors and medical students should maintain a cold distance from their patients. Adams starts to visit the patients, however, and his humorous and compassionate approach begins to make a great difference to them during their stay in the hospital. Then the dean of studies forbids him to visit the patients. Meanwhile, Adams is attracted to Carin, another medical student who refuses his romantic attention. When Adams begins a free hospital called the Gesundheit Institute, two friends, Carin and Truman, join him in order to practice their own unique brand of medicine outside the rigid regime of medical school.

Adams despairs of God and his life when one of the patients murders Carin. He is summoned to appear before the dean to answer charges of misconduct, and his supporters rally behind him. He makes a powerful case for dealing with patients as people rather than merely as "numbers."

COMMENTARY

Patch Adams was very popular at the box office despite the fact that many critics accused it of gross sentimentality. London's *Daily Telegraph,* for example, commented: "To like the film would strike a massive blow to any cineaste's credibility." It is true that *Patch Adams* is a film that presses all the emotional buttons. Though some may find certain sequences very "sugary"—the butterfly on the cliff as Adams contemplates suicide, and the children wearing the red noses Adams had given them at his hearing—*Patch Adams* has a great deal to say about healing.

The movie is quite critical of medical school pedagogy and current health practice in the United States. The dean is portrayed as a villain-doctor who teaches students that they must never lower themselves to the level of their patients, because patients only want professional expertise. He appeals to the tradition of time-honored rules and systems, whereas Patch Adams takes a more creative and personalized stance.

Robin Williams has played a number of healers and educators in, for example, *Dead Poets Society, Awakenings,* and *Good Will Hunting.* Tom Shadyac, known for *Ace Ventura,* directed the film. The screenplay was written by Steve Oedekerk and is based on the book *Gesundheit: Good Health Is a Laughing Matter* by Hunter Doherty Adams (the real "Patch" Adams) and Maureen Mylander.

DIALOGUE WITH THE GOSPEL

Focus: Jesus shows his love through healing. Patch Adams, despite his own personal suffering, shows that joy as well as loving commitment is possible in healing professions.

Early in the opening chapter of Mark, Jesus begins to heal people. Not only does he cure friends, like Peter's mother-in-law, he heals the numerous strangers who plead for help. Even when he retires to a lonely place to pray, the crowds come flocking and Jesus cares for them. The Gospel journeys of Jesus are journeys of healing.

Patch Adams, like Jesus, has the ability to draw people to himself. Adams treats patients with joy and love: people who experience his energetic "power" of love and happiness are reassured, enabling the healing process to begin.

Patch Adams' cheerful support of people takes its toll on him, and when Carin is killed, he despairs. He had already found an isolated "lonely place" to build his center for the sick. Now, in his depressed state, he retreats to a cliff's edge where he berates God for creating human beings and allowing them to suffer. This is the desperate prayer of a man completely given over to healing others.

In his despair at the beginning of the film and when Carin dies, Adams can be compared to Job in the first reading. He, too, believes that happiness is indeed fleeting. Through humor and communication with patients, Patch Adams becomes "all things to all, to save at least some," as St. Paul describes his own ministry in the second reading.

KEY SCENES AND THEMES

- Patch Adams in his hospital room desperate, depressed, and even suicidal; his ability to make his fellow patient laugh and the effect this discovery has on him.

- Dean Walcott as a doctor and a teacher, his talk of professionalism; his hostile interviews with Adams; the people going to the Gesundheit Institute, the self-sacrifice of all Adams' friends who work there.

- Adams at the cliff's edge, his sense of despair and his prayer to God; his speech to the medical board justifying his beliefs and practices; his supporters and the verdict.

1. Dean Walcott gives a lecture to an admiring class of medical students; he tells them that for professionalism's sake, he must "train the humanity out of you to make you something better: a doctor." How might Walcott's approach embody what seems to be wrong with managed care in the United States today? How do the elements of story and character development in the film work to make Dean Walcott almost a stereotype for bad doctoring?

2. Many films have been made about the medical profession or sick people who rely on the medical profession for healing. Compare the films *The Doctor,* *Lorenzo's Oil,* or *John Q* with this quote from *Patch Adams:* "You treat a disease, you win, you lose. You treat a person, I'll guarantee you'll win." How do they compare on personal, professional, and social levels? In the more than thirty years since the events in *Patch Adams* transpired, what has changed about the medical profession? In your experience, how does the medical profession define the human person? Was Patch Adams justified when he questioned the status quo and the authority of educators and broke the rules? Why or why not?

3. Dean Walcott noted in Adams' file that he possessed "excessive happiness." There is a mighty cheer at the end of the hearing when the dean is advised by the head of the medical board to try to get some of this

excessive happiness for himself. How important is humor to living a Christian life? What role does it play in your life and spirituality?

Prayer

Jesus, at the beginning of your ministry healing flowed from you and gave new life and wholeness to many people. Teach us the joy of healing and be with us as we serve the needs of others. Amen.

Molokai: The Story of Fr. Damien

Belgium, 1999, 120 minutes
Cast: David Wenham, Peter O'Toole, Leo McKern,
Derek Jacobi, Sam Neill, Kate Ceberano, Kris Kristofferson,
Alice Krige, Tom Wilkinson, Chris Hayward, Aden Young
Writer: John Briley
Director: Paul Cox

Molokai: The Story of Fr. Damien

Jesus Became Leper

SYNOPSIS

Fr. Damien is a young Belgian missionary of the Congregation of the Sacred Hearts of Jesus and Mary who ministers in Hawaii in the 1870s. He volunteers to be the parish priest at the leper colony on the island of Molokai.

When Fr. Damien arrives, he exercises a zealous and sometimes harsh attitude toward the people. He is hard on them because they live in squalor and do not help themselves. Many live in sin and they have little hope. After initial clashes with a number of the lepers, Fr. Damien builds a church and gathers the people together as a community.

Fr. Damien has his own personal struggles and makes many spiritual sacrifices to serve the lepers. He is not allowed to leave Molokai, and so he goes without the benefit of the sacrament of Reconciliation for long periods of time. An opportunity for confession comes one day when a bishop visits Molokai, but is not allowed to leave the ship. So Fr. Damien, from the wharf, shouts his sins to the bishop in French, the only privacy available.

Fr. Damien's provincial superior in Honolulu is unhappy with him because of his demands that government officials secure better treatment for the lepers. This puts a strain on relations between the officials and the missionaries. The governor, originally Fr. Damien's supporter, now regards him as a troublemaker. When Fr. Damien writes a letter to his brother in Belgium, it makes headlines in the world press and Damien becomes something of a celebrity. Doctors come to inspect and study his work, and donations begin to pour in.

Fr. Damien mellows as he grows older. He is more understanding of the people and more tolerant of their behavior. A group of sisters arrives to assist Fr. Damien, as does an American layman, Joseph Dutton. They also dedicate their lives to helping the lepers and take over Fr. Damien's work when he is diagnosed with leprosy. As his earthly life comes to a close, he acknowledges his own weakness and finally dies of the disease.

COMMENTARY

John Briley, who also wrote the screenplays for *Gandhi* and *Cry Freedom*, wrote the script for *Molokai: The Story of Fr. Damien*. The film was directed by Dutch-born Australian Paul Cox, whose previous work includes *Man of Flowers, Vincent, Exile, Innocence,* and *The Diaries of Vaslav Nijinsky*. Shot on location, Molokai and Honolulu provide spectacular backdrops to the action.

The movie boasts a large international cast. Australian actor David Wenham, who plays Fr. Damien, is a down-to-earth and sometimes cantankerous saintly man.

This is a moving story of a holy man who in his own time had a worldwide reputation for his charity and compassion for lepers. Pope John Paul II beatified Fr. Joseph Damien de Veuster (1840–1889) in 1996. It is also a serious film about social justice, the impact of leprosy in the nineteenth century, and the beginning of efforts to eliminate the disease. Viewers growing up in the mid-twentieth century will perhaps remember the 1954 biography, *Damien the Leper,* by writer and director John Farrow, that helped make Fr. Damien a household name. *Damien: the Leper Priest,* a made-for-television movie featuring Ken Howard as Fr. Damien, was released in 1980.

DIALOGUE WITH THE GOSPEL

Focus: In Mark's Gospel, Jesus heals the leper who came to plead for cleansing. Fr. Damien of Molokai has become the patron and hero for people who suffer from leprosy and those who care for them.

The treatment of lepers in the Book of Leviticus is not so different from that of the nineteenth century. In both worlds, lepers were exiled to the margins of society and were recognized only by their affliction. In the Scriptures, all maladies of the skin were considered leprosy, and those judged to be lepers had to identify themselves as "unclean" whenever they came into contact with others.

When Jesus touched a leper, as he did in today's Gospel reading, he would technically have been a leper himself until the time of quarantine passed. Jesus would have been bound to stay away from people, sharing the suffering and humiliation of the lepers, although we have no scriptural confirmation that he did this. Likewise, when Fr. Damien wanted to go to confession, he was prevented from personal contact with the bishop. Fr. Damien was quarantined for life, sharing in the isolation of those he served.

Fr. Damien acknowledges, as did Jesus, the role of authority in declaring who was well or not. He obeys the health laws for the sake of the greater community and the care for the lepers themselves. For himself personally, however, he interprets the law more leniently in order to follow Jesus' example. He stays close to those who suffer from leprosy, eats with them, and is not afraid to touch them. Fr. Damien is a significant Christ-figure, because he took on and shared the illnesses of others, eventually dying for them.

- Fr. Damien's initial zeal in volunteering for Molokai and starting his ministry from scratch; his friendships; conversations with the government official; listening and learning how to understand and relate to the lepers.

- Fr. Damien's attempts to stop immoral behavior on the island and passing judgment on the people; the antagonism between priest and people, his gradual understanding of himself and the needs of the lepers; his confession to the bishop.

- Fr. Damien's final illness; performing the wedding, how he mellows and identifies with the lepers; his self-sacrificing life and death.

KEY SCENES AND THEMES

1. Since 1990, the World Health Organization has been working to reduce the occurrences of leprosy (Hansen's disease) in 120 countries to one per 10,000 people. It has reached this goal in ninety countries. The biggest challenge, however, is the stigma attached to Hansen's disease, which is similar to that of the human immunodeficiency virus (HIV) that causes AIDS. What can we learn from the life and example of Fr. Damien as we seek to live the Gospel in today's world, still afflicted by disease? What is our response to the call for help and a cure from those who are sick and perhaps outcast among us?

2. The film for the Fifth Sunday of the Year was *Patch Adams*, a movie that stressed sanity, compassion, and healing among the sick. How can the attitudes and approaches of Patch Adams and Fr. Damien toward the sick be compared? How do each of these men define the human person through their actions? Is

FOR REFLECTION AND CONVERSATION

the dignity of the person an issue for both health care and human relationships in general? Why or why not?

3. Power and power relations are dominant elements in the Fr. Damien story, as the film documents so well. In fact, much of the drama comes from the portrayal of power clashes. Identify the characters and sequences in the film that concern power and power relations. How can power be a force for good, or is this question an oxymoron? Do abuses of power occur in the story? What kind of power, ability, or skills can believers develop in order to be Christ-followers for today?

Prayer

Jesus, your heartfelt response to the leper was to reach out, touch, and heal him. Give us the grace to share your deep healing love with others. Amen.

SEVENTH SUNDAY OF THE YEAR
Isaiah 43:18–19, 21–22, 24–25;
2 Corinthians 1:18–22; Mark 2:1–12

My Left Foot
U.K., 1989, 103 minutes
Cast: Daniel Day-Lewis, Brenda Fricker, Ray McAnally,
Fiona Shaw, Ruth McCabe, Hugh O'Conor, Cyril Cusack
Writers: Shane Connaughton, Jim Sheridan
Director: Jim Sheridan

My Left Foot

Paralysis of Body and Soul

It is Ireland in 1959 and Christy Brown, at the age of twenty-seven, is a celebrated writer and painter with a severe form of cerebral palsy. He arrives at a fund-raising event to give a lecture. As people wait for Christy to speak, a nurse, Mary Carr, reads his recent autobiography, *My Left Foot,* while he sips whiskey from a bottle he has hidden in his coat pocket.

SYNOPSIS

Going back in time, we learn that Christy was born in 1932 to the Browns, a working-class family in Dublin. The father is a bricklayer, and the mother stays at home to care for their large family. Because of his affliction, Christy is barely able to communicate. The only part of his body that moves under his control is his left foot. Most of the family assumes that he is mentally retarded, except his mother who can see intelligence and humor in his eyes. The family resolves to keep him at home rather than send him to an institution.

One day, when he is about seven years old, Christy takes a piece of chalk between his toes and writes the letter *a* on the floor. Then he astounds his mother by writing the word "mother." His proud father shows off his son to his friends at the pub—the only way he knows how to express his love for his afflicted son. Christy eventually learns to speak.

Dr. Eileen Cole comes to the Brown home to teach Christy speech communication. She introduces him to literature and, after some time, organizes an exhibition of his art. Christy becomes infatuated with her. When he realizes she is engaged to the gallery owner, he throws a terrible tantrum, attempts suicide, and falls into depression. During this time he also begins to drink.

His loving family builds a studio for him in the backyard so that he can have some privacy to write and paint. After his father dies, he writes an autobiography, typing each word with his toe. He offers the royalties he earns to his mother as a gift.

The film returns to the present, where Christy gives his lecture and then persuades the nurse, Mary Carr, to stay with him. They later marry.

COMMENTARY

My Left Foot was one of the surprise commercial and artistic successes of 1989. It was a modest British production filmed in Ireland, starring character actor Daniel Day-Lewis. It was nominated for five Academy Awards, including Best Film, Best Director, and Best Adapted Screenplay. Daniel Day-Lewis won the award for Best Actor and Brenda Fricker won for Best Supporting Actress.

The screenplay was adapted from Christy Brown's autobiography, *My Left Foot*. Its courage and humanity are similar to the 1984 Australian movie, *A Test of Love*, about fourteen-year-old Annie O'Farrell. She is a cerebral palsy patient who is rescued from a state institution, learns to communicate, and finds a home.

My Left Foot portrays the startling poverty of Dublin families in the 1930s. Ray McAnally dominates the household as Mr. Brown. Brenda Fricker went on to an international career after her touching portrayal of Mrs. Brown. Daniel Day-Lewis consolidated his star status and went on to collaborate with Jim Sheridan on two movies about Northern

Ireland, *In the Name of the Father* in 1993, and *The Boxer* in 1997. More recently, he starred in *Gangs of New York* in 2002. Day-Lewis is a chameleon-like actor who completely becomes his character. Many audiences assumed that the man playing Christy Brown in *My Left Foot* actually had cerebral palsy.

Focus: Christy Brown is a paralytic who needs healing. Today's readings, especially the Gospel, focus on forgiveness of sins and the healing of the body.

DIALOGUE WITH THE GOSPEL

Isaiah 43 tells of God's personal love for each of us and that he will wipe out our sins and remember them no more. This theme is reinforced by the responsorial psalm and its request that God heal our souls. The verses of the psalm show the relationship between healing and forgiveness.

Mark's version of the well-known story of the paralytic who is lowered through an opening in the roof is presented in specific detail. When Jesus sees the man, he heals his soul by forgiving his sins. This is particularly apt when considering *My Left Foot*. The movie is not simply the story of an innocent, physically challenged child. It is the story of a man who has suffered through relationships, depression, alcoholism, and who has even attempted to kill himself. He needs his sins to be forgiven and his soul to be healed. In Mary Carr, he finds someone whose love will continue to heal him.

The scribes, the interpreters of the religious law, found it difficult to accept Jesus as one who could forgive sins. Jesus is aware of these unspoken suspicions. He offers a physical healing, not as an absolute necessity for the paralytic's future, but as a sign of God's healing forgiveness.

The man healed in today's Gospel did Jesus' bidding, picking up his stretcher and walking. Christy Brown's movements are still limited by the cerebral palsy, but he learns to write, paint, and speak, so that everyone is amazed and can say, like the crowds in the Gospel, "We have never seen anything like this."

KEY SCENES AND THEMES

- The Brown household, the uncommunicative, hard-working father, the harassed mother; the father with his friends at the pub, Mrs. Brown's dedication; Christy at home and the acceptance and love of his family, writing with his foot for the first time, Mrs. Brown's joy and Mr. Brown taking his son to the pub, rejoicing.

- Christy and his art; his infatuations, especially with Dr. Cole, the exhibition and his discovery of her engagement; his drinking, depression, and attempt to kill himself.

- His recovery and lingering depression, his father's death; writing his autobiography; the lecture, his trust in Mary Carr, and his hope for the future.

FOR REFLECTION AND CONVERSATION

1. Mothers wanting to integrate their disabled children into every phase of life rather than institutionalize them began the United Cerebral Palsy foundation (www.UCPA.org) more than fifty years ago. The Brown family was ahead of its time. They refused to commit Christy to an institution and included him in everything possible, as the film shows. We don't know what caused the afflicted man's disability in today's Gospel, but he had friends who cared enough to bring him to Jesus for healing. How do these examples challenge us today?

2. Noted *Chicago Sun-Times* film critic Roger Ebert wrote about *My Left Foot:* "It is not an inspirational movie, although it inspires. It is not a sympathetic movie, although it inspires sympathy. It is the story of a stubborn, difficult, blessed, and gifted man who was dealt a bad hand, who played it brilliantly, and who left us

some good books, some good paintings, and the example of his courage. It must not have been easy." Do you agree with Ebert's evaluation? Why or why not? Which event or character in the film stands out for you as the most blessed, and why?

3. What can the themes of *My Left Foot*—body self-image, caregivers, family, communication, disability, human dignity, alcoholism, hope, faith, love, healing, and humor—contribute to a dialogue about forgiveness and healing within personal relationships and community? How do you integrate forgiveness and healing in your own life?

Prayer

Lord, you can read our hearts. You know the healing we need in both soul and body. Be compassionate, heal us, and give us the fullness of life. Amen.

EIGHTH SUNDAY OF THE YEAR
Hosea 2:16, 17, 21–22;
2 Corinthians 3:1–6; Mark 2:18–22

Bed of Roses

U.S.A., 1996, 87 minutes
Cast: Christian Slater, Mary Stuart Masterson,
Pamela Segall, Josh Brolin
Writer: Michael Goldenberg
Director: Michael Goldenberg

Bed of Roses

Time to Be Sad, Time to Rejoice

SYNOPSIS

Lisa is a successful financial consultant. When she receives word that her adoptive father has died, she has unhappy memories of childhood abandonment and being the victim of abuse. She does not even know her real birthday.

One day at her office, she receives a beautiful flower arrangement. She wants to discover who sent the flowers and meets Lewis, who eventually confesses that he saw her one night and followed her. She spends a day delivering flowers with him and visits his rooftop garden.

Lewis falls in love with her, and a few days later Lisa moves in with him. She is reticent about her personal life, while he explains that his wife died giving birth. He persuades her to visit his family for Christmas. Lisa is overwhelmed by the happiness in the house, and, when Lewis proposes to her in front of everyone, she cannot accept such happiness and flees back to New York.

After three months, her friend Kim persuades her to ask for Lewis' forgiveness. She visits his apartment, apologizes to him, and moves to the door as if to leave, hoping that he will ask her to wait. Finally, he does.

Bed of Roses was a Valentine's Day release, indicating how the distributors saw this romantic tale. It is a modern love story. A young woman without any experience of family gives herself completely to her work and success; a widower opts out of a Wall Street firm to cultivate flowers. They meet, fall in love, and after overcoming some obstacles, live happily ever after.

Mary Stuart Masterson portrays her character's tentative love and apprehension convincingly, and this elicits the audience's understanding of and sympathy for her fears and dilemmas. Christian Slater brings warmth and gentleness to his portrait of a grieving man rediscovering love. Michael Goldenberg wrote the screenplay and, the following year, the script for *Contact.*

There are references to love stories, fairy tales, and Prince Charming in the film. Lisa's best friend, Kim, puts on a play where a talented but frightened little girl takes on the role of Sleeping Beauty. As Lisa watches, she becomes aware of the parallel to herself. The dialogue talks of perfect roses, and it also refers to the need of thorns to make a realistic world. This is an attractive and entertaining movie.

COMMENTARY

Focus: Today's readings use the language of love and covenant within the context of weddings. Many people are unable to change from an old to a new way of life until they experience love, as Bed of Roses *demonstrates.*

The Gospel includes sayings of Jesus about weddings and fasting. It ends with the now commonly quoted passage, which warns against putting new wine into old wineskins, because the old skins will burst and the wine will be lost. It's the same with love. We have to change and grow to receive the love that can change us even more.

The entrance antiphon, "He saved me because he loved me," is also the theme of the reading from Hosea, a prophet

DIALOGUE WITH THE GOSPEL

who searched for a wife and offered her gifts of integrity, justice, tenderness, compassion, and faithfulness. Lewis illustrates these biblical ideals when he offers Lisa love, stability, and the embrace of a warm and loving family.

In the second reading, Paul shows his tenderness toward the Corinthians, though we know from his first letter that they exasperated him to no end. Now he recognizes them as a "letter" written on his heart, an expression of God's covenant. Both Paul and his fellow apostles are ministers of that covenant of love.

The Gospel speaks about a time to rejoice and a time to fast, especially in the context of a wedding celebration. The bridegroom is the image of Jesus himself. Lewis experiences great joy because of his love for Lisa, especially when he proposes to her. He suffers when she runs away from his love, and he grieves at losing her as he did over the death of his wife.

Images of the new and old cloth, the new and old wineskins, fit Lisa's experiences. She has been trapped by the lack of love in her life. This is her old cloth, her old wineskin, so to speak. When Lewis offers her a new life made of new cloth and new wine, she is unable to receive it. Only when she lets go of the old by visiting her adoptive father's grave is she able to open herself to a relationship with Lewis. Now, she has new wineskins into which she can pour the new wine of their love.

KEY SCENES AND THEMES

- The contrast between Lisa busy at her desk and Lewis working with and delivering flowers; listening to the reader of the children's stories.

- Lisa and her response to the flowers; delivering them with Lewis; the rooftop garden; the perfect roses in her apartment.

- Lisa going to visit Lewis' family, her running away when he proposes; Kim's advice; Lisa going to Lewis with the flowers, apologizing, and hoping he will say, "Wait" before she walks out the door.

1. *Bed of Roses* is largely a film about the effects of emotional dysfunction, not unlike Israel's relationship with God, symbolized in Hosea's relationship with Gomer (the focus of the entire Book of Hosea). What are Lisa's problems and how do they affect her choices? Who are the past and present characters Lisa must deal with in order to respond to love and enter into a relationship and marriage covenant? Lisa and Lewis have sex, but what is missing? Why isn't this enough to establish a true covenanted relationship?

2. Romantic literature grew out of medieval prose and poetry, and was devoted to legendary or supernatural subjects with characters involved in amorous situations. Romantic cinema follows this development. Romanticism is a reaction to rationalist philosophy that seeks truth through emotional experiences. How does *Bed of Roses* exemplify both romantic literature and romanticism? Is the film only a Valentine flick, or does it challenge us regarding love and covenanted relationships? What is the "truth" in the film, and how do the protagonists arrive at it? What kind of response does it seem to seek from the audience?

3. *Bed of Roses* uses obvious symbolism to tell its story: flowers, the garden, stars, music, and so forth. The Scriptures today also use symbolism to convey God's truth to us. What are these symbols, and how do they compare to those in the film? What is the role of

symbolism and metaphor in storytelling and the Word of God?

Prayer

Lord, we all know times of sorrow. Help us not to remain stuck in our sadness, but to recognize the freeing power of love in our lives. Amen.

1919-115

Brock Peters in *To Kill a Mockingbird*.

Deuteronomy 5:12–15;
2 Corinthians 4:6–11; Mark 2:23—3:6

To Kill a Mockingbird
U.S.A., 1962, 129 minutes
Cast: Gregory Peck, Mary Badham, John Megna, Philip Alford,
Brock Peters, Robert Duvall, Narration by Kim Stanley
Writer: Horton Foote
Director: Robert Mulligan

To Kill a Mockingbird

A Just Man and the Law

SYNOPSIS

Jem and Scout Finch are two children living with their widowed father, Atticus, in a small Alabama town in 1932. Atticus is a good man and a well-respected lawyer. He brings up his children according to principles of justice and respect for all human beings.

Jem and Scout are afraid of their strange, hidden neighbor, Boo Radley, but find small indications that Radley might be friendly.

Atticus agrees to defend an African-American man, Tom Robinson, who is accused of raping a white woman, Mayella Ewell. This stirs up racial bigotry among the citizens. The night before Tom's trial, fearing trouble, Atticus guards the jail. A vigilante group confronts him, but Scout eases tension when she joins her father. The crowd disperses.

During the trial, Atticus shows that the prosecution witnesses, Bob Ewell and his daughter Mayella, have lied. Tom Robinson's left hand had been severely injured in an accident, so he could not have assaulted and raped the woman as described in testimony. Atticus' closing statement is an eloquent plea for justice for African-Americans. Nevertheless, the jury finds Tom guilty. When Tom is later shot dead, the sheriff claims he was trying to escape.

Ewell is angry at Atticus for defending Tom Robinson. It is obvious that Ewell—who is right-handed—is the real culprit who assaulted his own daughter. One night Ewell retaliates by attacking Jem and Scout, but he is killed by a mysterious assailant: Boo Radley, who has been looking out for the children.

COMMENTARY

To Kill a Mockingbird is one of the best-loved and admired films ever made in the United States. Based on the celebrated novel by Harper Lee, it was adapted for the screen by playwright Horton Foote in an Oscar-winning screenplay. Foote's distinguished writing career for stage and screen includes credits for *The Chase, Tender Mercies, The Trip to Bountiful, 1918, Valentine's Day,* and *Of Mice and Men.*

Robert Mulligan, the director, made a series of sensitive dramas during the 1960s: *Love with the Proper Stranger, Baby the Rain Must Fall* (also written by Foote), and *Up the Down Staircase.* Mulligan's creative collaborator was producer Alan Pakula, who made the transition to directing in the late 1960s with memorable movies like *Klute, All the President's Men,* and *Sophie's Choice.*

Movie buffs will be interested to see Robert Duvall in his first screen role as Boo Radley. Young Mary Badham received a Best Supporting Actress nomination for her role as Scout. The character of Dill is based on Truman Capote, a childhood friend of Harper Lee's. Gregory Peck won the Academy Award for Best Actor for his role as Atticus Finch.

Though the events in the film take place thirty years before the Civil Rights era in the United States, the film acted as a catalyst for change.

Focus: Atticus Finch is a lawyer trying to break through the legal and social injustices afflicting African-Americans. Jesus tells the Pharisees that the law was for people's welfare, and not the other way around.

DIALOGUE WITH THE GOSPEL

If we were to consider only the reading from Paul to the Corinthians today, there would be more than enough parallels between Paul's words about light shining out of darkness and *To Kill a Mockingbird*. Atticus Finch is an earthen vessel holding a great treasure of light, goodness, and justice. He might be perplexed and persecuted, but he is not constrained or driven to the darkness of despair.

The readings from Deuteronomy and the Gospel turn our attention to Atticus' profession: the law. The first reading lays down the law of Sabbath rest, stating that even male and female slaves should share in the rest and worship of God, their Master. The Sabbath law does not condone slavery, but reminds the people that observing the Sabbath rest is an opportunity for everyone to remember the saving act of God that made them who they are.

Unfortunately, later interpreters of the Law forgot its basis in the experience of God's saving power. Rules governing external behavior sometimes received more attention than the actual meaning or spirit of the Law. The Pharisees condemned the disciples for picking the heads of grain on the Sabbath. Jesus was impatient with such quibbling and pointed out that the Law is for our welfare; it is not meant to enslave us to minutiae and self-righteous applications.

Scout embraces her father's advice to practice sympathy and understanding and demonstrates that her experiences with hatred and prejudice will not sully her faith in human goodness. Atticus Finch's main attribute is his dedication to the meaning of the law and its social function to preserve human rights and dignity. Former laws of segregation dictate what we see in the courtroom scene: African-Americans sit in the balcony apart from the white townspeople. We also see how the underlying social and cultural segregation made it impossible for the jury to find a black man innocent despite the overwhelming evidence. Atticus Finch breaks through this prejudice and teaches his family and the community about justice, restraint, and honesty.

Today's Scripture readings and film profoundly call us to conversion of both heart and life.

KEY SCENES AND THEMES

- The Finch family and their place in the town; Atticus the widower caring for his children, bringing them up according to strict but just principles; Atticus explaining that their neighbor, Boo Radley, is not scary; justice for Tom Robinson and not killing a mockingbird.

- The children and their perspective on the townspeople; the hearings at the courthouse, the children watching the trial; Atticus' vigil at the prison; Scout talking to Cunningham.

- Tom Robinson as a victim of malice and prejudice; Atticus' eloquent defense, the guilty verdict; the unlikely cause of Tom's death; Boo Radley as a victim, his care for the children, saving Jem and Scout, the children walking hand in hand with Boo.

FOR REFLECTION AND CONVERSATION

1. Between the end of Reconstruction after the Civil War (1877) and desegregation in the 1960s, African-Americans were subjected to the humiliating "Jim Crow" laws in states south of the Mason-Dixon line, which kept white people and black people publicly separated. St. Thomas Aquinas wrote, "Human law is law

only by virtue of its accordance with right reason, and by this means it is clear that it flows from Eternal law. Insofar as it deviates from right reason, it is called an Unjust law; and in such a case, it is no law at all, but rather an assertion of violence." How is this true in *To Kill a Mockingbird?* What is the cause of racism, and how is it perpetuated in law and in cultures? What can we do to teach human dignity, respect, and tolerance in our own homes first of all? When God's law and human law are at odds, how are we to respond as believers?

2. Some recent films comment on racism, the fallout of the many years of legal segregation in the United States. *American History X* is a shockingly brutal yet honest film about a father teaching racism to his sons and the dire consequences in a post-segregation world. *Pleasantville* refers back to the black and white film, *To Kill a Mockingbird,* when it recreates the balcony scene in a courtroom, thus commenting on the evil of distinguishing between people because of their color. *A Time to Kill* questions the possibility of a black man receiving a fair trial in America. How do these films comment on racism of any kind? How do entertainment and information media represent the people of various ethnic or cultural groups in your area?

3. *To Kill a Mockingbird* is filled with gothic images: the unseasonal snowfall, the burning of Miss Maudie's house, the gloom and darkness, and the children's superstitious fears of Boo Radley. Through these images we see the contrast between good and evil, the role of parents in the education of their children, and what it means to be a human being. What other images and symbols are present, and how do they create

meaning in the film? Is *To Kill a Mockingbird* a "white man's film" because a white man tries to save a black man? How might this be a film with a message for any time, for any group, in any place that believes itself superior to others?

Prayer

Jesus, open our hearts to the meaning of your law. Help us to avoid rigid observance of the law and judging others; rather, help us to embrace its spirit. Amen.

Bram Stoker's Dracula

U.S.A., 1992, 128 minutes
Cast: Gary Oldman, Anthony Hopkins, Winona Ryder,
Keanu Reeves, Richard E. Grant, Tom Waites,
Sadie Frost, Cary Elwes
Writer: James V. Hart
Director: Francis Ford Coppola

Bram Stoker's Dracula

Symbol of the Diabolical

SYNOPSIS

The Prologue: It is 1462 and Prince Vlad Dracula is victorious in battle at Constantinople. When he returns to Transylvania he finds that his enemies have shot an arrow into his castle with a letter to his wife, Elisabeta, stating that Dracula is dead. In despair, his wife dresses in her wedding gown and throws herself from a tower and dies. When she is refused Christian burial by the very Church he has been defending, the grief-crazed Dracula throws a lance at a cross, drinks the blood that flows from it, and declares that, after death, he will rise and avenge his wife.

In 1897, a British businessman, Jonathan Harker, arrives in Transylvania to sell some London real estate to the reclusive Count Dracula. Dracula sees a photo of Mina Murray, Harker's fiancée, and becomes obsessed with the idea that she is the reincarnation of Elisabeta. He imprisons Harker and sails to England. Before arriving, he destroys the ship's crew and drinks their blood.

In England, Dracula moves around by morphing into creatures. He pursues Mina in the guise of a charming Eastern European prince, and she is attracted to him as well.

Dracula preys on Lucy Westenra, Mina's friend, and turns her into a vampire.

Dr. Seward attends an ailing Lucy and calls in Dr. Van Helsing, a blood specialist, to try to explain her illness. Van Helsing is a vampire hunter. Meanwhile, Mina travels to Transylvania to marry Jonathan, who has escaped from Dracula's palace. (Jonathan has not been "infected" or bitten by a vampire.)

Van Helsing, Seward, and a group of Lucy's admirers rouse Dracula at the abbey, where he spends his days sleeping in soil he brought from home. Dracula comes to Mina's room, and they vow eternal love while drinking each other's blood. He then flees and the group pursues him back to Transylvania. Van Helsing hypnotizes Mina to find out where Dracula is. When Dracula emerges from his coffin at sunset, they set upon him. Harker cuts his throat and tries to destroy him. Even as she kisses him, it is Mina who drives a knife through Dracula's heart.

COMMENTARY

Irish author Bram Stoker published his famed novel in 1897, and it has never been out of print since. F. W. Murnau filmed the story as *Nosferatu the Vampire* in 1922, using German expressionist styles of light, darkness, and shadow. Coppola is indebted to Murnau's style for this film, as was Werner Herzog for his 1979 version, *Nosferatu the Vampyre*. The "classic" screen Dracula was played by Bela Lugosi in the 1930 film version of the story. Also of interest is *Shadow of the Vampire*, which premiered in 2000 (about the filming of Murnau's original *Nosferatu the Vampire*).

Writer James V. Hart has provided a historical prologue with information about Count Vlad Dracul, nicknamed "The Impaler," and the religious background leading to his becoming the notorious Dracula.

Francis Ford Coppola has made a number of significant films including *The Godfather Trilogy, The Conversation, American Graffiti*, and *Apocalypse Now. Bram Stoker's Dracula* was advertised with the caption, "Love never dies," and was presented as a romance as much as a horror story. Gary Oldman's performance, Hart's writing, and Coppola's direction make this a credible and involving drama using symbols of diabolical evil.

Focus: The reading from Genesis as well as the Gospel shows images of evil and the devil. Dracula has long been a symbol of diabolical evil.

DIALOGUE WITH THE GOSPEL

Apart from the Gospel narratives of Jesus' temptations in the desert, it is only in Cycle B that the Church gives us readings that focus on evil and the devil. These include the exorcism Gospel for the Fourth Sunday of the Year and today's discussion about the presence of the devil in the world.

The Genesis reading reminds us of the archetypal story of temptation and sin. The serpent is the seducer, an intelligent being that takes animal form in order to tempt the humans who occupy the garden. The story also highlights the confrontation between the man and the woman and the tension between the woman and the devil; it is ultimately she who will conquer him. The responsorial psalm reminds us that no matter how low the depths into which we fall, God promises redemption.

The scribes in the Gospel are the exorcists of their day. Jesus appears casting out powerful devils, and he incurs the jealousy of the religious professionals who accuse him of using the devil to cast out the devil. Jesus replies, however, that Satan cannot stand if divided against himself.

Dracula is a tormented and divided devil. His inner conflict and division is symbolized in his love for Mina that does not prevent him from seeking to destroy her life at the same time. As the prologue of the movie shows, Dracula is divided against himself. He despairs of God, blasphemes against the Holy Spirit, and rejects forgiveness—things he could not do unless he believed.

Mina, who kills Dracula, is the Eve-figure, the woman who was tempted and finally crushes the evil one. Mary, the Mother of Jesus, has always been considered the new Eve, who crushes the head of the serpent. Mary appears at the end of today's Gospel, not merely as mother, but as the one who does not succumb to temptation. She does the will of God. She is the model of all who try to be faithful to God's will and reject the temptations of the evil one.

KEY SCENES AND THEMES

- The prologue: Vlad the Impaler, fifteenth-century Romania, the silhouettes of the battle; the role of the Church, the Turks, the fall of Constantinople, Vlad's victory, kissing the cross, the false information, Elisabeta's suicide; Dracul piercing the cross, the blood flowing, his vow against God and rising from the grave to avenge his wife.

- Dracula the diabolical monster, his eyes and the sky, his face over Lucy and Mina; the undead, evil, and blood.

- Van Helsing, his background, his quest against evil, his confrontation with Dracula; the destruction of the diabolical monster.

FOR REFLECTION AND CONVERSATION

1. *Bram Stoker's Dracula* is not for everyone. It is an explicit horror film in the full sense of the term, but the story's century-old tradition in film, and this rather avant-garde rendition, make it worth seeing. There is evil and blood everywhere. In what some considered a surprising move, the 1922 silent version of Dracula's story, *Nosferatu the Vampire,* was placed on the list of the Vatican's "Forty Important Films" under the category of art. The list was published in 1995 to mark the centenary of cinema's beginnings. *Nosferatu the*

Vampire deserves to be compared to this version of the story. Using the Gospel dialogue above as a context, why is Dracula's story a religious one, despite some of its explicit scenes? Why do you think the Vatican's Pontifical Council for Social Communications would place the Dracula story on a list of important films?

2. *The Catechism of the Catholic Church,* numbers 407–412, and 410 in particular, refer precisely to today's Genesis reading, humanity's struggle with evil, the question of sin and redemption: "This passage in Genesis is called the 'Protoevangelium' (first gospel): the first announcement of the Messiah and Redeemer, of a battle between the serpent and the Woman, and of the final victory of a descendent of hers." How do the forces of good and evil confront each other in *Bram Stoker's Dracula?* Why is the woman as savior so significant to the story?

3. Why do people go to horror shows? At an interview sponsored by "Reel Spirituality" in October 2001 in Los Angeles, horror film director Wes Craven *(Nightmare on Elm Street, Dracula 2000)* told interviewer Scott Derrickson that people go to horror movies already afraid, and that these kinds of films are a way to process their fears. They also go because they already have a sense of being lost and threatened, and a horror film puts the threat of chaos into a narrative with control over its beginning, middle, and end. Do you agree with Craven's rationale? Why or why not? If what Craven says is true, can there be a point of integration between fear of evil, horror films, and Christian faith? If so, how? If not, why?

Prayer

Mary, full of grace, you said yes to God's will for you. Help us to say yes as you did and to reject the temptations of evil. Amen.

ELEVENTH SUNDAY OF THE YEAR

Ezekiel 17:22–24; 2 Corinthians 5:6–10;
Mark 4:26–34

Finding Forrester

U.S.A., 2001, 130 minutes
Cast: Sean Connery, Rob Brown, F. Murray Abraham,
Anna Paquin, Busta Rhymes, Michael Nouri
Writer: Mike Rich
Director: Gus Van Sant

Finding Forrester

The Gift of a Mentor

SYNOPSIS

Jamal Wallace is sixteen years old and attends a South Bronx high school. Jamal plays basketball with his friends in a parking lot and accepts a dare to go into the apartment of a recluse they know is watching them through binoculars. When Jamal does, he is caught. He runs away in fright, leaving behind his notebooks and his backpack.

When the recluse returns his backpack, Jamal finds comments written on his essays, and a strong friendship begins between Jamal and the crusty, vulnerable man. Jamal learns that he is William Forrester, the winner of a Pulitzer Prize for his only novel, published in the 1950s. Forrester becomes Jamal's creative writing mentor.

The school's literature teacher, Robert Crawford, is suspicious of Jamal's writing ability and accuses him of plagiarizing an article written by Forrester.

Forrester comes out of his seclusion to help Jamal. He reads one of Jamal's essays and Crawford, believing the work to be Forrester's, is humiliated to learn that Jamal is the author.

Forrester returns to Scotland where he eventually dies. In his will he leaves everything to Jamal, including the manuscript of a novel, *Sunset,* for which Jamal is to write an introduction.

COMMENTARY

Finding Forrester director Gus Van Sant also directed *Good Will Hunting,* a film about a brilliant young man who resisted mentoring in mathematics, but found a kind of spiritual mentor when he confronted his personal problems in therapy. *Finding Forrester,* Van Sant said, is a natural extension of *Good Will Hunting.* Both films show students whose creative gifts grow side by side with their inner development because of mentors who cared.

Some reviewers rejected *Finding Forrester,* cynically calling it "high-minded" and "preachy." Hopefully, audiences will disagree and find this appealing story both inspiring and encouraging. Talents should not be hidden, and if we are unable to develop them ourselves, it is a gift to find someone who will draw them out.

Sean Connery credibly portrays a character that is simultaneously irascible and vulnerable. Rob Brown has a natural talent for the screen. When he turned up to audition as an extra with no previous acting experience, he won the role of Jamal. He and Connery work well together, and we can believe in the reality and depth of their friendship.

DIALOGUE WITH THE GOSPEL

Focus: A person's talent may seem slight because of one's fear of recognition; it requires nurturing to make it fruitful. The main characters in Finding Forrester *call to mind the grain and the tree-like mustard plant in today's Scripture.*

Ezekiel offers the image of a towering cedar. Its vast branches provide shade and shelter for "every winged thing." William Forrester, an acclaimed and revered award-winning author, has not published anything since the Pulitzer Prize fifty years before. While his growth has been stunted by the sorrows in his life and his hermit-like existence, he is able to offer Jamal a refuge in which he can develop. Forrester is a strong, wise, aging cedar to Jamal's youthful, vague, mustard seed-like talent, waiting in the field of his soul.

Jesus' parables, as in today's Gospel, were often metaphors for the kingdom of God. After he spent time exploring the parables' meaning with his disciples, Jesus enabled them to grow and teach others. When Forrester becomes Jamal's mentor, he shares his talent and vision with him. The seed planted may have been small, but the crop will be abundant. Jamal will eventually grow into a great tree, like Ezekiel's cedar; like Forrester, Jamal will be able to offer shade and shelter to others, as the mustard seed will eventually do.

- Forrester in his apartment, looking at the basketball players with his binoculars; his initial encounter with Jamal, writing comments on his work; talking about creative writing, opening up to Jamal and telling him his life story.

- Jamal and his writing, hiding his intelligence from his friends; the offer of a scholarship; his response to Forrester and to his classes; the clash with his lecturer, Crawford, and his conduct in the literary competition.

- Forrester leaving his apartment; reading Jamal's essay and supporting him against Crawford; the letter from Scotland and leaving his house, books, support, and his new novel to Jamal.

KEY SCENES AND THEMES

1. Just as the parables offer reflections on God and the kingdom, so does *Finding Forrester*. William Forrester is an all-knowing God-figure, watching the world on his three televisions—all on at the same time, but on different channels. He sits literally "on high," watching the boys play ball in the street. Forrester is complex—judgmental, harsh, kind, challenging, and good. He is a father figure to a young man sorely in

FOR REFLECTION AND CONVERSATION

need of one. As the film proceeds, our understanding of Forrester grows and changes. What is your image of God? How, if at all, has this image grown and changed over the years? What might account for this change?

2. The dominant theme of the films chosen for this volume of *Lights, Camera...Faith! A Movie Lectionary* centers on the dignity of the human person. Today's film addresses the human attributes of talent and genius. The school invites Jamal to become a student because of his talent for basketball rather than who he might really be. How often in real life is a young person seen for his or her "talent," rather than for who he or she is as a person? What does this say about how society sees and values young people in general?

3. In *Finding Forrester,* William Forrester's mentoring changed Jamal's life. In 1997, the Center for Applied Research in the Apostolate (CARA) of Georgetown University (www.georgetown.edu/research/cara) published the results of a survey on vocations to the religious life and priesthood. One significant factor contributing to fewer people entering ministries was found to be a lack of religious and clergy available for mentoring. Because they are so involved in administrative tasks, mentoring is not a priority. How can this challenge be overcome so that mentoring can become a priority in the Church? What does it mean to truly mentor another?

Prayer

Lord, help us to discern the mustard seeds of talent you have planted within us. Grant us the help of wise and affirming persons so that our gifts may grow. Amen.

Titanic

U.S.A., 1997, 186 minutes
Cast: Leonardo DiCaprio, Kate Winslet, Bill Paxton,
Gloria Stuart, Kathy Bates, Billy Zane,
Frances Farmer, David Warner, Victor Garber
Writer: James Cameron
Director: James Cameron

Titanic

Master, Do You Care? We Are Going Down!

In the 1990s, modern deep-sea technology allowed the exploration of the wreck of the mythic *Titanic*. Rose, now 101 years old, is a survivor of the disaster who identifies herself as the wearer of a fabulous diamond seen in a surviving drawing that the divers recover. The exploratory team is resolved to find the diamond.

SYNOPSIS

The movie flashes back to 1912. The *Titanic* prepares to sail from Southampton, England. Captain Smith and the crew are urged by the company chiefs to break all the speed records to arrive in New York early. The engineer who designed the ship, Thomas Andrews, has grave reservations. The wealthy passengers assemble and move into their luxury cabins. Among these are Rose DeWitt Bukater, her moody fiancé, Cal Hockley, and her mother. Meanwhile, a penniless artist named Jack Dawson and his friend win tickets for the voyage in a card game and hurry aboard.

Jack is an enthusiastic young man, full of life. When Rose, in despair over her coming marriage, attempts to jump from the ship, Jack saves her. A romance blossoms between Jack and Rose, and he sketches her wearing the diamond necklace. Cal becomes fiercely jealous.

The ship strikes an iceberg south of Newfoundland and the *Titanic* begins to flood. Passengers rush to fill the insufficient number of lifeboats. The struggle for survival is a mixture of heroics and selfishness. Cal traps and shackles Jack below deck, but Rose searches for him and frees him. They escape from the doomed ship by jumping overboard. Rose floats on some debris and Jack holds on, waiting for rescue. Jack dies in the freezing water while Rose survives.

Back to the present, the elderly Rose throws the diamond, which she has kept all these years, into the sea.

COMMENTARY

Titanic was a movie event that more than satisfied audiences around the world. It won eleven Academy Awards, including Best Film, Best Director, Best Cinematography, Best Musical Score, and Best Song.

James Cameron is well known for action and special-effect films such as *The Terminator* movies, *Aliens, The Abyss,* and *True Lies.* In *Titanic* he reinforces his reputation for creating on-screen spectacles. *Titanic* is an epic film, running nearly four hours long. Its enormous budget had to cover the cost of a new built-to-scale ship that was only somewhat smaller than the original *Titanic.* Once the plotline moves to the story of the *Titanic* itself, audiences are overwhelmed by the re-creation of the ship; the extraordinary re-enactment of the sinking is a powerfully emotional experience.

The human story is conventional, especially the contrast between the wealthy elite and the steerage immigrants. Billy Zane, David Warner, and Frances Fisher do what is expected, and Kathy Bates is a vigorous and believable "unsinkable" Molly Brown. At the center of the action are the two young actors who make their variation on the Romeo-and-Juliet theme come alive. Leonardo DiCaprio proves he is versatile and talented and Kate Winslet complements him effectively.

Titanic is a mighty cinematic experience, and video and DVD audiences continue to respond to its theme of undying love.

Focus: When the storm arose on the lake, Jesus taught his disciples that they needed more faith. The passengers on the Titanic *are tested. Some show themselves selfless, and others selfish.*

DIALOGUE WITH THE GOSPEL

When built, the *Titanic* was the best-designed and most luxurious ship to ever sail the Atlantic. It had been proclaimed as "unsinkable," yet it had not even been sailing for a week when it sank. Over the decades, it has become a symbol of human pride and what it means to be brought low.

The first reading from Job is God's challenge to human pride: "Thus far shall you come, but no farther, and here shall your proud waves be stilled." The imagery of immense pent-up waves about to be unleashed reminds us of God's omnipotence.

The Gospel about the calming of the storm would have been familiar to many of the *Titanic's* passengers. It must have seemed to them that God was asleep, allowing them to perish in the waters of the Atlantic. Yet, as the ship sank, the band played *Nearer, My God, to Thee,* and the film shows many of the people facing their death with devout faith.

Jack had already saved Rose from suicide, and his love for her made her want to live. As they float in the freezing waters, with only space for one person on their makeshift raft, he saves her life again when he makes her promise to keep on living no matter what happens to him. Jack's love and self-sacrifice have overtones of the words of Paul in the second reading. Jesus' love for us is overwhelming, expressed most clearly in his dying for us. He died so that we would no longer live for ourselves. Jack died so that Rose could live on in his love.

KEY SCENES AND THEMES

- The initial view of the sunken ship and the information given by the computer-graph demonstration; the return to 1912 and the majestic ship, its engineering, beauty, and luxury; the iceberg and the sudden destruction of the ship.

- The cross-section of passengers: the wealthy, the working-class people, the immigrants, the distinction between the social classes; the disaster cutting through class divisions and showing heroism, cowardice, and fear among everyone.

- Jack and Rose, their meeting, their love for each other; Jack saving Rose from suicide; life on deck; his saving her life in the freezing waters; the band playing *Nearer, My God, to Thee.*

FOR REFLECTION AND CONVERSATION

1. In general, the Hebrew people were not seafaring because they lived inland. References to ships and the sea are almost always associated with mystery and disaster (cf. *Dictionary of Biblical Imagery*, 1998, InterVarsity Press). Christians will always associate St. Paul with a shipwreck. Noah's ark, a refuge and place of safety, on the other hand, became a symbol of the Church to the Fathers of the Church. St. Ambrose (d. A.D. 397) saw a cross in the masts of the ships of his day. Using a concordance, research some of the Scripture citations about ships, boats, and the sea. How do the symbolism of ships and boats and these references make today's Scripture readings, through the story of the *Titanic,* more meaningful? What parallels, if any, can be drawn?

2. Cameron's very successful use of a romance in *Titanic* was a magnet to people young and old. One young woman said she and her boyfriend watched the movie

several times and their relationship grew in kindness and respect as a result of seeing how Jack treated Rose. Others fault the film for the sexual encounter between Jack and Rose, which they believe typifies today's lack of respect for chastity before marriage. What do you think is the message of the film and the place of the love story in it? Could the sexual relationship work as a metaphor for the lack of intimacy in the lives of Jack and Rose? How might today's reading of Paul's Letter to the Corinthians shed light on and speak to the morality of the love story in the film?

3. Human freedom, that is, interior freedom, is another theme in today's readings. At one point, Rose says, "I know what you must be thinking. 'Poor little rich girl, what does she know about misery?'" And Jack responds, "No, no, that's not what I was thinking. What I was thinking was, what could've happened to this girl to make her feel she had no way out?" Who is a "free" person in *Titanic*? Is *Titanic* "just another love story," or is there more to it? What transcendent values, if any, did the movie seem to convey?

Prayer

Lord, when we find ourselves in the midst of life's overwhelming storms, increase our faith in your provident care. Amen.

A Test of Love (Annie's Coming Out)
Australia, 1984, 93 minutes
Cast: Angela Punch McGregor, Drew Forsythe,
Tina Arhondis, Monica Maughan, Simon Chilvers,
Wallas Eaton, Charles Tingwell
Writers: John Patterson, Chris Borthwick
Director: Gil Brealey

A Test of Love (Annie's Coming Out)

She Is Not Dead

SYNOPSIS

Jessica Hathaway is a social worker in Australia, newly employed by a state hospital for severely disabled children who are assumed to be mentally retarded. Her manner is concerned, vigorous, and compassionate toward the children, and she immediately begins to make changes. She adjusts the layout of the ward, brings in posters and pictures, and takes the children into the facility's garden. She treats the children as if they are intelligent rather than retarded. The authorities are wary of her innovations and methods.

Annie O'Farrell, a fourteen-year-old who has cerebral palsy and suffers from debilitating spasticity, attracts Jessica's attention. She finds ways of testing whether Annie can understand her or not. Using a letter board for Annie to spell out words by pointing to them, Jessica tries to persuade the doctors that Annie possesses above average intelligence. She takes Annie home with her and on outings to art galleries. Jessica's boyfriend, David, is supportive, but finds that his life is being taken over by Annie and by Jessica's preoccupation with her.

Government officials are increasingly suspicious of Jessica, and the head of the hospital, Dr. Rowell, refuses to see Annie any differently despite her progress. Jessica and David approach a lawyer who takes the case to court in order to contest Annie's detention in the hospital for the mentally handicapped. The sympathetic judge gives Annie a test, which she passes. The verdict is in Annie's favor, and she leaves with Jessica.

COMMENTARY

A Test of Love was originally titled *Annie's Coming Out* when it was released in Australia. It is based on a book by Rosemary Crossley and Anne McDonald about Crossley's experiences in Melbourne during the 1970s. The movie is a slightly fictionalized account of an actual case.

A Test of Love is a plea for the consideration of handicapped children with conditions like cerebral palsy, who may seem to have low intelligence and are maintained without affection or a chance to develop intellectually. Five years after this movie, audiences worldwide responded sympathetically to the life of Irishman Christy Brown, who also suffered from severe cerebral palsy, portrayed in *My Left Foot*.

There are some very powerful scenes at the opening of the movie when Jessica goes through the wards and sees the children for the first time. The film also contains sequences that show clashes of opinion about the status of the children's quality of life and how easy it is to dismiss and/or deride them.

Annie's Coming Out won the Australian Film Institute awards in 1984 for Best Film, and Angela Punch McGregor, one of Australia's leading stars of the 1970s and 1980s, won for Best Actress. She gives a spirited performance, carrying audience sympathy along with her.

**DIALOGUE WITH
THE GOSPEL**

*Focus: People laughed when Jesus said the daughter of Jairus
was not dead but asleep. People laughed when Jessica said that
Annie was not retarded, but intelligent. Each girl was given
the gift of new life.*

The fifth chapter of Mark's Gospel is one of the most
compassionate portions of all the Gospels. It contains two
stories about Jesus' life-giving ministry: the woman who had
been hemorrhaging for twelve years and Jairus' daughter
being raised to life.

Overall, this Gospel narrative focuses on the child. Jessica might be seen as both a figure of the woman with a
hemorrhage and a Christ-figure. Jessica is like the bleeding
woman as her heart bled with compassion, and she finds satisfaction at the end of her efforts. She is a Christ-figure
because she extends healing power to Annie, just as healing
went forth from Jesus.

Annie O'Farrell is not dead, but is treated as if she were.
There seems to be no reason to bring her to a fuller life. In
fact, like the crowd who scoffs when Jesus tells them the child
is not dead but asleep, the nursing staff treats Jessica's attempts to communicate with Annie and the other children
with contempt. Even Annie's parents are against Jessica. Yet,
Jessica perseveres and raises Annie to life.

The basis of this compassion is to be found in the reading from Wisdom; death is not God's doing. God takes no
pleasure in human suffering and death, "the destruction of
the living." All human beings are created in God's image, for
"he fashioned all things that they might have being." Compassionate caregivers are able to discern wholeness in those
who are sick and enable them to live a better life.

Paul speaks of a rationale for Christian benevolence and
a balance for those who work for the relief of the afflicted.
Helping others is not about impoverishing oneself, but about
giving so that everyone may be equal. The movie dramatizes

Jessica's struggle as she almost loses David's support because of her obsession with Annie. As Annie needed Jessica, Jessica needed Vera and David. Wholeness of life is God's desire for all.

KEY SCENES AND THEMES

- Jessica's tour of the wards and seeing the neglected children, their illnesses, disabilities; Jessica's realization that the children are alert and her suspecting their actual intelligence; the lack of compassion on the part of most of the staff; Dr. Rowell's statement that the children had to get by without affection.

- Jessica's work with Annie, discovering a way to help her to communicate "yes" and "no"; the visit to the art gallery and Annie's laughing at the caricature; Annie's use of the letter board and her comment on David while Jessica is out of the room, Annie's response to education.

- The indifference of the staff; Vera's mixed attitudes toward Jessica, her report; Dr. Rowell's hostility, the government official; the lawyer's investigations, the court hearing, the defense and prosecution arguments; the judge's test, the verdict, and Annie's freedom.

FOR REFLECTION AND CONVERSATION

1. Caring professions require people with well-adjusted personalities capable of being compassionate and living their own personal lives at the same time. As Jesus felt the power go out of him in the healing of the woman with the hemorrhage, so caregivers can feel their power diminish if they do not take the means to renew themselves. Jessica came close to burning out when her love and attention became so obsessively focused on Annie that she nearly destroyed her personal life. Why was saving Annie the one thing Jessica

had to do? Was she right to sacrifice so much of herself for Annie? Why or why not? How can caregivers stay strong for the sake of those they serve?

2. In 1972, television reporter Geraldo Rivera went into the Willowbrook State School in Staten Island, New York, and filmed a story exposing the horrible conditions that resulted from budget cuts: patients were sick because of the filth they lived in, the small staff could not cope. Rivera's report shocked the nation and began a series of actions that changed legislation and improved the quality of life for the disabled. How can journalists, filmmakers, and communicators of every kind become means of healing for those in need? Recall other news stories or films that have been the means of social reform and healing for justice (e.g., *Cry Freedom*). Why is respect for the dignity of the person at the heart of all human activity, especially healing?

3. Compassion is sympathy for the plight of others combined with the desire to do something to help. What saints are known particularly for their part in healing others, spiritually and physically? How did they do this? Who are some contemporary people whose lives personify the compassion of Jesus?

Prayer
Lord, people came to you in their desperate need for healing and life. Show your compassion to those who are neglected in their sufferings. May they be given the care they need and deserve. Amen.

Raul Julia in *Romero*.

FOURTEENTH SUNDAY OF THE YEAR

Ezekiel 2:2–5; 2 Corinthians 12:7–10;
Mark 6:1–6

Romero

U.S.A., 1989, 105 minutes
Cast: Raul Julia, Richard Jordan, Harold Gould,
Tony Plana, Ana Alicia
Writer: John Sacret Young
Director: John Duigan

Romero

A Prophet Rejected

SYNOPSIS

A right-wing military junta governs the Central American country of El Salvador during the civil war of the 1970s. Fr. Oscar Romero is a quiet, rather reserved and bookish priest working in the capitol, San Salvador. In a move that surprises many, Rome appoints Fr. Romero archbishop of San Salvador and primate of the country. It is expected that his episcopate will not have a great impact and that he will support the status quo.

At the instigation of his friend, Fr. Grande, Archbishop Romero soon begins to look more closely at the social situation of the country, but he does not openly criticize the government and its repression until the outspoken Fr. Grande is killed. This murder so saddens and enrages Romero that he becomes more actively involved in the fight for justice.

Criticized by the government and military, he is arrested and tortured, but continues to speak out. He makes an impassioned radio broadcast appealing to the military to stop the repression. Instead, they plan to kill him. On April 20, 1980, Archbishop Romero is shot while celebrating Mass.

Romero was produced by Fr. Ellwood "Bud" Kieser, a Paulist priest who produced the popular television *Insight* series for many years, as well as *Entertaining Angels: The Dorothy Day Story* and several made-for-television movies.

The screenplay is by John Sacret Young, the originator and writer of the television series, *China Beach.* Australian John Duigan directed *Romero.* Other films that he wrote, directed, or produced include *Far East, The Year My Voice Broke,* and *Flirting.*

Raul Julia gives an impressive performance as Archbishop Romero. The movie is fairly straightforward in style as a popular biopic of a clergyman whose reclusive and academic ways are challenged by the social unrest and atrocities in El Salvador. He comes to realize that God has chosen him to be a martyr.

The stereotyping of the aristocracy and the persecuted people is a weak point in this otherwise earnest narrative. The film invites audiences to appreciate the challenges that life presented to a man like Romero. It communicates the atmosphere of social injustice in Latin America, especially in El Salvador. *Romero* was shown to the American Congress to provide background for a debate about Central America.

Focus: Jesus preached the Good News to the poor and was rejected by his own people. Oscar Romero's life and death can be understood in the light of the example given by Jesus.

Oscar Romero was officially anointed a servant of the Lord when he became archbishop of San Salvador. He surprised himself and his people by becoming a prophetic voice proclaiming the truth about injustice and calling for justice instead. Today's reading from Ezekiel aptly describes what happened to the shy and scholarly priest. The spirit of the Lord entered into him, and he found the strength and conviction to confront the oppressors of his land. The words of

Paul in the second reading come alive when we observe Archbishop Romero. God's grace was sufficient for him because "power has been made perfect in weakness" and "when I am weak, then I am strong."

In three short years, Archbishop Romero was able to announce with increasing conviction that his mission and that of the Church was to relieve the suffering of the people of his country. This is the language of authentic liberation spirituality. In the eyes of such a corrupt regime the consequence of this mission was death. Just as Jesus was criticized in Nazareth, so the Salvadorian establishment turned against Romero and the government sponsored his execution.

While Archbishop Romero was actually killed after Communion, the film chose the more dramatic moment after the Consecration for the murder—when the newly consecrated wine, now the Blood of Christ, joined with the blood of the martyr.

The witness of Oscar Romero echoes the ending of the reading from Ezekiel: "And whether they heed or resist—for they are a rebellious house—they shall know that a prophet has been among them."

KEY SCENES AND THEMES

- Romero as a quiet clergyman, dressed in a cassock; his friendship with Fr. Grande, their conversations, ideas, the question of some clergy being communists; the revolutionaries, the portrait of Jesus Christ the Revolutionary; Romero named Archbishop of San Salvador, the hostility of the priests to his appointment, his episcopal ordination; the bishops' conference, the meetings, the sinister whisperings of the bishops; the factions.

- Romero changing, the radio broadcasts, the decision about the celebration of Mass, the interdict, going to get the Blessed Sacrament from the altar, the shooting of the altar; the hostages, betrayal, arrest, the experience in jail listening to the torture, the deaths; his wandering in agony, stripped of everything.

- The bishops, their opinions, military chaplains; the divided clergy mocking Romero; fighting for the people; the Galedo family, their status and lands, present at Romero's episcopal ordination, their role in government; the civil authorities, the president; Romero's final broadcast, vesting for the Mass, the soldiers drawing lots, the archbishop shot, and the wine falling from the chalice.

FOR REFLECTION AND CONVERSATION

1. The first thirty minutes of *Romero* lend themselves to theological reflection in a particular way as the Archbishop sincerely begins to learn from his own experience. He slows down to listen and attend to what people are telling him and what is happening around him. He enters into dialogue with others to gain insight. He discerns, prays, and then, with a vision that gives him a dynamic new perspective on his vocation as a human being and follower of Christ, takes action. How can *Romero* become part of our own theological reflection process?

2. Once again, we are offered a film to contemplate along with the Sunday readings that together parallel the Christian's obligation to witness to and work for social justice. How does a film like this evoke the Gospel message and the example of Christ? What do you think is at the heart of the Gospel message for all people of all times?

3. Justice is about rightness, fairness, and giving each person his or her due. Justice is also about commu-

nity over individualism. Through the many major motion pictures that tell stories of heroism, why do you think so few, whether based on fact or fiction, have women (or other minorities) as the protagonists? Martin Luther King, Jr. wrote in 1963: "Injustice anywhere is a threat to justice everywhere." How and why might this be true of representation regarding both entertainment and information media?

Prayer

Jesus, today we ask the intercession of Oscar Romero, holy man and martyr, to listen to the pleas of the poor to whom you came to preach Good News. Amen.

The Magnificent Seven.

The Magnificent Seven

U.S.A., 1960, 126 minutes
Cast: Yul Brynner, Steve McQueen, James Coburn,
Horst Buchholz, Robert Vaughn, Charles Bronson,
Brad Dexter, Eli Wallach
Writer: William Roberts
Director: John Sturges

The Magnificent Seven

Casting out Evil

The townspeople of the remote Mexican village of Ix-catlan grow their own crops and lead a peaceful and self-sufficient life. A bandit chief named Calvera leads his gang into the village, subjugates the people, and takes what he needs to maintain his men. With a power base and supplies, he leaves to attack other villages.

SYNOPSIS

The desperate villagers approach an American, Chris Adams, who promises to find some gunfighters to defend them and eliminate Calvera.

Chris recruits six others who sign on for minimal wages, each for his own reasons. There is the rugged Bernardo O'Reilly who befriends some of the village boys and who will die protecting them. Britt is a knife expert, and Lee suffers from nightmares—he is on the run and has an alcohol problem. Vin is second-in-command and has a calming influence on the group. Chico is a Mexican who falls in love with one of the local girls. Harry is a mercenary who believes there is more money involved.

The seven men teach the villagers how to shoot and they build a trench and walls to hide behind while fighting. Calvera comes to the village saying he wants to negotiate, but instead attacks. The seven fight off Calvera and his forty men, but as

235

they pursue him, they are betrayed by a fearful villager. Calvera moves back into the village while they are gone and captures the seven when they return. He takes their guns and expels them from the village. The villagers, who had hesitated to continue with the plan to fight Calvera, finally decide to act. They take guns to the seven and they return to the village. There is a desperate battle. In the shootout, four of the gunmen sacrifice their lives for the villagers. Calvera is also killed.

Chico stays in the village to marry the girl he fell in love with and to work with the villagers to rebuild the town and the farms. Chris and Vin ride away.

COMMENTARY

The Magnificent Seven is a movie classic that comes from a Golden Age of Westerns that began in the 1950s and extended to the mid-1960s. *The Magnificent Seven* director, John Sturges, also directed several other fine Westerns including *Bad Day at Black Rock, Gunfight at the O.K. Corral,* and *Last Train from Gun Hill.*

The source for *The Magnificent Seven* was Akira Kurosawa's 1955 classic, *The Seven Samurai.* Kurosawa was pleased that his film was used as a basis for an American Western, because his own movie was the result of his love for Westerns.

The Magnificent Seven consolidated Yul Brynner's reputation as a star and set some of the others, especially Steve McQueen, Charles Bronson, and James Coburn (who would win an Oscar thirty-eight years later for *Affliction*), on to high-profile screen careers. Elmer Bernstein's score remains one of the most instantly recognizable because it became the theme of Marlboro cigarettes commercials, which have not aired since they were outlawed in 1971. There was an attempt in 1998 to make *The Magnificent Seven* into a television series, but only twenty-two episodes were produced before it was cancelled. Three low-budget, routine sequels followed the original film.

Focus: As the Twelve are sent by Jesus to cast out devils, so the magnificent seven have a mission to cast out evildoers and defend the villagers from oppression.

DIALOGUE WITH THE GOSPEL

One might say that this is a Gospel about the Magnificent Twelve. As they go out two by two, their mission is, primarily, to cast out evil. They have "authority over unclean spirits." They are sent to villages and homes plagued by evil, to be accepted or rejected.

The seven gunfighters are not apostles; nevertheless, they have undergone, or are undergoing, a kind of transition in their lives that might be called a conversion. When they are hired to protect the villagers, they make a commitment to do something good. For several it means sacrificing their lives.

The seven men are welcomed into the village. The people, in the spirit of the Gospels, share with them what little they have. The hostility of the gang and its leader have dominated the poor villagers through violence. The village, possessed by the evil Calvera and his gang, needs these "devils" to be cast out from among them.

The confrontation between the seven and Calvera's men calls to mind the scenario portrayed in the first reading. Amaziah, the priest of Bethel, berates the outsider-prophet, Amos. Although Amos was a shepherd and a "dresser of sycamores" from the countryside, he was called by God and sent to the town to fiercely confront the oppressive authorities. They sneer at him and tell him to leave; it is no business of his to be taking a moral stance against them. Amos remains firm in his convictions and proclaims the truth of God's justice.

Today's Scripture readings and film tell of brave men sent to communities oppressed by evil in order to liberate them. They can impel us to question our own participation in carrying out Jesus' command to cast out evil in our own lives.

KEY SCENES AND THEMES

- The formation of the seven; their diverse backgrounds and past careers, their need for change; Chris as the leader and forming his group into a dependable band.

- The villagers and their need for the seven, Calvera taking their food; his swagger and taking it for granted that he can do what he likes, his presumption about buying off the seven and his disbelief that they would stay to defend the people.

- The decisions that the men make to stay with Chris and defend the people; their mixed motives: a desire to help, wanting to settle down, overcoming fear, friendship with the children, falling in love; the heroism in fighting and dying for the oppressed.

FOR REFLECTION AND CONVERSATION

1. *The Magnificent Seven* is a tale all about the evil nature of guns and violence. The serious filmgoer will no doubt link John Sayles' *Men with Guns* to *The Magnificent Seven* since its title and theme almost certainly come from it. Chico, one of the seven, asks, "But who made us the way we are, huh? Men with guns. Men like Calvera, and men like you...and now me." Bernardo O'Reilly gives a moving testimony about who the real heroes are: the men without guns. In the context of the gun culture in the United States today, including school shootings, what does the message of this film mean? What can we learn from it? What is the source of our national tolerance for guns? Is it ethical, even if legal?

2. For a forty-year-old film, *The Magnificent Seven* is somewhat ahead of its time, because of its sensitivity to contemporary issues such as the Aztec Indian heritage of the Mexican villagers. Chico, a Mexican like the villagers, emerges as a hero. On the other hand, only a

few Hispanic names appear on the cast list itself, and it is a predominantly white group that sets out to save the poor Mexicans. What other issues does the film propose for our reflection? Social activists and media educators continue to work for a more just racial, ethnic, and cultural representation in cinema (and other media productions). How is fair representation an issue of justice and concern for all people of good will?

3. There is a significant amount of religious symbolism and references in the film. What do you think is the reason for setting the film in Mexico rather than in the United States? What is the underlying ideology of the film, and how is it manifested? What do the symbolism, the dialogue, and the music say to you against the background of the readings and the responsorial psalm that prays, "Lord, let us see your kindness, and grant us your salvation"?

Prayer

There are so many oppressed people in our world, Lord. Call courageous men and women who are willing to sacrifice their own lives to work for justice and peace. Amen.

Dances With Wolves

U.S.A., 1990, 180 minutes
Cast: Kevin Costner, Mary McDonnell, Graham Greene,
Tantoo Cardinal, Robert Pastorelli
Writer: Michael Blake
Director: Kevin Costner

Dances With Wolves

The Inner Frontier

SYNOPSIS

In the middle of the Civil War, 1863, John Dunbar is badly wounded and the doctors want to amputate his leg. Instead, almost in despair, he leads a suicide charge into the Confederate lines. It becomes a victory ride; he is hailed as a hero. When given his choice of assignments, he asks for a posting to the frontier.

When he arrives at the outpost accompanied by a half-mad trader, he finds it abandoned. He sets it in order and meticulously follows daily army regulations as he waits for the cavalry to arrive. He begins to write a journal.

Dunbar befriends a wolf that he names Two Socks because of the white markings on his legs. Curious Indians of the Lakota Sioux visit him and try to steal his horse. Dunbar comes across a grieving Sioux widow, Stands with a Fist, only to discover she is white. When Dunbar accompanies her back to the native village, barriers between himself and the Indians come down, and he gradually becomes part of the tribe.

Dunbar rides with the Sioux as they hunt buffalo for the winter. He is increasingly attracted to Stands with a Fist. The

240

Indians accept him and name him Dances With Wolves, remembering when they saw him playing with Two Socks. The Sioux ask Dunbar how many white people will come to the frontier, and he tells them as many as the stars in the sky and warns them to move away.

Dunbar prepares to leave with the Sioux, and when he returns to the outpost for his journal, he is captured as a traitor. When he refuses to lead the cavalry to the Indians, he is put on a train to be taken for trial and execution. The Sioux attack and rescue him. He warns them that the army will continue to hunt them down, and, worried that they will be the cause of harm to the Indians, Dunbar and Stands with a Fist go on their solitary way.

COMMENTARY

By 1990, Kevin Costner was emerging as a major star. He had already and would go on to make a number of popular movies: *No Way Out, The Untouchables, Bull Durham, Field of Dreams, Tin Cup,* and *Thirteen Days. Dances With Wolves* was his personal project and his amazing directorial debut. Costner's friend, Michael Blake, the author of the original novel on which the script was based, adapted the screenplay. The movie was nominated for twelve Academy Awards and won seven for Best Film, Best Director, Best Adapted Screenplay, Best Cinematography, Best Music, Best Sound, and Best Film Editing.

Critics referred to the film as "a liberal Western" because it espoused the cause of the Native American Indians and the environment. It told American history from the point of view of the Sioux, rather than that of the white settlers. This had been done twenty years earlier in such "breakthrough" Westerns as *Little Big Man, Soldier Blue,* and *A Man Called Horse.*

Dances With Wolves is a long film that combines the contemplation of an indigenous way of life with traditional Western action.

DIALOGUE WITH THE GOSPEL

Focus: When Jesus looks for some seclusion, the crowds seek him out and he is moved by compassion. John Dunbar wants to move away from society, but he discovers the Sioux and is drawn into their way of life.

The reading from Jeremiah comes from a time of upheaval for Israel. Enemies were threatening invasion. The people were scattered and afraid. They hoped for security from their God, who would shepherd them more carefully than any of their kings had done. *Dances With Wolves* portrays a time of upheaval when the Civil War divided America. The movement of the cavalry ahead of the new wave of settlers meant upheaval for the Indians and destruction of their way of life.

In the reading from Ephesians, Jesus is the man of peace who brings together in himself those who are apart, "breaking down the dividing wall of enmity, through his flesh, abolishing the law with its commandments and legal claims." John Dunbar, too, breaks through a dividing wall and identifies with those who had formerly been his enemies.

The Gospel shows that Jesus and his apostles need to withdraw from the crowds in order to recuperate. Jesus must retreat, too, but he does so only for a short time, because the people soon clamor for him. He is moved by compassion for them as he sees them scattered and leaderless. He gives himself completely to them.

John Dunbar's experience is like that of Jesus, though he is not a Jesus-figure. Dunbar needs to retreat from the world he has known to gather strength. Soon, his encounter with the Sioux Indians draws him out of himself. As he learns their way of life, he gives himself to them completely. He also suffers arrest, interrogation, and beating on their behalf, and he must leave them in order to protect them, recalling aspects of Jesus' self-giving love for us.

- John Dunbar's battle wounds, the threatened amputation, his suicidal charge; moving west, the commanding officer's suicide; Dunbar's arrival at Fort Sedgwick, relishing his time alone, fulfilling his military duties; his "dancing" with the wolf.

- The way of life of the Sioux, the buffalo hunt, the warriors, Stands with a Fist; Dunbar and his encounters with the Sioux, joining them and being accepted as one of them.

- Dunbar taken by the garrison soldiers, interrogated and beaten; his decision to leave the tribe with Stands with a Fist.

KEY SCENES AND THEMES

1. Spiritual retreats have gained great popularity in North America since the late nineteenth century. The purpose of a retreat is perfectly articulated by Jesus, who invites the apostles, "Come away by yourselves to a deserted place and rest awhile." Today, there are more than 600 Christian retreat centers in the United States and Canada, and the majority are operated by religious orders that share their spiritualities through the retreat experience. Solitude forced Dunbar into a retreat situation, which he embraced and which led him to change his life. Have you ever made a retreat or course of spiritual exercises? What led you to decide to make a retreat? What did you learn from your experience and how did you carry it over into your everyday life?

2. The purpose of a major motion picture either based on historical fact, or a fictionalized story about a certain historical period, is both to entertain and perhaps teach the audience about the worldview or

FOR REFLECTION AND CONVERSATION

ideology of the filmmakers. Films such as *Dances With Wolves* try to engage the imagination to fill in the blanks that history leaves out. They rely on some kind of stereotype for the audience to connect with the story. What did you think about the characterization in the film? Although the events in *Dances With Wolves* are fictional, what meaning did you create from the story? Do you think the film is an attempt at revisionist history, revisionist filmmaking, or just storytelling? Why?

3. *Dances With Wolves* can be described as a politically correct film because it "rewrites" Hollywood film-making about how the West was won and incorporates all the attitudes of acceptable—and desirable—behavior today. Last week's film, *The Magnificent Seven*, could be called the last of the traditional Westerns. It questioned the traditional Wild West's gunslinger-heroes image by acknowledging that the true heroes were the people who kept their commitments and cared about others. It took the glamour away from being a gunman. How do these two films, *Dances With Wolves* and *The Magnificent Seven*, compare on the levels of ideology and historical truth? How might these films be said to create new myths, reinforce old ones, or question existing ones?

Prayer

Lord, you are always moved by compassion when you see your people harassed and dejected. Continue to look on us with kindness and be our Good Shepherd. Amen.

The Spitfire Grill

U.S.A., 1996, 117 minutes
Cast: Alison Elliot, Ellen Burstyn, Marcia Gay Harden,
Will Patton, John M. Jackson
Writer: Lee David Zlotoff
Director: Lee David Zlotoff

The Spitfire Grill

Give the People Something to Eat

SYNOPSIS

While serving a five-year prison sentence for manslaughter, Percy Talbott works for the Maine tourist authority, advising people over the phone. On release, she chooses to start fresh in Gilead, a town she learned about while doing her job. Gilead is a backwoods town that needs new jobs to sustain itself.

The local sheriff asks Hannah, who runs the local diner, the Spitfire Grill, to hire Percy and give her a room. Percy enjoys working at the diner and becomes friendly with Joe, to whom she reveals her past. Every night, Hannah leaves a sack of food by a woodpile outdoors, which is gone in the morning. Nahum, Hannah's nephew, regards Percy with suspicion.

Nahum is a mean-spirited and overbearing man who continually belittles his wife Shelby in public and private. Shelby helps out at the grill when Hannah falls and breaks her leg. Shelby gains a sense of achievement, and she and Percy become friends. Percy takes charge of putting out the canvas sack of food at night and glimpses a wild-looking man taking it.

Hannah begins to realize she can no longer handle the diner, and considers selling it. Percy hears about a diner in another town being raffled off in an essay contest with an entry fee of $100. Percy suggests that Hannah do the same. The raffle is very successful and draws the community together.

Nahum is increasingly suspicious of Percy and hides the money from the raffle in one of the canvas sacks to prevent her from stealing it. Unaware, Percy fills that sack with canned food and sets it out on the woodpile. She learns that the man who takes the food is Eli, Hannah's son, a town hero who went off to Vietnam and supposedly never returned. He lives alone in the forest.

A manhunt for Eli follows. When Percy goes to warn Eli, she drowns in the river. At her funeral Nahum confesses his guilt in not trusting her and inadvertently causing her death. Later, a young woman with a child arrives, the new owner of the grill.

COMMENTARY

The Spitfire Grill is a moving story about women. The title refers to a diner—a reminder of the Whistle Stop Cafe with its fried green tomatoes, and the gently humorous *Bagdad Cafe*.

Alison Elliott is persuasive as a young woman released from prison who gets a job helping the prickly Ellen Burstyn as Hannah at the diner. Hannah's nephew, played by Will Patton, portrays his role as the demeaning husband with realism. Oscar-winner Marcia Gay Harden (for Best Supporting Actress in *Pollock*, 2000) gives an effective performance as his wife, Shelby. The music is by James Horner.

The resolution of the conflict and the end of the movie are not quite what we might expect, since the beginning seems formulaic and plot developments are signaled ahead of time. At the end of the film, however, we are left in a thoughtful frame of mind about the film's characters and themes.

The Sacred Heart League, a Catholic organization, funded the movie with the desire to create a film that would make a positive contribution to the culture. *The Spitfire Grill* received the Audience Award at the Sundance Film Festival and consequently received worldwide release. Although not all critics appreciated the film, calling it manipulative and improbable, it remains a favorite among religious groups.

DIALOGUE WITH THE GOSPEL

Focus: No matter how difficult the situation, Jesus responds to the needs of the crowds, even when it means feeding them. They follow him enthusiastically, but will eventually turn on him. The story of Percy Talbott at the Spitfire Grill reminds us of some of the events in Jesus' life.

Jesus feeding the five thousand is not exactly the equivalent of mealtime at the Spitfire Grill. However, one might make some fruitful comparisons since the action takes place around a meal—actually several meals.

Jesus' personality, compassion for the sick, preaching, and healing attract the crowds, and so they follow him. They need him and his message. The people of Gilead are in the midst of a recession, and the past is vanishing along with the jobs. They experience some sense of continuity, community, and hope at the grill as Hannah provides for their needs. When Percy joins Hannah, she brings a new spirit to the diner and to the customers because she is a catalyst for good. This can be seen especially in Shelby's transformation into a more confident woman.

Percy, in her own way, is a Christ-figure in Gilead. She embodies some of the qualities of life and grace outlined in the Letter to the Ephesians, especially humility, gentleness, patience, and bearing with one another in love.

The people appreciate Percy—just as people appreciated Jesus in his own time—and she will undergo trials, even death because of her good works. Nahum's hostility toward Percy and his attempt to frame her for a crime remind us that Jesus also was the victim of plots. It is through her death when she attempts to warn Eli about the lynch mob, however, that she shows what giving one's life for others is like. We note that the single mother who comes at the end of the movie to take over the Spitfire Grill follows in the tradition of Percy. She is an outcast woman who gets an opportunity to start again by serving meals to the community. And the community—like the community of Jesus—is drawn together around a table to share in the life provided.

KEY SCENES AND THEMES

- Percy as a good, young woman; telling Joe her story and the revelation of how she had been victimized by her stepfather and by the system; her tourist work in prison, and her decision to come to Gilead.

- Hannah and her welcome; Percy at work at the grill, meeting and influencing people; Shelby and their friendship; organizing the raffle for the grill; Nahum's hostility and hiding the money in the sack.

- Percy helping Eli with the food; warning him about the search, giving her life as she drowned; the next young woman arriving in Gilead to run the grill.

FOR REFLECTION AND CONVERSATION

1. Taking a break from Mark's Gospel, the Gospel for this and the next four Sundays present the sixth chapter of John's Gospel for our consideration. The theme of John 6 is the Bread of Life, the Eucharist. Today's reading is the story of the multiplication of loaves—the only miracle recounted by all four evangelists. Bread was a staple in the biblical diet, and it was part of the religious ritual of the Jewish community. How is food the focus of *The Spitfire Grill?* How does the Spitfire Grill become the center of the community's life, sustaining it not only with food, but also through communication, friendship, generosity, and sacrifice? How do the "secular" and the "religious" become one in *The Spitfire Grill?*

2. An icon is a symbol that is immediately understood or a sign that points to another meaning. *The Spitfire Grill* is full of natural and religious iconography. What are some of these icons (bars on windows, the ax and wood, the forest, water, birds and feathers, the church, the cross, hands, etc.), and what do they mean in the context of the film? How are the biblical names in the film like icons, and what meaning do they evoke? How did the film's elements—the music, cinematography, plot, characters, and icons—work for you?

3. When Percy kills her stepfather in self-defense, she is punished. When Percy unknowingly uses the wrong bag for food, she is accused of theft. Yet, neither of these things deters her from risking and, ultimately, giving her life to save her friend. How does she save the community, and how does the community save her? How is Percy a Christ-figure?

Prayer

Jesus, you showed your human and divine compassion in feeding the hungry. You were also prepared to give your life for them. Help us to understand and put into action your law of love. Amen.

Stanley & Iris

U.S.A., 1990, 105 minutes
Cast: Jane Fonda, Robert De Niro, Martha Plimpton,
Swoosie Kurtz, Jamey Sheridan, Harley Cross,
Feodor Chaliapin, Jr.
Writers: Harriet Frank, Jr., Irving Ravetch
Director: Martin Ritt

Stanley & Iris

Food for Thought

SYNOPSIS

Iris King is a widow with a teenaged daughter, Kelly, and a young son, Richard. Her sister, Sharon, and Sharon's out-of-work, abusive, and alcoholic husband, Joe, are living with her until they get back on their feet.

Iris works on the assembly line at the local bakery and rides a bicycle to work. One day, when a thief tries to snatch her bag with her paycheck in it, a co-worker named Stanley Cox helps her. A few days later, Iris encounters Stanley, who works in the canteen at the bakery, when she is looking for aspirin. He offers her a variety of medicine bottles and she discovers that he can't read. Because his father was a traveling salesman, he was never in one place long enough to settle into school when he was growing up. He now looks after his elderly father. Though he is obviously interested in Iris, he is shy around her.

When the canteen manager realizes Stanley is illiterate, he fires him, saying, "You can't tell sugar from roach powder…you're dangerous." Iris wants to see Stanley again, but does not know where he has gone. He takes odd jobs but does not earn enough to support his father, so Stanley takes him to a home for the aged where he dies. Besides illiteracy, Stanley has another secret. He invents "contraptions" in a garage where he lives and has a workshop.

Stanley asks Iris to teach him to read. Despite difficulties at home, especially coping with her daughter's pregnancy, she manages to tutor him. Stanley makes progress, but disappears again when, unable to read the road signs, he gets lost.

Iris finds him. They go to Boston for the holiday weekend that she has always dreamed of, but memories of her deceased husband prevent a romance from developing. After returning home, they do not see each other for a time. Life goes on for Iris, but Stanley, unbeknownst to her, patents one of his bakery inventions and sells it. After a few months, he returns to bring Iris and her family with him to Detroit.

COMMENTARY

The veteran husband and wife team of Harriet Frank, Jr. and Irving Ravetch, whose credits include *Hud, Hombre, Conrack, Norma Rae, Backroads,* and *Murphy's Romance,* wrote *Stanley & Iris*—all of which were directed by Martin Ritt. Martin Ritt died in 1990, and *Stanley & Iris* was his last movie. He was a victim of the Hollywood blacklist and director of the 1977 blacklist exposé movie, *The Front,* starring Woody Allen. Swoosie Kurtz plays Fonda's sister, Martha Plimpton is her daughter, and Feodor Chaliapin, Jr. is De Niro's father. *Stanley & Iris* is based on the novel *Union Street,* by Pat Barker.

Jane Fonda is a strong screen presence and dominates the movie. Robert De Niro plays against type and is convincing as the shy and illiterate Stanley. The star power of Fonda and De Niro did little for the movie at the box office. The love story is engaging, but the illiteracy theme doesn't quite work in the film, and according to most critics, the script is not up to par. Yet, it is a humane movie, the kind people say "they don't make" any more, but should.

DIALOGUE WITH THE GOSPEL

Focus: Stanley and Iris both struggle to make ends meet working at a bakery. Their mutual help and love are images of God's gift of life to those in need, symbolized in the Bread of Life.

Today's Gospel is the second of five successive Sunday installments from John, chapter six, focusing on Jesus as the Bread of Life. In this reading and in the story from today's first reading, we can see images of the Eucharist. In the first reading from Exodus, God provides the people with manna for bread and quail for meat to save their lives. In the Gospel, Jesus tells his followers that the manna given to the Israelites is also a sign of Jesus' gifts to them. He emphasizes that it was not Moses who gave the people the manna, but God himself. Both the reading from Ephesians and the Gospel reveal that Jesus himself, the Bread of Life, is the means to renew our lives.

Stanley, hungry for literacy skills and love, and Iris, so hard-working for so little and needing a loving relationship, live in a world that can serve as an image of the world of the desert exodus. They remind us, too, of the people who followed Jesus after he fed them, searching for signs of hope and life. Both Stanley and Iris work for food "that perishes" and do not have enough to sustain them or their dependents.

Jesus is present in our world through word and sacrament. Through the gift of words, Stanley and Iris gain new life against the backdrop of the bakery and food. Iris enables Stanley to communicate by tutoring him to read and write, and both their lives are renewed.

In the mutual gift of life, both Stanley and Iris can begin their lives again. Just so, the people begged Jesus for the Bread of Life to satisfy their hunger, and ultimately, to change their lives.

KEY SCENES AND THEMES

- Iris at work on the assembly line and the women she works with; riding the bike, taking the bus, Stanley giving her a ride; at home with her sister, her children; Kelly's pregnancy and Iris' reaction and advice.

- Stanley at work, cooking; the bond with his father; helping Iris, giving her the lift; his admission that he cannot read, getting fired, odd jobs, his inventions; learning to read and write and how this changes him.

- Taking Richard to the park; failing the test with the street signs, getting lost, disappearing; Iris finding him and building up his confidence; their future.

1. Food is everywhere in the Scriptures. In the Old Testament, food is involved in the fall of our first parents; it is the sign of God's providence and a source of pleasure. Food attains its fullest meaning in the New Testament in the person of Jesus Christ who is the Bread of Life and food from heaven. Jesus says, "Whoever comes to me will never hunger, and whoever believes in me will never thirst." In the film *Big Night*, Primo, the older brother, says that food is like God. In light of today's film, how might God and food be compared? Where do Iris and Stanley meet and work? Where does Iris tutor Stanley? Why? What religious significance does this evoke?

2. Some of the themes of this film are illiteracy, food, human relationships, love, loss, family, and work. How important is the love theme as compared to illiteracy in the film? What about the subplot of work? What is the relationship between work and literacy? How life-giving is the work at the bakery for Stanley, and how does this change once he is able to fully unleash his creativity when he becomes literate? At the end of the film, Stanley comes back not only for Iris, but also for

FOR REFLECTION AND CONVERSATION

her children. How is Iris' generosity and self-giving rewarded? What is the message of this film to you?

3. In today's film, Stanley was completely capable of creativity and verbal communication, but he could not read or write. What impact did this have on his ability to make his way in the world? In what way can it be said that knowledge is the Bread of Life? What do you know about illiteracy levels in your area? What are some ways you can contribute to a more literate community?

Prayer

Lord, in the daily grind of our lives, we often lose heart. Give the Bread of Life that is your life for the world. Amen.

NINETEENTH SUNDAY
OF THE YEAR

1 Kings 19:4–8; Ephesians 4:30—5:2;
John 6:41–51

Alive

U.S.A., 1992, 127 minutes
Cast: Ethan Hawke, Vincent Spano, Josh Hamilton,
Illeana Douglas, John Malkovich, Christian J. Meoli
Writer: John Patrick Shanley
Director: Frank Marshall

 Alive

Life-giving Food

SYNOPSIS

High on a mountain, a man reflects on the true experience of survivors of a plane crash who had to eat the bodies of the dead in order to survive. He likens it to the Eucharist, Jesus giving his body for the life of the world.

Flash back to twenty years before. It is October 13, 1972. A chartered plane carrying the Uruguayan rugby team crashes in the Andes. The plane breaks apart and the fuselage lands first. The snow on a mountainside stops the front part of the plane. A number of passengers are killed, but many survive. The captain of the rugby team, Antonio, takes charge. The group tries to make the plane's cabin warm and safe and they begin to ration the food.

After a week, they hear on a transistor radio that the search for them has been called off. A small party tries to reach the tail of the plane that dropped off some distance away, but they are too weak to make any progress. Roberto, a medical student, tends to the sick and wounded, including Nando who has come out of a coma. It is Nando who persuades Roberto that the only way to survive is to use the bodies of their comrades as food. With open discussion about their feelings and the morality of what they are to do, they overcome their natural repugnance for eating human flesh.

During the winter storms and avalanches, the nose of the plane is destroyed and more survivors die. Nando and Roberto set out for Chile. At first, they fail to make any progress, but they eventually reach a village. They come back with helicopters to rescue those still alive, seventy days after the crash. Sixteen men survive.

COMMENTARY

The crash of the plane carrying the Uruguayan rugby team and their decision to eat the bodies of the dead in order to survive made headlines in 1972. A small-budget movie directed by Rene Cardona was quickly made and released in 1976, called *Survive!* Many reviewers thought it sensationalized the events and the dilemmas of the tragedy.

British novelist Piers Paul Read wrote *Alive,* the book on which today's movie was based, and gave a more humane and respectful picture of the group and the decisions they made for survival. He integrated both the experience and a Catholic theology of the Eucharist with honesty and dignity. Playwright John Patrick Shanley wrote the screenplay for *Alive,* as well as for *Five Corners, Joe Versus the Volcano,* and the Oscar-winning *Moonstruck.*

At the time the film was made, the majority of the cast did not have big names to attract audiences. Ethan Hawke had already appeared in several successful movies, including *The Goonies* and *Dead Poets Society,* but was to become a star later in the 1990s. Vincent Spano played in *City of Hope* and continues to act in motion pictures and television, but has never attained marquee status. Frank Marshall, a former producer for Steven Spielberg, directed *Alive.* His past credits include *Arachnophobia* and *Congo.* The well-known John Malkovich portrays Nando sitting on a mountaintop, reflecting on the religious significance of the survivors' behavior twenty years later.

The crash landing is one of the most vivid in movie-making, and the film is noted for this. However, a great deal of the movie is taken up with ethical questions and their religious interpretations rather than the action. A documentary titled *Alive: Twenty Years Later,* directed by Jill Fullerton-Smith and narrated by actor Martin Sheen, was released in 1993.

Focus: Jesus offers his disciples a mystery to consider, that he is the Bread of Life and that this bread is his body. The survivors in Alive *reflect on what this means as they are faced with the question of their need for food and the bodies of their dead friends becoming life for them.*

DIALOGUE WITH THE GOSPEL

The reading from First Kings offers a parallel to the story of the survivors in *Alive*. Elijah, hungry and thirsty, is trapped in the wilderness and wishes he were dead. When he wakes from a deep sleep he finds that God has provided sustenance for him. With this food he is able to walk for forty days and nights and eventually reaches his destination, the mountain of the presence of God.

The film seems to point to the reading from Ephesians, as well. Those who are destined for God's freedom must not quarrel or be spiteful, but kind and forgiving. In acting like this, Christians will be imitators of Jesus who loved and sacrificed his life for his friends.

These elements construct the religious premise for the behavior of the rugby team in *Alive*. The dialogue about the Eucharist throughout *Alive* draws its meaning from the Gospel and Catholic Christian theology. Even special food like the manna in the desert is not enough to give eternal life, but there is bread that comes from heaven, the Bread of Life, which will enable those who eat it to live forever. The life of Jesus, received sacramentally, sustains and nourishes us spiritually.

Today, Jesus defines himself as the Bread of the Eucharist, his true body. Many disciples find this teaching intolerable and they leave him. The Eucharist is Jesus' flesh sacrificed for us. It is this reflection that encourages the survivors stranded high in the Andes Mountains to understand their experience as Eucharistic: their deceased friends are consumed so that others may live.

KEY SCENES AND THEMES

- Nando twenty years later, meditating on the meaning of life and death, sacrifice, the eucharistic undertones of surviving by eating flesh; the recurrence of these themes throughout the movie.

- The reality of the crash sequence, the later avalanche destroying the nose of the plane and those inside it; the attempts to trek across the snow for help; the hardships of the fall and winter in the Andes.

- The decision to eat their deceased friends; Nando giving his reasons, his persuasiveness, the ethical and religious discussions; the survival experience, the consequences, and their survival.

FOR REFLECTION AND CONVERSATION

1. Cannibalism is defined as humans eating the flesh of other humans for food or as part of a ritual action. Because of the ethical and moral issues involved in this incident, the Vatican studied what happened and released a statement that the men were justified in using the bodies of their dead companions for food. How did the survivors featured in this film convince themselves that eating the flesh of their deceased friends was moral? Was the man who would not eat justified in his refusal? What role did conscience play in the discernment that took place?

2. Religion was obviously a way of life for the people involved in the crash: the mother and sister who died early on, the agnostic who suddenly began praying when things got worse, and the people's vision of their actions as eucharistic. Although some myth studies connect primitive rites of cannibalism to Christianity, the Eucharist is not cannibalism. Rather, in the Eucharist, we receive the Body and Blood of Christ, who is risen and can no longer die. How well does the film's eucharistic connection work for you? What role does religious symbolism play in the film? How do the symbols, words, and music contribute to the religious ethos? How does *Alive* work as a film? Do you think it is believable? Why or why not? What did the film mean to you?

3. Leadership is another interesting theme in this movie and can be defined as taking people where they would not go by themselves. How many times does the leadership change during this saga? How is this film similar to or different from other survivor films such as *Lord of the Flies?* What difference does Christianity make in *Alive*, especially regarding leadership? Who is a hero in *Alive?*

Prayer

Jesus, you are the Bread of Life. Help us to understand what it means to be united to you when we eat your Body and drink your Blood in the Eucharist. Amen.

Twentieth Sunday of the Year

Proverbs 9:1– 6; Ephesians 5:15– 20;
John 6:51– 58

U.S.A., 1999, 95 minutes
Cast: Sarah Michelle Geller, Sean Patrick Flanery,
Patricia Clarkson, Dylan Baker, Christopher Durang,
Betty Buckley, Amanda Peet
Writer: Judith Roberts
Director: Mark Tarlov

Simply Irresistible

A Taste of Life

SYNOPSIS

Amanda has co-inherited her mother's restaurant in lower Manhattan, but not her mother's ability to cook. She and her aunt find themselves in financial difficulties when, unexpectedly, a strange man sells Amanda a basket of crabs at the market. The mysterious person seems to be her guardian angel.

While at the market, one of the crabs crawls up the leg of the suave and wealthy Tom. He is opening an upscale restaurant in a department store uptown, but has no chef. Later that day, Tom is accidentally dropped off by a taxi in front of "The Southern Cross," Amanda's restaurant, and is mysteriously enchanted by her food. One of the crabs has escaped and benignly watches over the action in the kitchen.

Not only does business begin to improve, so does Amanda's cooking. Then she is invited to cater the opening night at Tom's restaurant. She and Tom discover an attraction to one another, but don't get along very well. Nevertheless, she pours herself into baking and preparing the dishes for Tom's event. As she cooks, Amanda reflects on her life and begins to cry. A tear falls into the entree. When the guests consume the various courses they, too, experience the moods Amanda felt while cooking: first sad, then joyful, and finally

260

carefree. Tom tries to resist letting the meal's moods influence his relationship with Amanda, but he cannot help himself. They reconcile their differences and live happily ever after.

Simply Irresistible is a pleasant, but not particularly memorable, movie. It was a big screen vehicle for television's *Buffy the Vampire Slayer,* Sarah Michelle Geller. Her role here as the sweet restaurateur certainly helped to change the thriller image she projected in *I Know What You Did Last Summer, Scream II,* and as the villain in *Cruel Intentions. Simply Irresistible* is a movie with a "thirty-something" cast, featuring fashionable stores, restaurants, clothes, and a romantic storyline about successful men and women.

What makes *Simply Irresistible* a little different is that, despite the magical realism contributed by Amanda's guardian angel and the unusual crab, the movie highlights the profound effect food can have on people. It also emphasizes cooking as an art, requiring chefs to put all their talents, indeed their very selves, into the food they prepare. The meals in the movie transform those who eat them. Characters begin to say what they really think and share the cook's sadness; they are overwhelmed by silence, and they savor their food. This same theme of transformation was profoundly dramatized in *Babette's Feast.* Here, it is presented sincerely and with a frothy, light touch. Amanda's food is alive with her spirit.

COMMENTARY

Focus: In today's Gospel, Jesus says that he is the "living bread," and "Whoever eats my flesh and drinks my blood remains in me and I in him." The image and the result of Amanda filling the food she prepares with her spirit reminds us of just how profound Jesus' gift of self in the Eucharist really is.

DIALOGUE WITH THE GOSPEL

The first reading from Proverbs is about "Wisdom," personified as feminine. "She" sends out her maidens to invite guests to share the feast she has prepared: "Let whoever is simple turn in here." Those who lack understanding are urged to eat and drink. Those who are foolish will find that the meal will change their perceptions, for Wisdom exhorts them to "Forsake foolishness that you may live; advance in the way of understanding." In its own light and popular way, *Simply Irresistible* offers the same invitation.

This is reinforced by the responsorial psalm and its antiphon, for if God is tasted, then we can savor God's Wisdom: "Taste and see the goodness of the Lord."

John 6 is one of the most profound and mysterious chapters of all the Gospels. It develops the revelation that Jesus is the full nourishment sent by God. Jesus is life itself and he offers new life and resurrection to all who believe in him. The people had shared in the miraculous meal that fed the five thousand, but they found this teaching too difficult to understand.

Simply Irresistible imagines personal transformation in a breezy, romantic situation that appreciates the spirit that good food contains because the chef has put so much of herself into its preparation. Christian theology teaches that our sharing in the Eucharist can transform us spiritually if we are willing to open ourselves to the mystery of this sacrament, which is Jesus himself.

KEY SCENES AND THEMES

- Amanda as an unsuccessful cook, emulating her mother, assisted by the sous-chef and her aunt; the friendly crab and the ubiquitous "angel" as plot devices; Gene O'Reilly who watches over her and sends Tom into her life.

- The crab dinner prepared for Tom; his response to Amanda compared with his girlfriend's tantrum; Amanda's talent increasing, her self-confidence growing, the faithful, appreciative customers.

- The resignation of the French chef who has nothing to give, the skepticism of the assistant; Amanda's hopes, shedding a tear into the entrée; the response of the guests to the food, the manifestation of feelings; the truth about themselves confessed with honesty and their hopes for their lives, the changes wrought by Amanda's food.

1. At first, *Simply Irresistible* may not seem to fit into the growing genre of "food" films because it is too lightweight. *Babette's Feast, Big Night, Chocolat,* or *What's Cooking?* are films that lend themselves to comparison with the eucharistic mystery in the Christian community. How does *Simply Irresistible* convey the spiritual dimension of preparing food for others? How do the details and the spirit of *Simply Irresistible* really compare with other movies from the "food" genre?

2. According to wisdom, "a proverb never tells a lie," and the film opens with: "The wind from one door slamming opens another." What does this truth mean in the context of the film? How does food become a means of opportunity for Amanda, Tom, and the other characters in the film?

3. *Pastiche* literally means "mixture" (or "mess") in French. Scholars in our postmodern era, however, use it to mean various artistic elements from literature, the arts, and academic fields employed to construct a creative artifact. In this case, *Simply Irresistible* could be said to be an example of cinema *pastiche.* For example, the story involves a mixture of genres—fantasy, magic, romantic comedy, and food—to tell the story. Without seeing more to the movie than may

actually be there, what other story elements does the film employ to evoke a response from the audience (e.g., religion and spirituality)? How did the film work for you against the backdrop of today's Scripture readings?

Prayer

Jesus, you remind us that food is a gift and it contains within it the spirit of the giver. Help us to appreciate more deeply that you are the Bread of Life. Amen.

A Beautiful Mind
U.S.A., 2001, 130 minutes
Cast: Russell Crowe, Jennifer Connelly, Ed Harris,
Paul Bettany, Christopher Plummer, Judd Hirsch
Writer: Akiva Goldsman
Director: Ron Howard

A Beautiful Mind

A Sign of Contradiction

SYNOPSIS

John Forbes Nash, Jr. is a scholarship graduate in mathematics beginning his doctoral studies at Princeton University in 1947. His quiet, reclusive, eccentric manner make him the butt of jokes by fellow students. His incessant problem solving amuses and amazes people. Nash annoys other students because of his sense of superiority. However, he relates well to his roommate, Charles, whose attitude to life is more spontaneous and carefree.

Nash is a self-acknowledged genius obsessed with finding a totally original idea, and his thesis is accepted as a breakthrough in mathematics. During the 1950s, Nash works at a research institute connected to MIT and teaches some classes there. He is recruited by Agent Parcher for top secret code-breaking.

One of John's students, Alicia, is both attracted to and challenged by him. They date and, despite his hesitations about commitment, marry. Alicia gives birth to a son, and Nash is busy lecturing and working for Parcher. When he suffers a breakdown and is taken to a psychiatric institution, he is diagnosed with paranoid schizophrenia: Charles, Parcher, and others are figments of John's imagination.

Alicia devotedly cares for John, although it takes an emotional toll on her. Then she discovers that he is still code-breaking for Parcher—his hallucinations returned when he stopped taking his medication. Nash finally acknowledges that his companions are not real. Eventually, an old associate allows him to stay around the Princeton campus where he meets students, begins to tutor small groups, and to lecture.

Finally, Nash receives the tribute of Princeton's faculty, as well as the Nobel Prize for mathematics. In his acceptance speech he speaks of how love transcends logic, a tribute to Alicia.

COMMENTARY

A Beautiful Mind is an adaptation of the best-selling book of the same title by Sylvia Nasar. Although only broadly biographical, the film is a tribute to John Nash's life and work.

Director Ron Howard stated at the Golden Globe awards ceremony in 2002 that the challenge for him and screenwriter Akiva Goldsman was to portray the workings of such a beautiful mind on screen for the popular cinema-going public. As a consummate actor, Russell Crowe helped Ron Howard immeasurably in this endeavor. While Nash's mathematical thinking bewilders most of us, we are bedazzled by how Crowe communicates Nash's vigor and intellectual delight. However, the filmmakers also continually remind us that this is a love story of tremendous proportions, as revealed in Alicia's fidelity and perseverance.

A Beautiful Mind was nominated for eight Academy Awards in 2002, winning Best Picture and Best (Adapted) Writing. Jennifer Connelly had the role of a lifetime as Alicia, and with it earned the Oscar for Best Supporting Actress. Ron Howard won the Academy Award for Best Director with *A Beautiful Mind*, which is added to his substantial body of work, including *Parenthood, Apollo 13, Ransom,* and *EdTV.*

Focus: Today, Jesus is seen as a sign of contradiction. The disciples who have witnessed his miraculous signs find his teachings too hard and walk away. Peter and the Twelve, despite the hardships, affirm their faith in Jesus. John Nash can be seen as a sign of contradiction. He alienates many, but elicits love from his wife and friends.

DIALOGUE WITH THE GOSPEL

Today's Gospel is the climax of John 6. The crowds following Jesus have seen him feed the multitude and walk on water. Jesus had to withdraw to a mountain by himself because he "perceived that they were about to come and take him away by force and make him king" (RSV). After hearing Jesus' words on the Bread of Life and how he will give himself as this food, the crowds turn fickle. They find his teachings too difficult and walk away. Jesus asks the Twelve, "Do you too want to leave?" They remain with Jesus. Peter asks, "To whom shall we go?"

The Gospel echoes the first reading from the Book of Joshua. Joshua challenges the leaders of the tribes of Israel to declare their faith in God. They acknowledge the marvels that God has done for them and, like Peter in the Gospel, choose to serve him.

The attitudes of others toward them provide a kind of parallel between the life of Nash and Jesus (although Nash humorously states during the film that his savior-complex takes other forms!).

Nash was a genius whose thinking fed a multitude of scientists. His work on game theory enabled others to revolutionize and reframe economics. However, most people who experienced his strange behavior could not understand him. He was different, and his teachings were unusual. He did not meet people's expectations, and they walked away from him. His own hopes and ambitions were dashed.

Just as Jesus experienced the fidelity of those near to him, Nash experienced Alicia's love, which supported and saved him, and Martin's kindness in finding him a place at the university where he could continue to teach and discover more "disciples."

The love between Nash and Alicia is an example of how the reading from the Ephesians can be lived. The exhortation that husbands and wives respect and love each other is a metaphor for Jesus' love for the Church. Alicia's remarkable fidelity to Nash highlights this relationship and gives a contemporary ring to Peter's response of determined love, "To whom else shall I go?"

KEY SCENES AND THEMES

- Nash at his initial meetings with the professors at Princeton, his arrogance toward his fellow students; his obsessive solving of math problems on windows, his failure to meet his scholarship requirements, and his determination to find an original idea; developing game theory.

- His paranoid schizophrenia, the spontaneity of his roommate, the tender and childlike femininity of the little girl; Parcher and the wild danger, as well as Nash feeling his patriotic responsibility; the lecture at Harvard, the mental institution and treatment; the truth of his illness and how it became such a vivid part of Nash's imaginative life.

- Alicia's supportive love despite the demands on her; Nash's quiet decades at the university while still seeing the figments of his imagination; his achievement in academia and ways of relating to people; the acknowledgment of his work with game theory; the Nobel Prize in Economics and his final declaration about love.

1. One of the movie posters for *A Beautiful Mind* declares that the courage of a beautiful heart is more than a beautiful mind. Nash is drawn into loving Alicia. When he proposes to her, he asks her for some kind of proof of love, and she asks him whether he can prove that the universe is infinite. What does he reply? What does Alicia then say about the nature of love? What does Nash say about the relationship of love and logic at the end of the film? At what point in the film is Alicia's strength and determination most evident? Why? What cinematic techniques reinforce the message of that strength?

2. Mental illness can cover a wide range of human disorders that affect a person's thoughts, emotions, and behavior in mild to debilitating ways. What does *A Beautiful Mind* teach audiences about mental illness and our attitude toward those who see reality in a different way, as did John Nash? Who sets the standard for mental illness in the world? What is your attitude toward those who are mentally or physically handicapped or ill?

3. All biopics and biographical documentaries are subjected to the filmmakers' interpretation and creative license in order to tell a story that the audience will find believable and enjoyable. In doing this, choices always have to be made. Many professional and armchair critics were unhappy with Akiva Goldsman's screenplay and Ron Howard's interpretation of John Nash's life because it was not strictly factual. Howard explained that the film is based on Nash's life and is not a true biography. In real life, Alicia did remain

faithful to John Nash, but they lived apart for some time and even divorced. However, they were reconciled around the time of the Nobel Prize and have since remarried. How is *A Beautiful Mind* a truthful film, even if it is not factual? Why?

Prayer

Jesus, to whom shall we go? You have the message of eternal life. We believe. We know you are the Holy One of God. Amen.

The House of Mirth

Scotland/U.S.A., 2000, 141 minutes
Cast: Gillian Anderson, Eric Stoltz, Dan Akroyd, Laura Linney,
Elizabeth McGovern, Anthony LaPaglia,
Johdi May, Terry Kinney, Eleanor Bron
Writer: Terence Davies
Director: Terence Davies

The House of Mirth

To Cling to Human Traditions

SYNOPSIS

It is 1905 and Lily Bart is a twenty-nine-year-old woman of slender means who wants to find her place in New York society. She has a studious bachelor friend, Lawrence Selden, who wants to marry her, but is not a man of means. Lily has gambling debts and decides to woo a wealthy husband to solve her problems.

One day, she buys some letters from an acquaintance that reveal Lawrence's affair with Bertha Dorset, a married socialite. A lawyer, Gus Trenor, offers to invest Lily's savings so she can pay her debts. He also introduces her to a rich businessman, Sim Rosedale, who has seen Lily visit Selden in his bachelor apartment. Using this as leverage with her, Rosedale proposes an arrangement, but she rejects him. Everything fails for her when Trenor reveals that he has indeed paid her debts, but invested some of his own money with her savings and now demands it back. When he makes advances toward her, she refuses. He becomes an enemy.

While on a cruise with Bertha and George Dorset on the Riviera, Lily discovers that Bertha is using her to cover up her love affairs. When Bertha publicly accuses her of seducing George, Lily is rejected by society.

On her return to New York, she finds that her aunt, who has died, has left her $10,000, but it will be a year before she can receive it. Lily is committed to paying her debts. She goes to work as a secretary and then as a milliner, but she is not competent at either job. She starts taking pills to help her sleep. When the check from her aunt's estate finally arrives, she decides to put her affairs in order. She sends the money to Trenor and burns the incriminating letters. She then takes some sleeping pills. Selden, who had come to retrieve the letters, finds her dead.

COMMENTARY

An impressive and elegant version of Edith Wharton's novel, this interpretation of *The House of Mirth* has been adapted for the screen and directed by Englishman Terence Davies, who also has *The Long Day Closes, The Neon Bible,* and *Distant Voices, Still Lives* to his credit. *The House of Mirth* has a strong American cast. The movie's external scenes were filmed in Glasgow, Scotland, because the architecture resembles early twentieth-century New York so accurately.

No effort was spared for period costumes and decor. Davies has a painter's eye, and his scenes look like works of art, some even resembling a tableau. In *The House of Mirth*, a great deal of action takes place offscreen, with only some cues from the script to help us realize that time has passed and significant events and interactions have taken place. Davies gives us enough hints to appreciate the characters, and then makes us use our own imaginations to interpret the new events and developments in character. *The House of Mirth* is a very literary and literate movie.

Lily Bart is the central character, the naive rebel who wants to be in society, but misjudges characters and situations. Gillian Anderson, of *The X-Files,* plays her role with dignity and credibility.

Focus: Jesus condemns the hypocrisy of those who extol external morality while ignoring corruption of the heart. Lily Bart wants to find a place in society, but is destroyed by the hypocrites she admired.

Laws and regulations are important, and the reading from Deuteronomy is a tribute to the law. There is great value in keeping God's word through the active observance of God's law, the Torah, because, as Moses tells the people, this "will give evidence of your wisdom and intelligence to the nations."

The theme of the righteousness of the person who observes God's law is consistent throughout today's readings, including the responsorial psalm and its description of the person who "walks blamelessly and does justice." The Letter of James reinforces this with the advice to "humbly welcome the word that has been planted in you." In Mark's Gospel, Jesus condemns double standards, especially when making judgments about others.

Lily Bart has high hopes of finding a place in New York society and acquiring wealth and status. She believes that if she achieves this, her life will have value and meaning. Instead, she falls out of grace with people like the ones that Jesus describes in the Gospel, people whose criteria for acceptability are external and formal. Minute details of pedantic good manners and etiquette rituals governed decisions of who was "in" and who was "out." As with some of the Pharisees in Jesus' time, it was more important to *appear* clean than to actually *be* clean. *The House of Mirth* offers us a gallery of beautifully dressed and well-spoken hypocrites.

The House of Mirth could be interpreted as an allegorical display of the virtues and vices of which Jesus speaks in the Gospel which today's liturgy offers for our prayerful reflection.

KEY SCENES AND THEMES

• Lily Bart's meeting with Lawrence Selden but rejecting a relationship with him; misjudging him because of the letters she bought; his finding her body and realizing what might have been.

• The way Lily is treated by Trenor, Bertha, and Grace; their external respectability along with inner deception or harshness.

• The pathos of Lily's failure to enter society; her work as a secretary, as a milliner, her lack of financial security, her loss of friends, her dependence on sleeping pills, and her death.

FOR REFLECTION AND CONVERSATION

1. Jesus tells us in the Gospel today that "evil thoughts, unchastity, theft, murder, adultery, greed, malice, deceit, licentiousness, envy, blasphemy, arrogance, and folly" come from within a person and defile the community. These traits read like a laundry list of sins that can be attributed to the characters in *The House of Mirth*. To which persons do they apply and why? What are the consequences in the lives of the characters in the film, especially Lily?

2. Compare Edith Wharton with Jane Austen, who wrote romantic comedy with great insight and satirized the English culture in which she lived. Austen's works, such as *Pride and Prejudice, Sense and Sensibility,* and *Emma,* show the dilemma of women caught in the "no-man's-land" of a society in which a desirable marriage held the only hope for a secure future. Edith Wharton, writing in the United States a full century later, described the same dilemma in the new world, but through stories that had hopeless endings. Lawrence Selden asks Lily, "Isn't marriage your vocation? Isn't

that what you were brought up for?" If we accept that Christian marriage is a noble aspiration, what does it mean in this context? How and why can his question be understood as an indictment? Why are Lily's options so limited?

3. If there is one film that is easy to compare to *The House of Mirth,* it is James Cameron's *Titanic.* The era is the same, and Rose, the main character, is caught up in a situation similar to Lily's. She feels she is being forced to marry to save her family. What are the other similarities and differences between the two films? Why was *Titanic* such a commercial success, while *The House of Mirth* remained only a critical success?

Prayer

Jesus, some of your harshest words were spoken against hypocrisy. Give us the grace to live with integrity of heart and consistency of action. Amen.

Mr. Holland's Opus
U.S.A., 1995, 142 minutes
Cast: Richard Dreyfuss, Glenne Headley, Olympia Dukakis,
William H. Macy, Jay Thomas, Joanna Gleason,
Anthony Natale
Writer: Patrick Sheane Duncan
Director: Stephen Herek

Mr. Holland's Opus

Hearing the Music

SYNOPSIS

Glenn Holland starts teaching music in 1965, hoping to make enough money to support his wife and himself so he can compose on a full-time basis. Soon his wife, Iris, becomes pregnant, and they have a son. Mr. Holland's students are bored during class, while he thinks they are poor musicians. When he realizes that they should be enjoying the music they play, he changes his methods. Finally, he begins to communicate with them and to reach even those who seem unteachable.

The 1960s go by. One of his best students is killed in Vietnam. Iris discovers that their son, Cole, is deaf, and the parents are advised to treat him "normally." Iris is desperate to communicate with Cole, so she learns sign language. Mr. Holland becomes more involved in the school music program than in his family life. He avoids Cole and refuses to learn more than the bare minimum of sign language.

Throughout the 1970s he becomes more and more successful at school, although frustrated that his life as a composer remains a dream. When budget cuts threaten the music program, he stages a successful Gershwin revue. He is momentarily tempted to leave for New York with a student, a young singer named Rowena. When John Lennon dies in 1980, Cole confronts his father and forces him to face the reality that he is deaf. Through this encounter, Mr. Holland discovers how the hearing impaired can experience music through light and vibration. He realizes that he loves Cole and sings John Lennon's "Beautiful Boy (Darling Boy)" to his son.

Mr. Holland teaches music for thirty years at JFK High School, until the school's program is cancelled. Iris, Cole, and the past and present students pay tribute to Mr. Holland by playing his American Symphony in concert. At last, Mr. Holland realizes that his son and students are truly his "opus."

COMMENTARY

Although this film evokes an emotional response, its treatment of school and family themes is a bit sharper than in some of its predecessors. Richard Dreyfuss gives an energetic and engaging performance as Mr. Holland, supported by Glenne Headley as his wife. Olympia Dukakis is the sympathetic principal, and William H. Macy plays the stuffy vice-principal so well that he irritates the audience as much as he does Mr. Holland. The movie not only shows us educational values, but also offers a commentary on family relationships.

One of the attractions of the movie is the musical score, and the musical selections range from Bach to Gershwin to rock 'n' roll. This is a film that any audience can watch and thoroughly enjoy.

DIALOGUE WITH THE GOSPEL

Focus: When the Lord comes with divine recompense, the blind will see and the ears of the deaf will be opened. While few receive such a cure, Mr. Holland helps his son to "hear" music, and he finally gains insight to appreciate his life, family, and students for who they really are.

The reading from Isaiah is a canticle of joy. When the Lord comes, those who are afflicted will be healed, including the deaf whose ears will be unsealed. Among the many themes in *Mr. Holland's Opus* is that of the teacher who learns to listen to his students and arouse their enthusiasm for learning. The subplot about Cole's deafness makes the movie more challenging, for although Mr. Holland is a savior-figure for many of his students, he is not for his son.

Like the man in the Gospel, Cole Holland is deaf and cannot speak clearly, though he can communicate through sign language. All he wants from Holland is the acknowledgment that he is his son, an intelligent and capable young man, but his father is deaf to him and his needs.

When Cole challenges his father about knowing John Lennon's music, Glenn Holland's eyes and ears are opened, and he begins to speak authentically through words and signs with his son. He gives a class on Beethoven, his music, and his deafness. He then plays for the deaf and sings John Lennon's tribute for his son. Cole does not hear in the same way as hearing people do, but his father's gift of music and the acknowledgment that he is loved heals Cole and empowers him for the future. In today's Gospel, the deaf man was healed, but in the movie, it is not the deaf who needs healing. Instead, it is the deaf man who brings healing so that one who could already hear might become whole through the power of love.

KEY SCENES AND THEMES

- How Mr. Holland's classes bore the students, their poor test results; his introducing a range of music; the news that Cole cannot hear; his class on Beethoven and his deafness.

- His reaction to Iris telling him that she is pregnant, his inability to say anything to her, and her weeping; his hopes dashed about having time and money to compose and how this hinders his appreciation of his son; the parade and Iris's discovery that Cole is deaf; the expert telling them to treat Cole as a "normal" person; Iris and the scene of frustration in the kitchen, Cole learning to communicate, Iris interpreting sign language for her husband and his reluctance to learn how to sign.

- The confrontation about John Lennon; Cole's explanation of himself and the shock to his father; the school concert and Mr. Holland singing and dedicating "Beautiful Boy" to Cole; the tribute, Iris and Cole and Gertrude's speech that Mr. Holland's life has truly been wonderful.

FOR REFLECTION AND CONVERSATION

1. People are considered physically deaf, that is, disabled, when they find it difficult to understand speech, even with the help of a hearing aid. But sign language is considered a language like any other, because it is a means of communicating. The deaf community strives to let the hearing know that the deaf are simply different, rather than disabled. How important is communication in the Holland family and how is this portrayed? How does Mr. Holland finally learn to communicate?

2. Listen to the lyrics from John Lennon's "Beautiful Boy (Darling Boy)" and talk about the meaning of the song for Mr. Holland and Cole. How do these lyrics express the relationship between father and son?

3. In the cultural milieu of the United States today, the more difficult scenes in *Mr. Holland's Opus* stand out, such as Mr. Holland's temptation to run off with the young woman, or his vehement arguments with his wife over Cole. These scenes might make the audience uncomfortable, since such failings show that Mr. Holland is not perfect. Why do you think the writer

made them part of the story's plot? How does the film's thirty-year trajectory parallel the stages of a person's life? Think about the worldview of the filmmaker and director. How do they show Mr. Holland making or finding meaning in his life?

Prayer

Lord, you gave the deaf man the power to hear and speak. Continue to heal all of us so that we may be able to listen to and hear the needs of those around us. Amen.

A Simple Plan

U.S.A., 1998, 121 minutes
Cast: Bill Paxton, Billy Bob Thornton, Bridget Fonda, Gary Cole
Writer: Scott B. Smith
Director: Sam Raimi

A Simple Plan

Losing One's Soul and Life

SYNOPSIS

One snowy winter's day, a plane crashes in the Minnesota woods. Hank, his slow-witted brother Jacob, and their friend Lou, discover the plane and find four million dollars hidden inside. At first Hank is unwilling to take the money, but the other two want to keep it, rationalizing that it's probably drug money anyway. Hank's wife Sarah also wants to keep the money. Hank finally agrees and decides to hide the money until spring so no one will associate it with the crash.

But before they can act, a farmer approaches the plane wreck. Jacob attacks him, and Hank kills him. They then discover that the cash was ransom money belonging to two brothers who are indeed criminals, and the dead pilot is one of them. Jacob and Lou want to take some of the money immediately, and Lou threatens to blackmail Hank if he doesn't agree. Then, Hank and Jacob set up Lou, and he "confesses" on tape to the farmer's murder. When Lou realizes he has been trapped, Jacob kills him and his wife.

An FBI agent arrives to investigate the crash, and the local sheriff asks Hank and Jacob to help in the search. Sarah knows that the FBI agent is really the other criminal brother. During a confrontation in the woods, the imposter agent kills the sheriff, and then Hank kills the imposter. Jacob now wants to save Hank from the terrible mess they have created. He urges Hank to kill him and to make it look as if the agent had murdered both him and the sheriff. Hank does it.

When real FBI agents arrive, they reveal that the cash notes were marked. Hank must burn the money because he realizes he can never spend it without being caught. It has all been for nothing.

COMMENTARY

A Simple Plan was one of the most critically acclaimed movies of 1998. The versatile writer and actor, Billy Bob Thornton, who also starred in films such as *Sling Blade, The Man Who Wasn't There, Bandits,* and *Monster's Ball,* received an Oscar nomination for his performance as the slow-witted Jacob who gradually develops a conscience as the simple plan goes awry. This is one of Bill Paxton's best roles as a decent man who makes one bad decision opening up the way to perdition. Bridget Fonda's character is not so well developed as the others, but she is credible in her role as a moral chameleon.

The real surprise in the movie is director Sam Raimi. He is best known for *The Evil Dead* horror series; his thriller, *Darkman;* his Western, *The Quick and the Dead;* and for television versions of Stephen King's *The Stand* and *The Shining.* Perhaps even more extraordinary, Raimi's next movie was the sentimental baseball portrait, *For Love of the Game,* with Kevin Costner, followed by his return to supernatural drama in *The Gift,* and to the action film, *Spider-Man,* based on the popular comic-strip.

A Simple Plan is an austere and wintry movie without the flair of a thriller. It derives its power from its atmosphere, Danny Elfman's moody score, its performances, and the insight into human nature at its worst.

Focus: Jesus reminds us that human ways are not always God's ways, and we can lose our lives if we make the wrong choices. Is it worth gaining the world and losing our souls? A Simple Plan *is a stark, dark response to this Gospel question.*

While the first reading from Isaiah praises the Suffering Servant's fidelity, the reading from James challenges inconsistencies between faith and behavior. Faith, without the effort to live faithfully, is not enough. To declare what is good or evil is one thing, but to choose good over evil for the sake of Christ's love is to follow him in faith.

There are two parts in today's Gospel. The first is Peter's confession of faith that Jesus is the Messiah. Peter's is the kind of straightforward faith that might be found among the righteous townspeople, including Hank, in *A Simple Plan.*

The second part is the warning about temptation, the contrast between God's ways and human ways. This Gospel passage continues, but the Lectionary text stops just before some key words of Jesus: "What profit is there for one to gain the whole world and forfeit his life? What could one give in exchange for his life?" These words give meaning to his warnings about saving and losing one's life, and it is tragic that the characters in *A Simple Plan* do not remember them when faced with choosing between right and wrong.

Hank's journey is complex; he knows what is right, but chooses evil because it is attractive. This has dire consequences. He has numerous opportunities to turn back, to make the right choice and put an end to his folly, but never does. Hank wished to save his life, but in the end, he loses everything—"the whole world"—at the cost of the life he had known.

- The discovery of the money and the decision to steal it, the simple plan; the killing of the farmer; finding out the truth about the money.

KEY SCENES AND THEMES

- Hank and Jacob, their roles in the robbery; Hank falling into deeper trouble, Sarah's part in it; Jacob becoming more aware of the evil of their actions.

- The confrontation with Baxter, the killings; Jacob urging Hank to kill him, the terrible deed; the burning of the money.

FOR REFLECTION AND CONVERSATION

1. If the theme of Shakespeare's *Macbeth* is that unchecked ambition has the power to corrupt, then the same can be said of unchecked greed. Hank, Jacob, Lou, and Sarah seem to be fairly ordinary folk. If the plane with its load of illegal money had not crashed, who is to say how their uncomplicated lives may have continued? Were these people essentially greedy? It is said that twenty-three out of 100 people would steal if they could get away with it. Do you think this is true? Why or why not? What would you have done if you had been in the place of Hank, Jacob, Lou, or Sarah?

2. One of the most insightful facts highlighted by studies about entertainment and information media is that mainstream American movies and television stories almost always blame a "woman" as the cause for the dramatic moral failure on which the plot turns. What do you think the reasons for this might be? What is Sarah's role in the story? Do you think she is the main cause for Hank's failure? Is she a "Lady Macbeth"? Why or why not?

3. The first story of fratricide comes to us from the Book of Genesis, chapter 4. When God sees that Cain has killed Abel, the Lord promised to punish him by making him a restless wanderer on the earth. What do you think Hank's real reason is for killing Jacob? Does

burning the money resolve the moral conflict of the film? Does Hank, or any of the other characters, appreciate the consequences of their actions?

Prayer

Lord, give us the wisdom and integrity to make choices that will save our lives and not lose them. Amen.

Life Is Beautiful (La Vita è Bella)

Italy, 1998, 118 minutes
Cast: Roberto Benigni, Nicoletta Braschi, Giorgio Cantarini,
Marisa Paredes, Horst Buchholz.
Writers: Vincenzo Cerami, Roberto Benigni
Director: Roberto Benigni

Life Is Beautiful (La Vita è Bella)

Anyone Who Welcomes a Child

SYNOPSIS

In the late 1930s, Guido and Ferruccio pretend they are royalty as they drive to Arezzo, Italy, where the humorous and histrionic Guido hopes to open a bookshop. Through a bizarre car and bicycle accident Guido encounters a schoolteacher, Dora, and is smitten with love. Taking a temporary job at the hotel where his uncle works, Guido impersonates a fascist school inspector to get a glimpse of Dora. Then, riding his uncle's horse—painted green by anit-Semites—into the hotel, he literally sweeps Dora off her feet.

They marry and have a son, Giosuè. Five years later, toward the end of World War II, the Jewish Guido and Giosuè are arrested. As soon as non-Jewish Dora discovers this, she demands to be allowed to travel to the concentration camp with her husband and son. Though she gets on the same train, they are separated at the camp. Guido hides Giosuè so they can stay together.

In order to hide the camp's horrible reality from his son, Guido creates a game around their cirumstances. According to Guido, the first one to gain a thousand points wins a real

286

army tank. Giosuè has only to stay hidden and quiet to win points. Guido conceals Giosuè, finds him food, and manages to keep him happy. It takes all of his ingenuity to protect Giosuè. Always clever, he manages to play a music record that lets Dora know he is alive.

Before the camp is liberated, Guido is killed while trying to keep his son hidden. Giosuè emerges from hiding when the camp is liberated, and the American soldiers let him ride in their tank. He sees his mother along the road. The voiceover of the older Giosuè pays tribute to his father who loved enough to give up his life for his son.

COMMENTARY

Pleasing audiences has been the quest of Italian comedy actor Roberto Benigni (*Down by Law, Son of the Pink Panther, Johnny Stecchino*). Benigni has a gift for physical comedy and a face that can be gleeful as well as doleful. His Chaplinesque talent allows him to act in the tradition of clowns, alternating slapstick antics with the pathos of "the little man."

The comedic qualities are abundantly present in the first half of *Life Is Beautiful*. The second half, however, takes place in a death camp. Many commentators have declared that the Holocaust was too serious an event for Benigni to have made a comedy involving it. Others championed the movie and its attempt to show such deep humanity through humor, the only alternative in the face of such evil.

Life Is Beautiful won the Grand Jury Prize at Cannes, 1998, and went on to win Oscars for Best Foreign Language Film, Best Original Music for a Drama, and Best Actor for Benigni in 1999.

DIALOGUE WITH THE GOSPEL

Focus: Jesus told the Twelve, "Whoever receives one child such as this, receives me." Guido so loved his son, Giosuè, that he devoted his life to protecting and saving him in the midst of injustice and death.

The reading from Wisdom is one of the options designated for funerals. It can be read today as an elegy for Guido, a virtuous, decent, and light-hearted man, who is condemned by the "wicked." The "wicked" or "godless" say, "With revilement and torture let us put the just one to the test." Guido passes this test and nobly makes the supreme self-sacrifice for his son.

The first paragraph of the reading from James can also be used as a tribute to Guido, as it praises "the wisdom from above," which contributes to building peace. Ultimately, Guido is killed, but he was kind and considerate in the death camp. He struggled and worked for peace. The second paragraph in the reading from James summarizes the kinds of selfishness and ambition that lead to war and to atrocities like the Holocaust.

In the Gospel, the disciples failed to comprehend Jesus' words about his suffering and death. They avoided the serious issues by arguing about who was the greatest. It is in this context that Jesus rebukes them with a lesson on true authority, which means a genuine service of others. The image of this attitude of service is that of the little child.

Giosuè touches the hearts of the men in the camp, as well as those of the audience. His absolute belief in his father and his trust in "the game" epitomizes the simplicity of heart that Jesus urges his disciples to emulate. Guido is an example of someone who welcomes a child in God's name. Guido's love for his son proves his genuine authority as a father. By loving, protecting, and keeping his son alive in an impossible situation, Guido shows himself to be a man capable of welcoming God.

KEY SCENES AND THEMES

- Guido and his first meeting with Dora; his impersonation of the fascist school inspector and the mock explanation of racism; riding the horse into the banquet and asking Dora to marry him.

- Giosuè and his parents' love for him; the arrest and being put on the train for the death camp, Dora going with them, the separation of the family; Guido hiding Giosuè and the game to keep him hidden; joining the German children for food and the final hiding place that saves him.

- Guido's love for his son; the hard labor, Guido finding the shoes and the glasses, his new awareness of the killings in the camp; Dr. Lessing and his riddles, oblivious of the atrocities; Guido's protection of Giosuè and dying for him.

1. In his review of this film, Roger Ebert said, "*Life Is Beautiful* is not about Nazis and Fascists, but about the human spirit. It is about rescuing whatever is good and hopeful from the wreckage of dreams. About hope for the future. About the necessary human conviction, or delusion, that things will be better for our children than they are right now." If you were to write a paragraph about the film, what would you say the film was about? Why?

2. Of all the dramatic genres, comedy is performed most frequently, and its forms, whether farce or satire, demand a happy ending. *Life is Beautiful,* however, disregards this rule. In the first part of the film, we laugh until we cry. In the second part, we just cry. Yet, through our tears we feel hope because of a father's sacrificial love for his wife and son. How can this film still inspire hope in a post-September 11 world? What does such a world require in order to be a place where children everywhere can have a trusting relationship with their families and with God?

FOR REFLECTION AND CONVERSATION

3. On the way to the bookstore one morning, Giosuè asks his father about the signs that forbid Jews to enter certain places. Guido promises him that they will also post a sign on their store: "No spiders or Visigoths." What did he mean by this? How does Guido use humor as a defense against powers he cannot control? Why can humor be so powerful?

Prayer

Jesus, you showed yourself as our servant by laying down your life for us. Give us the simplicity and trust of a child so that we, too, will serve others as you did. Amen.

TWENTY-SIXTH SUNDAY
OF THE YEAR

Numbers 11:25–29; James 5:1–6;
Mark 9:38–43, 45, 47–48

Second Best

U.K., 1994, 105 minutes
Cast: William Hurt, Chris Cleary Miles, Keith Allen, Alfred Lynch,
Alan Cumming, Prunella Scales, Jane Horrocks, John Hurt,
Nathan Yapp
Writer: David Cook
Director: Chris Menges

Second Best

Leading Not Astray But to Love

Graham Holt, a forty-two-year-old local postmaster in a small Welsh village, cares for his bedridden father. Graham is an only child who strove all his life to please his parents, but never seemed able to do so. He decides he wants to be a father and applies to adopt.

Jamie is a disturbed ten-year-old, full of rage. He is devoted to his father, who is in prison for armed robbery and drug use. His most exhilarating memories are of camping in the woods with his father some years before. Bernard, who works for the welfare department, suggests that Graham take on Jamie with a view to adoption. The rather sardonic caseworker, Debbie, warns the reserved and gentle Graham of the difficulties involved in caring for the angry boy. In the meantime, Graham attends a number of courses to understand himself better and to prepare for Jamie's arrival.

Jamie visits Graham on a series of weekends. He is moody but sometimes shows great affection for Graham. At other times, he is deliberately cruel. He idealizes his father and is haunted by the memories of his mother's suicide and consequent abandonment.

Graham, a good and patient man, adapts to Jamie's moods. He takes him camping, and tries to make him feel welcome and at ease. When Graham's father dies, Jamie lovingly comforts him.

One day, while Jamie is at school, his father arrives at Graham's home. He has AIDS and only a few months to live. Graham invites the sick man to live in their home, which brings the relationship's crisis to a head. Graham wants Jamie to know the truth about his father and to love him, but he also does not want to be merely second best in Jamie's eyes.

COMMENTARY

Second Best is a little-known Welsh film that deserves a wider viewing. For fans of William Hurt, it is a must-see movie, as he takes on a Welsh accent, curly hair, glasses, and a baggy sweater to immerse himself in his character.

Chris Miles Cleary as Jamie is equal to the task of making audiences believe in his pain, anger, and hunger for affection and love. Celebrated British cinematographer Chris Menges, known for his work in *The Killing Fields* and *The Mission,* directed the film. He also directed *A World Apart,* the story of a white family in apartheid South Africa in 1963.

David Cook adapted *Second Best* from his novel of the same title. In some ways, *Second Best* is a story that initially may be open to misinterpretation given the prevalence of child abuse in our times. Like the authorities in the film, we may also question Graham's motives for wanting to adopt a boy. But the strength of the screenplay and performances allow us to see a man who genuinely wants a son to care for and love as a father.

DIALOGUE WITH THE GOSPEL

Focus: Jesus tells the disciples that everyone who acts in his name will be rewarded. At the same time, he has hard sayings regarding the consequences for those who scandalize little ones. Second Best *illustrates how a child can be harmed, as well as saved, by love.*

In the reading from the Book of Numbers, the people are conscious that they have been chosen. Yet they are puzzled when some who seem to be disobeying God are still filled with God's spirit. As the film demonstrates, even people who are underestimated by others can be instruments of God's love and power.

The Letter of James seems an introduction to the Gospel because James has tough things to say to the rich. They will be punished for oppressing those who are righteous; they will weep and wail over their impending misery.

Similar to Moses, Jesus challenges us in the Gospel with some very hard sayings when his disciples object to the unexpected do-gooders who cast out devils in Christ's name. In *Second Best*, Graham is like an outsider who wants to do good and, despite his own expectations and others' doubts, succeeds. In last week's Gospel, we are told that whoever receives a little one in Jesus' name, receives him. Children are truly the ones who belong to Christ, and they are models for all who would be Jesus' disciples.

Jamie reminds us that not all children are innocent and carefree. For some, life has meant bitter hardships. Jesus' rhetorical condemnation of scandalous behavior is not meant to be taken literally; when he says that we should pluck out our eyes and cut off our limbs if they are a source of scandal, he is indicating how serious is the scandal and abuse of children. *Second Best* takes us beyond Jesus' condemnations, however. It shows us beautiful and positive images of love for "one of these little ones," and encourages us to be a healing presence in children's lives.

- Jamie and his father in the woods and their love for each other; his father abandoning him as he goes back to prison; Jamie's memories, his father's letter; having to face his father's illness, approaching death, and

KEY SCENES AND THEMES

the question of forgiveness; the flashbacks to his mother's suicide and having to come to terms with it.

- Graham's relationship with his parents; his mother's death; his father, bedridden and refusing to communicate, the stroke, hospitalization, and death; Graham's memories of the holidays and being close to his father, his disillusionment at his father's hurtful words.

- Graham and Jamie together in the house and camping; Graham comforting Jamie; the moments of Jamie's anger and Graham's bewilderment, Jamie smashing everything and spitting at Graham, Jamie cutting himself; Jamie comforting Graham when his father dies, finally accepting Graham as a father and not "second best."

FOR REFLECTION AND CONVERSATION

1. State-sponsored foster care began in the United States around 1912. Its purpose is to protect children from abusive or harmful home situations. It is estimated that one out of every twenty children in the United States under the age of eighteen is in foster care. In 1989, the United Nations attempted to consolidate international law so that the rights of every child to survival, education, and protection from abuse and exploitation would be assured. What are the conditions of children in your parish and community? How can you become more involved in children's advocacy? What is your parish doing to support parents?

2. Graham tells Jamie, "I know where you've gone. I know where you're hiding. To have nothing, to feel nothing, to be nothing. It doesn't work, I've tried it. Anything's possible, Jamie, except feeling nothing. That's never possible." How is *Second Best* a story about

family and relationships, pain and healing? How does the film paint the similarities between Graham's and Jamie's stories? How are they salvation for one another? What did you think about Graham's decision to give a home to Jamie's father?

3. Part of what makes a film interesting is the art and symbolism used to tell its story. What is the meaning of the broken glass, the shell, and the old military medal in *Second Best*? How did the symbols work to create and evoke meaning and move the action along?

Prayer

Lord, help us to do good to children and never harm them by our actions or neglect. Show us how to love children as you loved them. Amen.

TWENTY-SEVENTH SUNDAY
OF THE YEAR

Genesis 2:18–24; Hebrews 2:9–11;
Mark 10:2–16

Disney's The Kid

U.S.A., 2000, 104 minutes
Cast: Bruce Willis, Spencer Breslin, Emily Mortimer, Lily Tomlin
Writer: Audrey Wells
Director: Jon Turteltaub

Disney's The Kid

Welcome the Little Child

SYNOPSIS

Russ Duritz, about to celebrate his fortieth birthday, is an image consultant who is ruthlessly confrontational with clients and relentlessly demanding on his long-suffering secretary, Janet. His assistant, Amy, is in love with him, but begins to despair of his ever becoming more humane toward others. Russ is hostile to his father.

A mysterious red plane is seen swooping down over Los Angeles. At the same time, an eight-year-old boy appears in Russ' house. Although Russ chases him away, the boy keeps returning. Russ eventually realizes that the boy, Rusty, is actually himself at eight years of age. Exasperated because Rusty is a chubby wimp, Russ tries to disown him. Amy and Janet like Rusty, but are mystified by him.

As Russ and Rusty approach their birthday, they revisit the past. When Russ was in school he could never defend himself, so one of Russ' friends shows Rusty how to box. Rusty successfully defends himself against the school bullies, but is brought before the school principal for fighting. His father comes to the school and angrily accuses the boy of doing things that have caused his mother's illness. Russ begins to understand his past, and realizes that his need to prove himself at work and his avoidance of commitments are a result of unresolved issues from his childhood.

Russ and Rusty go to an airport and find themselves in the future. There, they meet the seventy-year-old Russ, who has become what he really wanted to be, a pilot. Rusty recognizes Russ' wife, Amy.

The word "Disney" in the title of this movie indicates that it will be a feel-good, moral tale, as indeed it is. *Disney's The Kid* is a pleasantly sentimental, light fantasy about the meaning of life.

COMMENTARY

Bruce Willis continues to show his versatility by portraying an obsessive image consultant approaching middle age. Lily Tomlin is the entertaining secretary who brings a comic touch to Bruce Willis's humorless character. Emily Mortimer is his ever hopeful, always disappointed, assistant. An engagingly chubby Spencer Breslin plays Russ at eight years old.

The movie was directed by John Turteltaub, whose other films include *Cool Runnings, While You Were Sleeping,* and *Phenomenon.* Audrey Wells, who also scripted *The Truth about Cats and Dogs* and *George of the Jungle,* wrote *Disney's The Kid.*

The moral of the story is: you might wish to be wealthy, successful, powerful, and sensitive, but ultimately you can only be yourself, and the love of your life might be your ordinary assistant. In *Disney's The Kid* we enter midlife crisis territory and watch Russ getting in touch with his inner child, literally. As we journey toward the happy ending, Russ must learn to integrate the past into his present life, rather than suppress it, and eventually find his true self.

Focus: Jesus loved to have children come to him. He blessed them and said that God's kingdom "belongs to such as these." Russ has suppressed his past, his inner child, and must learn to welcome "the kid" within him.

DIALOGUE WITH THE GOSPEL

Jesus is approachable and welcoming, and parents confidently bring their children to Jesus for him to touch and bless. Jesus' command to let the children come to him is part of the message of the reading from Hebrews, which attests to how Jesus shared in what it means to be human.

Russ is like the disciples who rebuked those who brought their children to Jesus. As soon as he finds Rusty in his house, Russ' instinct is to turn him away. He chases him out of the house and disowns him in public. Russ has repressed the memories of his childhood so much, he cannot face the surfacing of his inner child.

Mark's Gospel continues the focus on children from the previous two Sundays and underlines Jesus' deep feelings for little ones. The lesson he gives his disciples about the real meaning of childhood is the lesson of the movie: there is a goodness about children, a purity that makes them the image of a sincere heart open to the kingdom of God. The movie reminds audiences, however, that childhood is not a perfect time. Children can experience painful and traumatic events that affect them into adulthood.

Jesus says that we must welcome the kingdom like a child. Russ, at forty, has become a self-centered, dominating professional with little capacity for welcoming any Gospel message. It is only when he embraces Rusty, his childhood self, that he is truly blessed.

KEY SCENES AND THEMES

- Russ' criticism of the woman on the plane, his clients, the politician, the dishonest sports manager; getting the children to ridicule the manager; throwing the video cassette away to please Amy and then secretly retrieving it; Janet and Amy's attempts to humanize him.

- Rusty in the house and Russ chasing him away; Russ realizing who Rusty is, yet disowning him in the restaurant; going back into the past, the fight in the school yard, his father's anger, and being blamed for his mother's illness.

* His discussion with Dierdre Lefaver in the bar and her good advice; the support of Janet and Amy; Russ and Rusty at the airport and seeing the future and its image of hope.

FOR REFLECTION AND CONVERSATION

1. Like Charles Dickens' *A Christmas Carol, Disney's The Kid* uses Russ' fortieth birthday as an opportunity to look at the past, the present, and the future with the possibility of change. Here, we discover that it is Russ' damaged inner child that is trying to get out and communicate with him. Why should Russ come to terms with his childhood? Why and how has it made him such an ogre? How does Rusty help Russ gain insight? What is the meaning of the red airplane?

2. Psychologist Daniel J. Levinson talks about the need to make a choice, especially at midlife, in order to continue "becoming" or growing as a person. What choice does Russ make? How does it involve Amy? Is there anything in *Disney's The Kid* that reminds you of yourself or someone you know? How so? How do moral integration and spiritual growth contribute to a person's "becoming" a true human being, no matter the age?

3. At one point, Rusty asks his older ego about the man he is supposed to become. "No dog? I grow up to be a guy with no dog?" Yes, says Russ. "What do I do?" the kid asks. "You're an image consultant," says Russ. The kid considers the situation. "So I'm forty, I'm not married, I don't fly jets, and I don't have a dog? I

grow up to be a loser?" Is Russ a loser? Is there hope for him yet? Why is "image" so important in the film? Why did Russ hide the video from Amy, only to retrieve it later? How might a midlife crisis be considered a blessing?

Prayer

Lord, people found you welcoming, and parents brought their children to you to touch and bless. Make our hearts like those of the children who confidently reached out to you. Amen.

The Godfather

U.S.A., 1972, 175 minutes
Cast: Marlon Brando, Al Pacino, James Caan, Robert Duvall,
John Cazale, Diane Keaton, Talia Shire, Richard Conte,
John Marley, Sterling Hayden, Al Lettieri
Writers: Mario Puzo, Francis Ford Coppola
Director: Francis Ford Coppola

The Godfather

Refusing an Offer

Guests are enjoying the Sicilian-style wedding of Don Vito Corleone's daughter, Connie, at his New York estate in the 1940s. Meanwhile, his youngest son, Michael, points out gangsters to his girlfriend, Kay. During the festivities, Don Corleone holds "court" as the godfather of the Corleone crime family. Petitioners come forward and the Don grants or refuses their requests.

SYNOPSIS

Enemies are terrorized and murdered in mobster style, and when a Hollywood producer refuses a key role to one of Don Corleone's acquaintances, he finds the head of his prized racehorse in his bed.

Traditional Mafia activities have included protection rackets, prostitution, and gambling, but the times are changing. Rival gangster Sollozzo wants Don Corleone's permission to create a narcotics business. Don Corleone disagrees, ostensibly condemning drug rackets, and gang warfare results. There is an attempt on Don Corleone's life and he is hospitalized.

The godfather's oldest son and heir, Sonny, takes over the running of the family business and relies on the advice of his father's *consigliere*, Tom Hagen. Sonny deals recklessly with business matters and people, especially Connie's husband Carlo, whom he beats up for assaulting her. In revenge, Carlo sets up an ambush at a tollbooth and massacres Sonny and his associates.

Michael Corleone is a decorated war vet who has been reluctant to serve in the family business. But once Sonny is killed, he opts for the family. He murders Sollozzo in revenge and goes into hiding in Sicily. There, he marries Apollonia, but she is soon killed. Michael returns to America because of his father's ill health. He marries Kay, they have a son, and the Don dies. While the family is at his son's baptismal ceremony, Michael Corleone's henchmen brutally massacre the family's rivals in New York, Las Vegas, and around the country. Michael has become the new godfather.

COMMENTARY   *The Godfather* has long been considered a classic. Based on Mario Puzo's bestseller, the movie was a risky venture as an epic gangster project that took place in the land of the Mafia (New York) and was produced during the 1970s—the years of the Mafia's greatest influence. It succeeded both critically and popularly, winning Oscars for Best Film and Best Screenplay in 1972. Marlon Brando, who had to audition for the role, received the Oscar for Best Actor, and Al Pacino is unforgettable as Michael Corleone.

The Godfather was acclaimed as a great movie, yet was criticized for glamorizing and mythologizing Sicilian-American gangster families. The Mafia had, in fact, already created its own mythology with its ethos of family and loyalty, its own code of law and *omertà* (conspiracy of silence), and sanctified it with the trappings of Catholic piety and rituals. The more earthy and "realistic" gangster movies of Martin Scorsese, *Goodfellas, Casino, Gangs of New York*, serve as a counterbalance to the mythic *Godfather* trilogy.

There is a great deal of moral and physical violence in the movie which may make many sequences too difficult to watch. Some of these are the scenes with the horse's head, the shootings on the bridge, and the baptismal scene that brought the Mafia and baptismal godfather theme together, with the massacre of the family's enemies.

Focus: Michael Corleone is the twentieth-century rich young man. When he chose power over an honorable life, it led to greed, violence, and betrayal. If ever there were a movie character that dramatized the Gospel's rich young man, it is Michael Corleone.

DIALOGUE WITH THE GOSPEL

It is impossible now to experience *The Godfather* without some prior knowledge of the plot. In 1972, watching the gradual corruption of Michael Corleone, the seemingly all-American innocent, was a shocking experience. The opening sequences set up the contrast between Michael and Don Corleone and cue us to the choices that will have to be made.

Like the young man of the Gospel, Michael obeyed the law; he had done everything he was supposed to do. He seemed to be open to a new life after the military, a life in which he would marry, raise a family, and have an honest career. In the opening scenes, Michael's character could be described by the first reading from Wisdom as prudent and wise. Michael reaches a point when he asks what more he can to do have a good life, like the rich young man in today's Gospel. Jesus saw great potential in the rich young man and challenged him to heroism and virtue, but the man's face fell and he went away sad, for he was very rich. Michael Corleone had the opportunity to live the Christian life, but turned away to follow his father's world.

When we watch the *Godfather* trilogy, we can see why Jesus emphasized how hard it is for the rich to be godly. No wonder the apostles asked who really could be saved, and no wonder Jesus replied that for men and women by themselves, it is impossible.

- Don Vito Corleone holding court, the petitions, the offers, the decrees; Don Corleone and his family, the importance of family, especially his sons inheriting his power.

- The journey of Michael Corleone; educated and independent of the family, his military service, his marriage and family; the influence of his father, loyalty, the assassination, his corruption, deceit, greed, and power.

- The Catholic trappings, rituals, and morality; the double standards of the Mafia, the culmination of Michael's evil choices when his son is baptized and his enemies massacred.

1. The word *Mafia* comes from the Arabic word for "refuge." The Mafia first began in Sicily as a secret society during feudal times to protect lands belonging to the wealthy and to preserve Sicilian culture from Arab invaders. The protection "black hand" racket was established in the 1700s to extort money from the wealthy. By the nineteenth century, the Mafia consisted of small independent groups of men who wanted to protect their families against political and economic oppression by the wealthy. They soon turned to crime and politics. The Mafia was established in the United States by the 1800s, and several crime families came into existence. What started as a response to oppression soon grew into a case of the oppressed becoming the oppressors. How might the

question of justice be at the root of the existence of such a group as the Mafia and other forms of organized crime? What is a Christian response to organized crime?

2. *Omertà,* the honor code of the Mafia, means never to reveal anything about the mob boss, to obey him blindly, to support the family members, avenge attacks on the family, and never go near the authorities. Why did Michael Corleone turn away from decency to embrace this alternate code of honor, a code of exploitation, violence, power, and greater wealth—a code of lies?

3. There is much ugliness in *The Godfather.* One of the most revolting aspects of the film is the implicit religiosity of mafioso "morality." The gangsters even invoke God's blessing. How is the integrity of the family and religion violated in the story, especially during the final, brilliant and shocking scenes of the baptism, intercut with the massacre of Corleone's enemies? How do more contemporary films and television shows, such as *The Sopranos,* compare with *The Godfather* on the issues of faith and family?

Prayer

Lord, you offered the rich young man the opportunity to go beyond the observance of the commandments to loving God and neighbor more completely. Help us to make right choices in our lives. Amen.

The Last Valley

U.K., 1970, 128 minutes
Cast: Michael Caine, Omar Shariff, Florinda Bolkan,
Per Oscarsson, Nigel Davenport
Writer: James Clavell
Director: James Clavell

The Last Valley

Pagan Authority in Jesus' Name

SYNOPSIS

The Thirty Years War (1618–1648) is nearing its end. The war has been fought in Germany and Western Europe between Catholics and Protestants. Local princes led the war in the name of their version of Christianity, and changed sides when political advantage suited them. Cities have been razed, peasants massacred, and villages destroyed.

Vogel is a wandering scholar who has escaped marauding soldiers and the devastation of the plague. Suddenly, a peaceful and prosperous valley opens up before him. Almost at once a band of mercenaries, under the stern but calm leadership of "the Captain," arrives with the intention of destroying the valley and taking its supplies. Vogel shrewdly persuades the Captain to spare the village, settle in for the winter, and escape from the war.

The villagers are Catholics under the leadership of a landowner, Gruber, and the local priest. The former is pragmatic, the latter fanatical. The Captain negotiates an agreement in order to maintain a balance between the Catholic villagers and Protestants in his band. This plan includes the allotment of some of the village women to the soldiers, for which Gruber offers to buy indulgences for their families. The Captain chooses Erika, Gruber's woman.

Their peaceful coexistence is upset when the Captain moves the shrine of Our Lady, which the villagers devoutly and perhaps superstitiously believe protects them. Vogel intervenes, relating a dream of how Mary wants the shrine moved. Both mercenaries and peasants believe him. Peace continues, until one of the soldiers attempts to rape Inger, a young woman who has been protected by Vogel. The soldier escapes but returns with a troop of soldiers, which the villagers ambush and defeat.

The priest thinks that Erika is a witch, and she is tortured and burned. An angry mercenary throws the priest on the pyre. After the winter has passed, the Captain leads his soldiers off to war again. Defeated in a bloody battle, he returns—only to be ambushed by Gruber and to die. Vogel, leaving the village to its temporary peace, continues his wanderings.

COMMENTARY

The Last Valley is one of the few films, including *To Sir with Love*, written and directed by author James Clavell. Clavell is especially known for his best-selling novels about the Orient. His *Shogun* became a miniseries, and *Tai-Pan* was made into a movie in 1986. Clavell's body of work demonstrates his versatility as the author of best-selling novels and literary screenplays. *The Last Valley* was adapted from the novel by J. B. Pick.

The movie is a striking visual presentation of the troubled times in the seventeenth century. Tyrolean mountain beauty and a score by John Barry enhance the experience. The themes of power and religion in *The Last Valley* drive the action forward: superstition, territorial greed, mercenaries victimizing peasants, religious bigotry, clerical celibacy and fanaticism, witchcraft and burnings. The movie is much more than action adventure. It is a glimpse into a painful period of

Christian history and a critique of the worst aspects of politics and religion controlled by fanaticism.

Michael Caine gives a well-controlled performance as the strong and practical leader. Omar Shariff matches him as the haunted, but shrewd, scholar. Per Oscarsson's intense priest looks, and sometimes acts, like Rasputin.

DIALOGUE WITH THE GOSPEL

Focus: The Last Valley *shows Christian history at its worst, with Catholics and Protestants trying to lord it over one another with pagan brutality. Instead, true leadership and authority is service in the pattern of Jesus' self-giving.*

A powerful image of the Church and its ministers since the Second Vatican Council (1962–1965) has been that of servant. The first reading from the fourth Servant Song of Isaiah offers us an image of the servant who suffers. He is crushed, he offers his life in atonement for evil, and takes people's sins on himself. The theme continues in the Letter to the Hebrews where Jesus is described as that very suffering servant. In *The Last Valley*, Vogel is a kind of suffering servant for both the villagers and the mercenaries.

Today's Gospel shows us the power struggle of the apostles James and John. Both wanted the prestige of sitting beside the Lord in glory, and the other apostles were indignant at the arrogance of the request. Jesus tells all of them, and us, "whoever wishes to be great among you will be your servant..."

Jesus' answer is well illustrated in *The Last Valley*, especially when Christians—whether civil, mercenary, or religious authorities—lord it over others and "make their authority felt." Jesus says that this behavior is the abhorrent conduct of non-believers, and that it cannot "be so among you."

There are many discussions in the movie about power and authority, and Jesus' teachings on these matters are unequivocal in today's Gospel. Jesus emphasizes his role as servant, for the "Son of Man did not come to be served, but to serve." Vogel, who came into the valley alone, leaves alone. He resembles a Christ-figure, because he has done his best to serve the people without distinction, and has asked nothing for himself.

- The symbol of the jeweled cross turning into warring soldiers; the massacres, the plague, displaced people, the war and its religious causes; the contrast between the war and the peace of the valley; the valley as a symbol of hope and survival.

- Vogel as a man of intellect and sensitivity, the Captain's strength and pragmatism; their differences in leadership; their motivation for staying in the valley and their differing attitudes toward the people; the experience in the valley, which gives Vogel some peace and the Captain some humanity.

- The Captain's return to the war, the fighting and bloodshed; the burning of Erika; a temporary peace before soldiers come to the valley and destroy it; Vogel's departure.

1. This is not an easy film to follow because of the obscure historical period and the complexity of the role of religion in the civil life of the people following the Reformation. Vogel describes how the members of his family died, especially his six-year-old sister—drowned as a witch. The Captain describes the slaughter in Magdeburg. Vogel is a philosopher who wants to find God. The Captain is a practical atheist who finally asks Vogel to remember him, should he ever meet God. What do these two characters stand for in the film? Is there a message in this film that transcends history? If so, what might it be?

2. Once again, Mark's Gospel presents us with the very human traits of Jesus' apostles. In a way it is amusing to see James and John bickering over who gets the best seat in heaven. How does today's Gospel take our focus off the tension between James and John and their companions, and move it once again to the issues of human dignity and respect? What do issues of power, status, and influence—whether religious, economic, civic, or political—mean for our understanding of authentic humanity? Do "power" and "religion" contradict each other? Why or why not?

3. Fanaticism is an extreme and irrational belief in a person or idea. British author Aldous Huxley said, "Defined in psychological terms, a fanatic is a man who consciously over-compensates a secret doubt." Talk about this definition and how fanaticism characterized the plot of *The Last Valley*. What causes fanaticism? What can prevent fanaticism, especially when it concerns religion and impacts the rights of others?

Prayer

Jesus, may we never lord religion over others in any way. Teach us how to be the servants you taught us to be. Amen.

At First Sight

U.S.A., 1999, 114 minutes
Cast: Val Kilmer, Mira Sorvino, Kelly McGillis, Steven Weber,
Bruce Davison, Nathan Lane, Ken Howard
Writer: Steve Levitt
Director: Irwin Winkler

At First Sight

That I May See

Virgil Adamson went blind when he was three years old, and he retains only vague memories of what it was like to see. Overworked architect Amy Benic takes a break at a resort where Virgil works as a masseur. At first, she does not realize he is blind. Within a short period of time they are attracted to one another. Jennie is Virgil's spinster sister who has cared for him for many years. She is apprehensive and jealous of Amy's relationship with her brother.

SYNOPSIS

After resisting Amy's concern and pushiness, Jennie persuades Virgil to undergo a new treatment to restore his sight. He moves to New York with Amy. He is afraid the procedure will be a failure, but it seems to be a success.

He has difficulty getting used to sight—reading and identifying objects and colors—and has to rely on his sense of touch. He struggles to adjust to a sighted world, and this puts a strain on the couple's relationship. He begins to work with a visual therapist.

Virgil also confronts his father who abandoned him and his sister when they were young. He leaves Amy when his sight begins to fade and he has to face blindness again. Amy realizes that she was too dominating, and finds Virgil again.

311

COMMENTARY

At First Sight is a very emotional movie based on the story *To See and Not See* by Oliver Sacks, author of *Awakenings*. This film can be seen as a parallel to the book and film version of *Awakenings*. Virgil Adamson is blind and regains his sight, but the recovery is only temporary. He goes blind again, just as the patients in *Awakenings* return to their coma-like state.

The movie is filmed in a glossy, studio style and relies on some typical Hollywood melodrama and the attractiveness of its stars to tell its story. Val Kilmer is more than usually sympathetic as Virgil Adamson. Academy Award winner Mira Sorvino plays the architect, Amy, and is a credible do-gooder. Kelly McGillis brings a harder edge to the film as Jennie, Virgil's older sister, who has sacrificed much of her life to care for him.

The film has a sharp moment when Virgil tracks down his father, played by Ken Howard, who deserted the family because he could not accept his son's blindness. Bruce Davison is the doctor who carries out the experimental surgery, and Nathan Lane is very good as the visual therapist, a role based on that of Oliver Sacks. Direction is by Irwin Winkler, a respected producer-turned-director whose credits include *Guilty by Suspicion*, *The Net*, and *Life as a House*.

DIALOGUE WITH THE GOSPEL

Focus: Before he healed the blind man, Jesus first asked what the man wanted him to do. Jesus does not impose; he responds to needs and requests. Vernon goes along with Amy's attempts to find ways to restore his sight. Both Virgil and Bartimaeus learn from their experiences.

Bartimaeus is a blind beggar who hears about Jesus and takes the opportunity to beg for compassion: "Have pity on me." Those who were near him scolded and rebuked him for bothering Jesus. Others encouraged him. Jesus' response to the blind man consists in some of the most important words for caregivers of the visually and hearing impaired. Instead of imposing his healing on Bartimaeus, Jesus prefers to ask him, "What do you want me to do for you?" Jesus respects the person and that person's wishes. He offers Bartimaeus the opportunity to articulate his plea, "Master, I want to see."

This contrasts with Amy's behavior. She is moved with pity, but does not consult Virgil about the treatment. She makes the arrangements without letting him know and without asking Jennie for more information and advice. While Virgil goes along with the treatment, he feels pressured into it and is scarcely prepared for the complexities of life afterward.

Bartimaeus has faith and is saved. His sight returns immediately, and he follows Jesus. Virgil, like the vast majority of us, does not experience the miracle he wanted, but he does learn from his experience to have faith in himself and in those who love him. He has his memories of sight and the confidence he needs to lead his life to the fullest. In his own way, he *has* been healed.

KEY SCENES AND THEMES

- Virgil playing hockey on the ice, massaging his clients, but not telling them he is blind; meeting Amy and her enthusiastic reading about treatment for the blind and acting on it without asking Virgil; preparation for the operation and its immediate aftermath.

- Jennie and how she gave her life to care for Virgil; her hostility toward Amy; Virgil's meeting with his father and being rejected by him again.

- Virgil and Amy communicating on the ice; Virgil's speech to the experts and the media announcing that he was going blind again; the finale: Virgil accepting his life and love for Amy.

FOR REFLECTION AND CONVERSATION

1. The film invites audiences into Virgil's experience so that we can identify with him and his situation. He is a well-adjusted young man and, though blind, has no difficulty navigating his life. Why does Amy automati-

cally assume that Virgil wants "saving," that is, to see like everyone else? Though well intentioned, was her approach the best way to advance the idea of experimental surgery to Virgil? Why or why not? Why did his ability to see strain their relationship?

2. Basic human communication has various definitions. In Korean, the word communication means "to be present to another." In English, it means to convey and receive ideas and information through words—spoken and unspoken—and gestures. Virgil gains information through touch, smell, hearing, and taste, and, for a little while, through vision. What did you think about the episode on the ice when Amy demonstrates and interprets body language for Virgil? How is Amy's communication a way to convey ideas and information? How aware are we of our body language? What does it communicate to others? How do Virgil and Amy finally become present to each other?

3. Blindness and vision are themes that the Scriptures and the arts address. Often, physical blindness is a metaphor for interior blindness, and the story of St. Paul's conversion on the way to Damascus (Acts 9:11) is one of the best illustrations. Talk about and compare other Bible passages and films about blindness and sight and what they mean to you. How is gaining insight into one's own reality a true gift and sometimes a miracle?

Prayer

Lord, you ask us what we want of you, and we respond, "that we may see." Amen.

THIRTY-FIRST SUNDAY OF THE YEAR

Deuteronomy 6:2–6; Hebrews 7:23–28; Mark 12:28–34

Keeping the Faith
U.S.A., 2000, 124 minutes
Cast: Ben Stiller, Edward Norton, Jenna Elfman, Eli Wallach, Anne Bancroft, Ron Rifkin, Milos Forman, Holland Taylor
Writer: Stuart Blumberg
Director: Edward Norton

Keeping the Faith

Torah and Gospel

SYNOPSIS

Fr. Brian Finn, a young priest in New York, confides his tale of woe to a sympathetic bartender. He remembers his school days, when he was part of a happy-go-lucky trio with his best friend, Jake Schram, and the vivacious Anna Riley. Suddenly, when they were eight years old, Anna moved out of their lives when her family relocated to San Francisco.

Brian decides to become a priest and Jake a rabbi. They remain close friends. At first they are tentative in their ministries, but they rapidly draw congregations to church and synagogue and get people involved in singing and in question-and-answer sermons. They also decide to start a club. They rent a hall and turn it into an interfaith karaoke lounge/senior center.

Just as suddenly as she left, Anna announces she is returning to New York. She has become a high-powered, workaholic executive. The three renew their strong bonds of friendship. Anna falls in love with Jake, and as they begin a relationship, they do not tell Brian. In their talks together, Brian explains to Anna why he is committed to his vow of celibacy. When Jake breaks up with Anna, she confides in Brian. He is shocked to discover that she has been involved

315

with Jake, and is just as shocked to realize that he, too, has fallen in love with her.

Jake is being pressured by his congregation to get married to a Jewish girl. He has not told them about Anna. Ruth, Jake's mother, realizes what has happened. When she has a slight stroke, she urges Jake to make his own decision. Anna is about to leave New York. During a Yom Kippur sermon, Jake confesses his relationship with Anna to his congregation. His honesty impresses the synagogue advisory board, and he is installed as the new rabbi. Brian realizes that celibacy is his vocation, and urges Jake to find Anna. Despite some comic obstacles, Jake succeeds.

COMMENTARY

A British Airways movie program synopsis of *Keeping the Faith* states, "A rabbi and a priest are friends, but fall in love with the same girl," which makes you wonder what you are in for. This is, in fact, an entertaining comedy, sometimes reminiscent of the contrived situations found in sitcoms, yet never cynical or sarcastic. The humor and clever one-liners are endearing rather than annoying. The screenplay is not meant to be realistic in the sense of what really goes on in either the Jewish or the Catholic community. Rather, the movie comically represents some of the struggles of religious people today.

Ben Stiller, best known for *There's Something About Mary* and *Meet the Parents,* is the intense rabbi Jake. Jenna Elfman, of television's *Dharma and Greg,* is the vivacious Anna. Edward Norton, Fr. Brian, has proven himself a versatile and talented serious actor in *Primal Fear, American History X, Fight Club,* and *The Score.* He not only acts in, but directs the movie.

DIALOGUE WITH THE GOSPEL

Focus: Love of God and love of neighbor are the greatest commandments. Rabbi Jake and Fr. Brian, despite confusion in their lives, keep the faith by living these two commandments.

The Gospel highlights the two commandments of love of God and love of neighbor that are necessary for a good life. The reading from Deuteronomy (quoted by Jesus) is a central text for the Jewish people, the declaration of the commandment for loving God, the "Shema Israel," "Listen, O Israel." What follows is the most fundamental declaration of Israel's faith in the one true God, which Jews, Christians, and also Muslims uphold. With its personalized, heartfelt style, Deuteronomy urges its readers to take the command to love God with your heart, mind, soul, and strength "to heart." The Letter to the Hebrews addresses priests of the Old and New Covenants, and mentions that human priests are "subject to weakness." It offers Jesus as the model of the perfect priest.

The themes of today's readings are readily identified in *Keeping the Faith*. The central characters are priests of the Old and the New Covenants, and both are "subject to weakness" in their love for Anna. Jake, first of all, has a sexual relationship outside of marriage with the non-Jewish Anna. When he begins to think of marriage, he does not admit the relationship to his synagogue community. Brian, meanwhile, struggles to cope with his commitment to celibacy when he realizes that he, too, loves Anna.

In the end, Jake is prepared to set aside his love for Anna for the love of God in order to be the rabbi he believes God has called him to be. Brian, having questioned his celibacy, comes away recommitted to it—something not often appreciated by Hollywood or audiences. The characters of Jake and Brian strikingly illustrate genuine faith and love of God and neighbor.

- Brian's story of his and Jake's vocations; their initial blunders; their commitment to preaching, helping their congregations, and initiating the club.

KEY SCENES AND THEMES

- Brian's story; contentment with his vocation, explanation of celibacy to Anna, and struggle with his commitment, Anna not responding to him; his discussions with the parish priest; his desire to help Anna, despite his hurt feelings; his sharing in the joy of Jake's appointment as rabbi and reunion with Anna.

- Jake's story; the Jewish congregation and its traditions, and inviting the Gospel group in to liven up the worship; the expectations for him to marry and his disturbed conscience because of his relationship with Anna; his harsh breaking off of the relationship for the sake of his ministry; his mother and her pressure on him; his clashes with Brian, their reconciliation and Brian's gift of the card.

FOR REFLECTION AND CONVERSATION

1. *Keeping the Faith* does indeed raise an important question for people who are committed to their faith: how do you communicate faith and religion to a modern TV and movie audience that may not be churchgoing or that may have unhappy memories? How can believers, ministers or lay, keep faith with "cultural" Christians or Jews, so that they in turn can keep the faith?

2. For Catholics, one of the strongest scenes in the movie is when Fr. Brian and the older pastor, Fr. Havel, discuss celibacy. Havel admits to falling in love several times during his life as a priest, but through prayer and ministry he has been able to recommit himself and not act on his infatuations. How does Fr. Havel's honesty influence Fr. Brian? Why is honesty about celibacy and sexuality always positive? How do the struggles of the clergy in this film compare to that of

Fr. Shore in *The Third Miracle,* or to clergy characters in other films you have seen? What can all believers learn from a film like this?

3. *Keeping the Faith,* though lighthearted, offers a model for interreligious dialogue, and walking ahead together toward the one, true God. It also questions, from the Jewish perspective, the wisdom of a husband and wife having different faiths. Various difficulties may arise, especially regarding the faith in which the couple's children will be raised. Talk about the sacrament of Marriage in the light of the *Catechism of the Catholic Church* (Part II, n. 7), and *Keeping the Faith.* What might it take for an interfaith marriage to work?

Prayer

Lord, help us to find authentic ways of putting your commandment to love God and neighbor into practice day by day. Amen.

The Long Walk Home

U.S.A., 1990, 97 minutes
Cast: Sissy Spacek, Whoopi Goldberg, Dwight Schultz,
Ving Rhames, Dylan Baker; Lexi Randall
Narrator: Mary Steenburgen,
Writer: John Cork
Director: Richard Pearce

The Long Walk Home

Giving All She Had

SYNOPSIS

The Long Walk Home is based on the historical events that took place in Montgomery, Alabama, in 1955. Rosa Parks, a black woman, refused to give up her seat to a white man and began the strike that led to the integration of city buses—which contributed significantly to the Civil Rights movement in the United States.

A wealthy, white family lives comfortably in the South. Miriam is a devoted wife and mother. She, like other affluent white women in Montgomery, is busy with her social life and supervising domestic arrangements. She does not question the status quo and relies on her black servants to run her household. Black servants are treated politely, but always considered beneath the white people.

Odessa is Miriam's servant. She works diligently all day and returns home to her own neighborhood. Odessa and her husband struggle with finances and bringing up their children. When the bus strike begins in protest to segregation, Odessa and many of the servants choose to walk to work. The long walk is their way to protest the injustices of racism. One day, Miriam sees Odessa walking to work and she begins to drive her to and from work. She also joins the demonstrators and experiences police brutality as well as slurs from her husband, family, and friends. Together, Odessa and Miriam discover the common ground of human dignity.

The Long Walk Home offers a serious dramatic study of United States race relations in 1955. It is a critique of the past, and it offers hope to create and strengthen bonds between people of different races, and, by extension, different cultures, creeds, social status, genders, and ages. Sissy Spacek brings conviction to her role as the well-meaning wife who employs a black housekeeper.

The film belongs to Whoopi Goldberg, who is at her dignified best as the middle-aged servant, Odessa. She plays a woman older than her actual age, and her performance is reminiscent of her roles in *The Color Purple, Clara's Heart,* and *Corinna Corinna,* rather than her wonderfully funny characters in such films as *Ghost* and *Sister Act.* In 1996, she played activist Medgar Evers' wife in *Ghosts of Mississippi.*

Richard Pearce directed the movie. A number of his movies reflect social awareness, and these include *Heartland, Country,* and *A Family Thing.* He was also one of the directors for the short-lived 1997–1998 television drama, *Nothing Sacred,* about a parish priest in the inner city.

Focus: The widow who gave everything she had for the upkeep of the Temple won Jesus' admiration. Odessa, a servant to a white family, gave everything she could for civil rights in Alabama during the 1950s.

In today's Gospel the "widow's mite" is translated, "two small coins, worth a few cents." The context is that of Jesus teaching the crowds to avoid the hypocrisy of the religious authorities in Jerusalem. He condemns the way they stand on their dignity, display their status by what they wear, and expect people to defer to them. They have a prominent social life and are conscious of keeping up appearances in society while neglecting those in dire need.

Odessa finds herself in a situation similar to that of the Gospel's widow. Odessa is a good woman who supports her husband and children. After a long day at work, she is ready to face their complaints and problems. She seems already to be giving all she has. Odessa's deeply held beliefs about human dignity are sorely tested when the buses in Montgomery are boycotted. She cannot give up her work, because she needs the money to support her family—but she cannot condone the racism underlying segregation. Like the widow of the Gospel, Odessa was prepared to risk everything she had to live on for the support of the "temple" that is human dignity.

KEY SCENES AND THEMES

- Montgomery, Alabama, in 1955; the world of the affluent whites, their homes, social events; the world of the blacks, their homes, neighborhoods, and singing spirituals; Martin Luther King, Jr., his presence in the background of the film, his arrest.

- The need for buses in Montgomery; Odessa and the buses, the boycott, and her willingness to walk; her daughter going on the bus and the attack by the white boys, the Christmas dinner and the rude comments of the family; Miriam changing her attitude because of the boycott, her conversations with Odessa and sharing her memories; going out and driving the black women, making a stand against racism; her transformation.

- The boycott and Odessa's options; walking, the pain, riding with Miriam, their friendship, Odessa's ultimate achievement.

1. When Rosa Parks refused to give up her seat on the bus, she was not new to civil rights activism. Her husband, Raymond, had long been involved in the NAACP, and she also joined the organization. Both Rosa Parks and her husband lost their jobs as a result of the bus boycott and were harassed and threatened. Finally, in 1957, they moved to Detroit. Rosa Parks is often called the "mother of the Civil Rights movement" because of her actions that day on a bus in Montgomery, Alabama. The film tells the story through the eyes of two characters and families that we come to know well. How well do you think the film is able to recount the story of an event that changed a nation? Why? What other films use seemingly insignificant characters to tell a larger story? Consider *Titanic, Born on the Fourth of July, Men with Guns, The Killing Fields, To Kill a Mockingbird,* and *Pleasantville.* Are they as successful as *A Long Walk Home*?

2. One of the interesting dimensions of *A Long Walk Home* is the unnecessary voice-over narration by Miriam's daughter, which some critics considered the producers' attempt to reassure white audiences. What audience do you think the film was made for? Would you have "walked the walk" as Odessa did? Are there people in your neighborhood or parish who are being treated unjustly because of race? What are you doing about it?

3. Christian feminism has its origin in a theology rooted in the experience of women. It considers the historical and cultural role that theology and the treatment of women have played in that experience. *A Long Walk*

FOR REFLECTION AND CONVERSATION

Home invites us into the lives and homes of black and white women in the American South. The husbands in the story are demanding and difficult and think that women exist to fill certain pre-established roles. How is there a feminist subtext to *A Long Walk Home?* What is the idea of God that comes into focus through the experience of women? How do the women in the film deal with their situations? How is discrimination against women or any person a form of racism? What would a Christian response to discrimination be?

Prayer

Jesus, the unobtrusive and completely generous widow caught your attention and evoked your admiration. Help us to recognize the people in our midst who are like the generous widow so we can learn from their example. Amen.

**THIRTY-THIRD SUNDAY
OF THE YEAR**

Daniel 12:1–3; Hebrews 10:11–14, 18;
Mark 13:24–32

Thirteen Days

U.S.A., 2001, 145 minutes
Cast: Kevin Costner, Bruce Greenwood, Steven Culp,
Dylan Baker, Bill Smitrovich, Stephanie Romanov
Writer: David Self
Director: Roger Donaldson

Thirteen Days

The End of the World

SYNOPSIS

October 1962 saw one of the greatest crises of the Cold War. United States reconnaissance flights over Cuba reveal the presence of Soviet missiles on the island. Teams of local and Russian experts are readying them for action.

The Kennedy administration initiates a diplomatic confrontation with the Russian ambassador to Washington. Russia denies the existence of the missiles. The Pentagon wants more direct action and promises retaliation if any American plane is fired on during missions over the missile sites. Attorney General Robert Kennedy supports and advises President John F. Kennedy. Their chief political advisor is Kevin O'Donnell. Adlai Stevenson, the ambassador to the United Nations, suggests negotiation and compromise. Robert Kennedy considers him soft and dismisses his suggestion.

A blockade, diplomatically called "quarantine," is set in place with the United States Navy blocking Russian ships carrying missiles. The President addresses the nation. The United States and the Soviet Union are on the brink of war.

At the last moment, the ships turn around. Meanwhile, the Russians in Cuba continue installing nuclear warheads. The Pentagon demands air attacks, but the president resists.

Premier Khrushchev sends a private message to the United States suggesting a way out that allows both sides to save face. Adlai Stevenson calls the bluff of the Soviet ambassador to the United Nations, and Robert Kennedy communicates the compromise solution to the ambassador in Washington. Nuclear war is averted.

COMMENTARY   *Thirteen Days* is a historical, political thriller directed by Australian director-producer Roger Donaldson, known for such films as *No Way Out, Dante's Peak,* and *The Farm.* The script, written by David Self, was based on the book, *The Kennedy Tapes: Inside the White House During the Cuban Missile Crisis,* by Ernest R. May and Philip D. Zelicow. With *Thirteen Days,* we have the opportunity to bypass the private world of the Kennedys and concentrate on what proved to be one of John and Robert Kennedy's greatest contributions to world peace.

Bruce Greenwood plays John F. Kennedy, and there is even a slight physical resemblance. His portrayal shows Kennedy's presidential qualities, exhibiting a mixture of strength and hesitation as he asserts his authority. Stephen Culp looks like the boyish Robert Kennedy, and believably communicates his shrewdness and intense moral support of his brother.

This is an entertainment film rather than a documentary. The filmmakers have chosen to tell the story of this moment in Cold War history through the experience of a minor character, Presidential Advisor Kenneth O'Donnell. Kevin Costner is in the starring role as O'Donnell, a relatively unknown member of the Kennedy White House. For those who know or remember this period, all the key personalities are portrayed on screen: Secretaries Dean Rusk and Robert McNamara, Vice President Lyndon Johnson, Generals LeMay and Maxwell, Press Secretary Pierre Salinger—and Andrei Gromyko, the Soviet Foreign Minister.

Focus: The warnings of the Scriptures about the end of the world seemed to be coming true in October 1962 during the thirteen days of confrontation between the United States and the Soviet Union. These were days of tribulation in a very real sense.

The readings for this Sunday speak of a catastrophic end of the world. October 1962 was a time when the world at large seemed on the edge of a nuclear apocalypse. By means of modern communications technology, everyone, especially in the United States, could see that this was "a time unsurpassed in distress since nations began" (Dn 12:13).

Jesus uses the same imagery when he speaks of the disastrous cosmic event that will mark the coming of the Son of Man. The last words of the Gospel are a reminder of the limits of human knowledge and of human fallibility. The alleluia verse reprises this theme with its warning, "Be vigilant at all times."

The world was spared in 1962 when acknowledgment of the finality of a nuclear war finally prevailed. The readings today emphasize God's providence and care, rather than human wisdom in a crisis, which seems to contradict John F. Kennedy's final words in the film. But the readings promise us that no matter what disasters befall us, God loves us and will be faithful. Jesus will come again, he will gather those who are faithful, and they will be saved—by God.

KEY SCENES AND THEMES

- The reality of nuclear destruction with scenes of atomic explosions; the installation of the missiles in Cuba; the reconnaissance flights and the photos; the blockade of the convoy, torpedoes and bombs on alert.

- John F. Kennedy, his authority and responsibility; the briefings, the arguments, the tactical discussions; hawks and doves in the Pentagon and at the United Nations; President Kennedy's decisions, Robert Kennedy and the final diplomatic meeting with the Russian ambassador.

- The media communicating the crisis to the public; fear, panic, frantic buying of food and supplies, the shelters; the church with twenty-four-hour confessions, Kenny O'Donnell getting into line; prayer for peace.

FOR REFLECTION AND CONVERSATION

1. The "Cold War" describes the time between the end of World War II and 1989, when its symbol, the Berlin Wall, tumbled. The Cold War was the political, economic, and ideological conflict between the United States and its allies with the Soviet Union and its allies. The United States stood for democracy and capitalism, the Soviet Union for communism and Marxism. If you know someone who remembers that era—and the Cuban Missile Crisis in particular—ask them to describe what it was like to grow up with the imminent threat of a nuclear holocaust. Why is nuclear war still possible? How did negotiation and diplomacy work, according to the film? Why might these methods, more than others, be good for all seasons?

2. The apocalypse is described in both the Hebrew Scriptures and in the New Testament. According to Scripture scholar Celia Sirois, the difference between the two is the central role that the New Testament gives to Christ in the "unfolding end-time drama." Talk about and compare some apocalyptic "end of time" films such as *End of Days* and *The Seventh Sign,* which use religion as their point of departure, with films about the possibility of a real-life apocalypse such as *Thirteen Days, On the Beach, The Omega Man,* or *The Postman.* What is the difference between the two approaches to the end times, and why are their themes

worth thinking and praying about? What is the role of Christ, the Alpha and Omega of all that exists, in our salvation and the events that seem to be foretold for the end of the world? What do the mainstream Christian churches and the Catholic Church teach about the apocalypse?

3. Advent is two weeks away, and the seasons are changing: to winter in the northern hemisphere, to summer in the southern hemisphere. How do the readings today reflect both fear of the unknown and God's care and providence? How do the liturgy and the liturgical year keep pace with our faith development and the rhythm of life? And finally, what is the message of hope in today's readings?

Prayer

Lord, you are a God of peace. May your loving and providential care save us from the conflicts between nations and peoples. Grant the world peace and protect everyone from terror, disaster, and fear. Amen.

Absence of Malice

U.S.A., 1981, 112 minutes
Cast: Paul Newman, Sally Field, Bob Balaban, Melinda Dillon,
Barry Primus, Wilford Brimley, Luther Adler, Don Hood,
Josef Sommer
Writer: Kurt Luedtke
Director: Sydney Pollack

Absence of Malice

Belonging to the Truth

SYNOPSIS

During a Department of Justice murder investigation involving Florida gangsters and union leaders, press officer Elliot Rosen leaks information to the press. He reveals that Michael Gallagher, the son of a mafioso, is a suspect. However, Gallagher seems innocent and confronts the journalist, Megan Carter, who wrote the story.

Assuming his guilt, Megan becomes interested in Gallagher and has lunch with him aboard his yacht, intending to tape him and have him photographed. When he explains himself to Megan, she believes him. Gallagher will not give his whereabouts at the time of the murder because he wants to protect a close friend, Teresa, the vice-principal at the local Catholic school. Teresa makes an appointment with Megan and reluctantly reveals that she had had an abortion on the day of the murder and that Gallagher had accompanied her. She begs Megan not to print names, but Megan publishes the story and the details. A depressed Teresa kills herself.

Gallagher meets with the district attorney, Quinn, who is running for office in a local election. Gallagher makes a deal with Quinn, offering information about the murder in exchange for a public statement that will clear him of suspicion. Quinn agrees. Megan gives prominence to the story of Gallagher's innocence.

Gallagher then sets up an elaborate plan to incriminate all those who conspired against him, including Megan, even though he has had a brief affair with her. He donates money anonymously to a Florida charity that is backing Quinn in the election. He plans a meeting with Quinn by phone, knowing that his phone is bugged and is being taped by the FBI. When Rosen exposes Quinn as having been bribed by Gallagher, Megan also prints that story.

During the ensuing recrimination, a federal official, James J. Wells, conducts a hearing with all the protagonists present. Quinn resigns, Rosen is given thirty days to leave the department, and Megan loses her job. Gallagher has achieved his retribution on all those who conspired against him.

Absence of Malice probed the journalistic ethics and the morality of revenge and was a very popular movie in 1981. It received three Oscar nominations: Paul Newman for Best Actor, Melinda Dillon for Best Supporting Actress, and Kurt Luedtke for Best Screenplay.

COMMENTARY

Director Sydney Pollack has to his credit a significant number of entertaining dramatic movies with social overtones. His extensive filmography as a director, over a more than forty year career, includes: *The Slender Thread, The Way We Were, Jeremiah Johnson, Tootsie, Out of Africa* (which was also written by Kurt Luedtke), and *The Firm*. Pollack has also acted in and produced many films in the United States as well as in the United Kingdom.

Absence of Malice was also popular because of its stars. Paul Newman had already become a screen icon dramatizing American values, not always necessarily in a clean-cut, upstanding way, but in a search for honesty and integrity. Sally Field had already proven that she was not merely a pretty face on television or in light comedy, having won Oscars in 1979 for *Norma Rae* and about to win another in 1984 for *Places in the Heart.*

DIALOGUE WITH THE GOSPEL

Focus: Jesus speaks the truth and tells us "everyone who belongs to the truth listens to my voice." Absence of Malice *is a movie about truth: reporting it and exposing lies.*

There seem to be two different dimensions to this year's celebration of the feast of Christ the King. On the one hand, the emphasis of the readings from Daniel and the Book of Revelation is apocalyptic. They focus on the last days of the world when all will be accomplished and Jesus comes again as Lord of all creation. In other words, they describe the cosmic kingship of Christ.

The Gospel focuses on the suffering of Jesus on Good Friday when Pilate judges him. Pilate's justice is of "this world." Pilate challenges Jesus, who up to this point has been silent. Jesus will not defend himself and seems to ignore the accusations brought against him. It is in this context of Jesus' condemnation that the Gospel question about the nature of truth is asked, although the lectionary has chosen not to include it here. After Jesus admits he is a king and that everyone who listens to the truth listens to him, Pilate utters the sometimes trivialized but profound question, "What is truth?"

Absence of Malice is a movie about truth and integrity. If one listens to the dialogue, "truth" is one of the most frequently used words. In the film's context, the question about what exactly *is* the truth is startlingly valid. The movie shows that truth is often exploited and manipulated, and that the integrity of truth, of which Jesus speaks, is expedient.

Jesus was not a victim of the media, but he experienced official misrepresentation; the truth about his ministry was twisted and he was sentenced to death. Michael Gallagher asks Megan Carter at the beginning of the movie, "What do you write when the investigation is over and a man is innocent?" Apparently no one is interested. Michael Gallagher went to ingenious lengths to trap those who conspired against him, and he vindicated himself. Jesus, on the other hand, though he was king, did nothing to prove his innocence. He emptied himself in order to experience the sufferings and injustices of this life so that truth would prevail in the end.

KEY SCENES AND THEMES

- Megan Carter's journalistic curiosity, pumping people for information, reading the document on Rosen's desk and leaking it; her justification to herself and to Gallagher that she was merely reporting; the support of Mac who questioned her as she wrote her articles; the newspaper wanting to report unconfirmed information, rather than be concerned about the truth.

- Michael Gallagher and his father and uncle's expectations of him; his explanation that his father wanted him to live honestly; telling the story of his father locking him in the cabin so that if he was to be a thief, he would know how a thief lived; his anger at Megan, confronting her with the truth.

- His plan to involve the officials; Megan, potential leaks, and Quinn; breaking the law and codes of conduct; Michael exposing how the professionals have lied.

FOR REFLECTION AND CONVERSATION

1. There are conflicting attitudes about truth in this film. We hear phrases such as "print the truth," "the public have the right to know," "create the impression of fairness," "is there an obligation to print the truth?" We ponder questions about people's right to privacy, and the media's responsibility to present the facts. The movie leaves us with a final query: "Do people believe what they want to believe?" In applying the Gospel

question about truth to the characters and the plot and subplots in the movie, what is your answer?

2. In July 2000, *USA TODAY* published a story on ethics and journalism that opened with, "Print and broadcast media should be guided by five values: honesty, independence, fairness, productiveness, and pride." The Radio-Television News Directors Association (www.RTNDA.com/ethics) issued an updated code of Ethics and Professional Conduct in September 2000. The main headings of the code include public trust, truth, fairness, integrity, independence, and accountability. How are these qualities present in *Absence of Malice?* What were Megan's and Quinn's code of ethics? Is one articulated and followed in the film? Why or why not? A mentally fragile woman was driven to suicide. Why did this happen? What could have prevented it?

3. The character of Michael Gallagher permits the plot to develop in more complex ways because he refuses to be passive. What does "truth" mean to him? Does he have a code of honor? Was he justified in avenging himself? What is the lesson in all this for media consumers? What is our code of honor regarding news and our desire for it? What does "truth" mean to us?

Prayer

Jesus, you spoke the truth. May we belong to the truth so that we may speak it and, in so doing, listen to your voice. Amen.

IMMACULATE CONCEPTION
Genesis 3:9–15, 20; Ephesians 1:3–6,
11–12; Luke 1:26–38

Unbreakable
U.S.A., 2000, 106 minutes
Cast: Bruce Willis, Samuel L. Jackson, Robin Penn Wright,
Spencer Treat Clark
Writer: M. Night Shyamalan
Director: M. Night Shyamalan

Unbreakable

Saying Yes to Goodness

In 1961, Elijah Price is born in a department store. The doctor discovers that he is very fragile and that many of his bones were actually broken during birth. Elijah grows up looking for his exact opposite: someone completely unbreakable.

SYNOPSIS

Almost forty years later, in the year 2000, David Dunn flirts with a passenger in a train, which suddenly derails and crashes. He is the sole survivor, and he emerges from the wreck without even one broken bone.

Elijah runs a museum-like comic book store filled with first editions. When Elijah hears about the train wreck and the sole survivor, he sends David an anonymous note to ask if he has ever been ill. David remembers surviving a car crash when he was in college, and his wife tells him that she has never known him to be sick. His son Joseph believes Elijah's theory that David is a hero and is, indeed, "unbreakable." David also recalls that as a child, he almost drowned in a pool, but managed to escape.

David finally accepts the gift of being "unbreakable." When he begins to allow people to brush against him, he discovers that he also has the ability to see the crimes others have committed. He follows a man who is terrorizing a woman and her children and rescues the children. Joseph sees the newspaper report and asks his father about it. David acknowledges what he has done.

When David shakes Elijah's hand, he realizes that Elijah is his exact opposite and has been involved in many accidents and disasters. Elijah spent his life trying to find a true hero, his opposite and complement to his brokenness, as a way to understand his own existence and destiny.

COMMENTARY

Such was the faith of Hollywood producers in the talents of writer-director M. Night Shyamalan after his unexpected success with *The Sixth Sense*, that they immediately began production on this psychological thriller. *Signs*, Shyamalan's newest contribution to the genre, was released in 2002.

Bruce Willis plays David Dunn, an ordinary citizen who is a chosen one. In the words of Scripture, "not a bone of his body is broken."

Samuel L. Jackson plays Elijah with great dignity, and every word is delivered with solemnity. Elijah is an expert on comics and comic heroes who believes that some comics are the repositories of popular wisdom concerning the struggle between good and evil.

While Shyamalan's filming style is "realistic," the plot can strain the audience's belief unless it accepts the basic notion that Bruce Willis is playing a superhuman, comic-strip hero, made recently aware of his powers. The audience must also suspend their belief in order to sympathize with Elijah, the evil-doing, broken man. He is a dark prophet who understands David and pursues the hero to persuade him to embrace and fulfill his powerful destiny—to be all that Elijah is not.

DIALOGUE WITH THE GOSPEL

Focus: Like Adam and Eve in the garden, we are tempted to say "yes" to evil. Mary said "yes" to God's goodness even though all was not clear. In Unbreakable, *David has to acknowledge his gift and say "yes" to goodness. Elijah instead chooses darkness. From time immemorial people have been faced with the struggle between good and evil.*

On this feast of Mary, the Immaculate Conception, we celebrate Mary as one who said yes. The Old Testament prophets, especially Jeremiah, were also graced to be open to receive the Word of God, and Mary is like these prophets. Her acceptance of her vocation brings forth divine goodness and salvation for the world.

In the film, David, too, is specially chosen. He is protected from harm so that he may eventually learn his true vocation in life. His call is to say "yes" to a gift that sends him out to protect and save those who suffer.

The Genesis reading reminds us of the sinful world we live in. The reading from Ephesians reminds us of God's loving plan for all people. We are part of a world where sin and evil co-exist with good. In *Unbreakable*, Elijah Price is an enigmatic figure. At first, he seems to be an angel of light. Gradually, and then with a final shock, we discover that Elijah is evil, a tempting and destructive devil incarnate, who manipulates David for his own satisfaction.

Though David struggles with his own personal weaknesses and estrangement from his wife, ultimately he chooses to do the right thing. He acknowledges that he has survived to help those in need. He says "yes" to goodness and helps life and redemption to enter the world.

Mary, by saying yes to God, is the archetype of those who say "yes" to their vocation.

- David's seemingly miraculous survival in the train wreck; his memories of the car crash; his bewilderment about being "unbreakable."

KEY SCENES AND THEMES

- Elijah's birth and his brittle bones; the adult Elijah, how he tracks David down; his explanations of comics and the perpetuation of myths; the final revelation of his destruction, his theory of opposites and David's reaction.

- David and his knowledge of those in need, his saving of the children; his sense of mission.

FOR REFLECTION AND CONVERSATION

1. *Unbreakable* draws the audience's attention to comics and the visual tradition of age-old myths. We can dialogue with the film to appreciate more deeply how God gives special graces to people who are able to put their lives on the line to rescue, protect, and serve others. Though they are heroes, they sometimes do not survive, succumbing to the very evil that threatens, whether the disasters are natural or man-made. What gives people the courage to choose heroism at the very moment they are needed? What makes a hero? Does everyone have the "gift" to be a hero? How does a person prepare to be a hero?

2. The family dynamic in *Unbreakable* seems very common. Communication breaks down between spouses, and the children suffer. How is this subplot a subtext to the film? What does the family's realization of David's indestructibility say about marriage and family? Talk about whether or not David's supernatural protection from physical brokenness might or might not protect his family as well. What good would David's gift be if he could not apply it to his personal brokenness and that of his family? What gifts does his wife bring to the story?

3. All M. Night Shyamalan's major films (*Wide Awake, The Sixth Sense, Unbreakable,* and *Signs*) reflect themes that are obviously important to him: children, parents,

family, and the influence of the supernatural. He uses colors and symbols to create atmosphere and convey meaning. These films take place in everyday life, but some characters move in and out of supernatural realms while others remain in the natural sphere, and everyone is trying to figure out life's bigger—and smaller—questions. How are the plot lines of these films alike or different? If Shyamalan has a message or purpose to his films, what is it? How does he use light and dark and other symbols to illustrate his "mythic" characters?

Prayer

Mary, you said yes to what God asked of you, and you brought salvation to the world. Help us to say "yes" to whatever God asks of us. Amen.

THE HOLY INNOCENTS
1 John 1:5–2:2; Matthew 2:13–18

Savior

U.S.A., 1998, 104 minutes
Cast: Dennis Quaid, Nastassja Kinski,
Stellan Skarsgard, Natasa Kinkovic
Writer: Robert Roe
Director: Predrag Antonijevic

Savior

Innocent Victims

SYNOPSIS

Joshua Rose, an American military officer and member of a bomb disposal unit, is on active duty in Yugoslavia during the 1980s. While he is on leave to visit his family in Paris, his wife and son die in an explosion almost certainly meant to kill him. Joshua vents his anger by taking a gun, going into a nearby mosque, and opening fire. With his friend and co-worker, Peter, he flees the country, changes his identity, and joins the French Foreign Legion. His new name is Guy.

In the early 1990s, Guy and Peter have returned to Yugoslavia to fight as mercenaries with the Serbian forces in Bosnia. Guy has become a skilled sniper without a soul. His partner is a local man, Goran, who is also a psychopathic killer. They receive orders to accompany Vera, a pregnant woman raped by opposition soldiers, back to her village. Angry at her for having been with a Muslim, Goran kicks her violently to cause her to miscarry. Guy kills Goran and then helps deliver Vera's baby—a girl. At first, Vera refuses to accept or to nurse the infant, but the baby's innocence and helplessness call to her. Guy takes Vera back to her family.

When they arrive at her home, Vera's Orthodox Christian father rejects her because of the baby's Muslim father.

When Goran's body is found, the local chief commands Vera's father to avenge Goran's death. He pursues Guy and wounds him. Guy, Vera, and the child flee the village.

Vera decides to try to return home once more, but she finds the village destroyed and her family imprisoned. Guy now wants to save Vera and her child. He manages to get a car to drive to safety in Split. When they run out of gas, Vera goes to look for a bus to continue their journey, but Croatians capture Vera and the other passengers before the bus reaches Guy. Because she is gone so long, Guy hides the child and goes in search of her—just in time to witness her brutal murder. Vera knows Guy is watching and signals to him to stay hidden so that he can live to protect her daughter. He retrieves the child and travels to Split. He decides to leave the baby in an ambulance, but a woman sees him. She persuades Guy to keep the baby.

COMMENTARY

By the late 1990s, several movies about the Balkan Wars were produced, especially in Serbia, such as *Underground* and *Pretty Village, Pretty Flame.* British director Michael Winterbottom's *Welcome to Sarajevo* and Greek director Theo Angelopoulos' *Ulysses' Gaze* were both made in 1997. *Savior* is an American production filmed in Montenegro. Like *Welcome to Sarajevo, Savior* was made principally for Western audiences. Despite an excellent performance by Dennis Quaid, the film failed to find wide release in the United States.

All of the movies mentioned above display an intensity of emotion that audiences, familiar with the atrocities of the war only through headlines and television news reports, found disturbing. Critics argued whether or not there was a pro-Serbian, pro-Bosnian, or pro-Croatian bias in the movies. Although *Savior*'s director, Pedrag Antonijevic, is a Serb, he does not hesitate to show the savage side of Serbia in the character of Goran. *Savior* is particularly hard-hitting in the opening sequences and at the end of the movie when several

Serbs, including Vera, are bludgeoned to death. In this film, only the women and children are innocent.

DIALOGUE WITH THE GOSPEL

Focus: Herod wants to destroy Jesus and so wreaks havoc on mothers and children in Bethlehem and its environs. The massacre of the innocent victims of war continues the image of this cruelty. The movie Savior *tells this story for our time using the Balkan wars of the 1990s as the context.*

The first letter of John speaks of innocence and goodness, of walking in light and truth and not in the darkness of sin and lies. In *Savior*, Vera's child is the symbol of this light and truth as well as of innocent hope for the future. Joshua/Guy, embittered by the savage murder of his family, dwells in darkness. He is finally redeemed when he decides to defend and rescue Vera and her child. Guy saves the child and, in another sense, the child saves Guy, who can now walk in the light.

Today's liturgy offers one of the most violent and vivid of Gospel stories. Jesus is the victim child who survives because of the Angel's warning to Joseph in a dream to flee with Mary and Jesus into Egypt. The title of today's feast, Holy Innocents, reminds us that for every child saved from perilous situations, there are many more who are killed or who die through war, abortion, abuse, or neglect. The grief of mothers whose children are violently taken from them is underscored when the Gospel quotes the prophet Jeremiah: "A voice was heard in Ramah, sobbing and loud lamentation; Rachel weeping for her children, and she would not be consoled, since they are no more."

Vera epitomizes mothers who are victims. She is raped, brutally kicked to bring on a miscarriage, suffers a difficult delivery on a roadside, and then, rejected by her family, must flee with her child to escape her enemies—echoing the flight into Egypt. Through body language, Vera silently communicates to Guy that she is prepared to die as long as her child lives.

Guy, like Joseph, took the child and mother on a journey toward safe haven. Even though he could not save the mother, he saves the child and the child saves him.

- The restaurant explosion and Guy's grief; the intensity of his attack on the mosque and shooting people; the effect on his life; his life as a mercenary sniper in Bosnia; the shooting of the boy with the goat.

- Goran and his brutality, kicking Vera, and Guy shooting him to protect her; the birth of her child, Vera rejected by her father, loved by her mother; saved by her brother and Guy; their flight to safety in a boat and car.

- The kind family who had lost their children in the war; the suddenness of Vera's capture; the bludgeoning of the captives; Guy almost suffocating the baby to protect her; his decision to abandon the child, and being saved by taking the child with him.

1. As modern communication technologies converge, so do their messages. And as often as we expect to be entertained by a film, we are constantly being informed. A war movie such as *Savior* gives us glimpses of violence, revenge, cruelty, ethnic bias, ethnic cleansing, and hate within an historic moment. At the same time, we see examples of simple kindness, loving humanity, the innocence of children, and the possibility for change and redemption. Why is it, then, that a story communicating a saving message with technical proficiency does not find an audience? What makes us avoid the reality of war, even in a fictional portrayal

in popular film? What kind of stories do we expect from the movies we choose to watch and why? What is the purpose of the cinema for people who share a belief in our common humanity?

2. From the beginning of the film, the crucifix becomes the visual symbol that silently ties the movie together. How effective is the use of this Christian icon in *Savior?* Talk about some other mainstream films that use the cross or crucifix to create meaning in the film (e.g., *Daylight, Saving Private Ryan),* and why Hollywood uses it and other religious symbols to help tell their stories.

3. We live in times that challenge and threaten humanity on all levels. Population control, threats to life in the womb, unjust living conditions and wages, domestic violence, lack of health care for the poor, the death penalty, ethnic cleansing, euthanasia, and waste of the environment are but a few. After the World Trade Center tragedy on September 11, 2001, a *Time* magazine editorial (December 1, 2001) suggested that both the West and the East need to engage in an examination of conscience so that all nations and people can make the changes needed for a better world. On this feast we commemorate the innocent victims who were slaughtered by the selfish and proud King Herod for his own benefit. Considering the feast and the story told by this film, what is the message for believers in a post-September 11 world? Where do we start to make a difference, to protect the innocent everywhere, both personally and as a community?

Prayer

Today, Lord, in the midst of our celebration of your birth, we remember the innocent children who are victims of the violence of our warring world. Give them your loving protection. Amen.

The Joy Luck Club
U.S.A., 1993, 139 minutes
Cast: Kieu Chinh, Tsai Chin, France Nuyen, Lisa Lu,
Ming-Na Wen, Tamlyn Tomita, Lauren Tom,
Rosalind Chao
Writers: Ronald Bass, Amy Tan
Director: Wayne Wang

The Joy Luck Club

Generations of Mothers

SYNOPSIS

June is preparing to visit China to meet her twin half-sisters for the first time. Suyuan, her recently deceased mother, had abandoned them along a roadside when fleeing the Japanese during World War II. In the United States, June's three aunts and mother had formed the Joy Luck MahJong Club and, over the years, their families met together to talk and share a meal. Now, the aunts bring their families to June's bon voyage dinner, during which each of the mothers and daughters remembers their past.

Aunty Lindo, betrothed at age five, is forced to leave her mother at fifteen for a loveless, unconsummated marriage. She shrewdly works out a plan to escape her unbearable situation.

Aunty Ying Ying, an impressionable young society girl, marries a charming philanderer. She becomes overwhelmed, outraged, and severely depressed over his callous behavior. One day, as she bathes her son, she drowns him in a desperate form of revenge.

Aunty An Mei's mother Sje is expelled from the family home after she is blamed for her husband's death. Sje then marries a wealthy man. Years later, she returns for her daughter, An Mei, but then finally confides that she had been raped and kills herself, leaving An Mei an orphan.

The daughters also remember their own difficult, but more mundane, pasts. Lindo's daughter, Waverley, was a child prodigy in chess who is now in a disastrous marriage. She always lacks confidence in the presence of her sharp-tongued mother.

Ying Ying's daughter, Lena, is married to an opinionated and self-absorbed architect. Ying Ying sees how Lena's marriage is destroying her and, in order to help liberate Lena, takes a stand.

An Mei's daughter Rose marries a wealthy man, but alienates him with her constant submissiveness. They have a child and are separated for a time, but are later reconciled.

June learns the truth about her own mother's self-sacrifice. As Suyuan fled China she became very ill. She was convinced that her twin daughters stood a better chance of survival without her and her "bad luck." In abandoning them, Suyuan had really been trying to provide for the twins in the best way she knew. June finally arrives in China and meets her sisters.

COMMENTARY

The Joy Luck Club was a bestseller for novelist Amy Tan. She collaborated with screenwriter Ronald Bass *(Rain Man, Snow Falling on Cedars)* on the adaptation of her book for the screen. The film is a tapestry of the stories of four Chinese women and, by extension, twelve others. It shows how the women came to the United States and built their lives and friendships through the Joy Luck Club. The harshness of their childhood and young adulthood influences the way they bring up their own daughters with unattainable expectations. Through flashbacks to childhood experiences, each mother recalls her earlier life, and each daughter reflects on her relationship with her mother. The final emotional drama of the movie centers on how the mothers learn to allow their daughters to be themselves.

The actors portraying the mothers render deeply felt performances, evoking sympathy for what these women experienced in the past and their frustration with the present. This film is notable for casting the most talented Asian and Asian-American actors working in the United States in the 1990s.

Direction is by Wayne Wang, who made such idiosyncratic Chinese-American movies as *Dim Sum* and *Eat a Bowl of Tea*. He later moved on to make more mainstream movies, including *Chinese Box* and *Anywhere But Here*.

DIALOGUE WITH THE GOSPEL

Focus: The Gospel gives us a picture of Mary, the mother who pondered great mysteries in her heart. The first and second readings speak of blessing and what it means to be filled with the Spirit. These are the themes of The Joy Luck Club *as well.*

Mary came from a culture that is not always familiar to Western or non-Jewish people. She was brought up according to Jewish traditions and lived as a Jewish woman. Mary's betrothal, Jesus' circumcision, the presentation in the Temple, and her "purification" were all part of that heritage. However, like the mothers in the film, Mary had to "move beyond" the religious culture she had inherited in some ways. She became pregnant while still a virgin and risked shame for accepting her role as the mother of the Savior. She had to flee to a foreign land to protect her child. When the four Chinese mothers in the film immigrated to the United States, they began new cultural traditions for their very American daughters. Mary, as mother of the Church, embraces children from all cultures, without distinction.

There is talk of "spirit" in the movie. Some of the mothers regret the "lack of spirit" in their daughters. Eventually they realize they must set their daughters free from their impossible expectations so they can discover "new spirit." There are echoes of these themes in the reading from Paul to the Galatians which reflects on the Spirit sent into the hearts of believers.

The reading from Numbers focuses on blessings that can overcome the weakness and sin experienced in life. In China, the four mothers experienced social sin as "bad luck" and curses. However, as these mothers begin a new life, start new families, and grow in their love for their daughters, these are transformed into blessings.

- The experiences of the mothers as girls and young adults; the Chinese traditions, family, arranged marriages, wives and concubines, illness, and having to abandon babies; the poignancy and sorrow of these memories.

- The experience of the daughters; growing up as Americans, their Chinese heritage, their mothers' expectations and their rebellion or being "crushed in spirit"; their own marriages and children.

- The aunties discovering the twins in China, June's impending visit; her father revealing the truth about her mother's illness and having to leave the children behind, but providing for them; the three sisters united.

KEY SCENES AND THEMES

1. The alternative opening prayer for today's Eucharist asks that "the gift of a mother's love be your people's joy through all ages" through Mary. Through the traumatic experiences lived by the women in *The Joy Luck Club*, exactly how does a mother's love sustain all the relationships established by the generations of mothers? How do family bonds of love transcend culture

FOR REFLECTION AND CONVERSATION

and religion? What is it that keeps these bonds alive or stifles them?

2. Today is also the World Day of Peace. There seems to be very little peace in *The Joy Luck Club*, though peace and joy, "luck," and blessings appear to be the goals that all the women seek. How is the film an exploration of family dynamics? In what ways does it help Westerners understand the social, cultural, political mores and world events that can impact the choices that individuals and families make? In what ways can family peace influence world peace? What kind of Christian dynamic would be involved?

3. Several films have already been featured in this year's movie lectionary that deal with mothers and the choices they make: *Angela's Ashes, Agnes of God, Savior,* and *The Seventh Sign.* What additional themes do these movies have in common? Does the genre make any difference to the messages conveyed? What would you have done if you had been in the same situation as any of the women in these films, especially the four main characters of *The Joy Luck Club:* An Mei, Suyuan, Ying Ying, and Lindo?

Prayer

Mary, our Mother, you gave us your Son as a blessing for the world. On this day when we celebrate motherhood, bless all mothers with peace, especially those who experience pain, weakness, and despair. Amen.

Mumford

U.S.A., 1999, 107 minutes
Cast: Loren Dean, Jason Lee, Alfre Woodard, Hope Davis,
Mary McDonnell, Martin Short, David Paymer,
Jane Adams, Ted Danson, Pruitt Taylor Vince,
Robert Stack, Dana Ivey, Kevin Tighe
Writer: Lawrence Kasdan
Director: Lawrence Kasdan

Mumford

All Things to All People

Mumford, a young man who claims to be a psychologist, has recently arrived in a town with the same name, Mumford. He has a growing and appreciative clientele, although he clashes and refuses to work with the town lawyer, Lionel. He is particularly friendly with Lily, his landlady, who runs a cafe in town.

His clients include a pharmacist with a poor self-image who is addicted to sex-fantasies; Althea, a housewife with a shopping compulsion; and Nessa, who is locked into a magazine fantasy world. Mr. Crisp asks Mumford to take his daughter Sophie on as a patient. She suffers from chronic fatigue syndrome. Skip Skipperton, a young skateboarding computer whiz, asks Mumford to be his friend rather than therapist, to help him overcome his loneliness.

Mumford is an excellent listener. He expresses himself through empathetic questions, as well as direct and challenging advice. Because he is not a real doctor, Mumford searches the Internet for sound advice when he is unsure of what to say. His work with Sophie gives her the strength to venture outside her home and walk with Mumford. She is gradually able to acknowledge how tyrannical her mother is. Mumford

SYNOPSIS

realizes he is falling in love with her. When Skip wants to confide a personal secret, Mumford takes the opportunity to confess his own story. He discloses that in his college days, he lived a promiscuous life and used drugs, then worked for the IRS and became addicted to cocaine. With the help of some monks, he was rehabilitated and began to exercise his special gift for listening to others, even though he had no training.

Mumford is now the town's favorite therapist. Even the other therapists in town come to him. While he helps one to break off an affair, another reports him to the authorities.

Government officials investigate Mumford, and his story is suddenly broadcast on Robert Stack's *Unsolved Mysteries*. On the advice of Lily and Skip, and with the support of Sophie who loves him, he tells the truth. Lionel defends him. Mumford is given a light prison sentence, and the police officer driving him to prison asks if he can run his problems by Mumford.

COMMENTARY

Mumford received very limited theatrical release and went straight to video in some areas—a pity, since it is one of the best examples of what attentive listening can do for troubled people.

The movie was written and directed by Lawrence Kasdan, best known for the movies *Body Heat, The Big Chill, The Accidental Tourist,* and *Grand Canyon.* Compared to Kasdan's previous films, *Mumford* is a small-scale movie. It focuses on the character of a single person, Mumford—played convincingly and with charm by Loren Dean *(Billy Bathgate, Space Cowboys)*. The first forty minutes are practically all therapy sequences where a cast best known for character acting portrays the clients. The second half of the movie moves more quickly toward the resolution of all the problems. More detail and expansion of the plot concerning Mumford's trial would have enhanced the movie.

Kasdan pokes some fun at the hang-ups of professional helpers as they get tangled in their own problems. His sympathy lies with those who have suffered, though he takes a fairly light touch to most of the problems experienced by Mumford's clients. Kasdan's main point is that those who really listen to what people actually say or don't say are the true healers empowering others to embrace their lives.

Focus: Paul's conversion is an experience of the risen Lord that enables him to change his life, become a follower of Christ, and proclaim the Good News to others. In his own eccentric way, Mumford experiences a conversion, and through listening and good words, helps other people.

DIALOGUE WITH THE GOSPEL

Paul's conversion is always considered rather "spectacular" and is described twice in the Acts of the Apostles. The road to Damascus has become the image of how God's intervention in people's lives can cause them to change dramatically. Mumford's conversion was less dramatic than Paul's, but a conversion nonetheless. He realized he was wasting his life, using people, and escaping through drugs. A major part of his own spiritual and psychological healing was the acknowledgment of his own God-given talents, which set him on the path of a new life at the service of others.

Conversion is not merely the initial change of heart, but more importantly, what follows. After his conversion Paul spent almost thirty years of his life proclaiming the Good News of salvation, listening, healing, challenging, and becoming all things to all people. However, conversion from sin is an ongoing process. Though we may lapse, as did Mumford, we can begin anew through the grace of Christ.

Paul reached out to devout and sometimes dysfunctional communities like Corinth, a city that could have used a few psychologists. Mumford also meets a range of clients in the town that bears his name. His converted, healthy self is available to them. He challenges others only when he senses it is the right thing to do.

The end of Mark's Gospel shows how the experience of the risen Lord "converted" and strengthened the Apostles so they could work wonders. Mumford had some experience of the risen Lord through the monks who took him in and gave him a second chance. Though brought low again, Mumford accepts responsibility for his recent wrong actions, and enters into his next conversion experience.

KEY SCENES AND THEMES

- The range of Mumford's clients and their problems, some petty, some disgusting, some profoundly disturbing; his capacity to listen, to empathize, to say the right word, to ask the right question; he is all things to all clients.

- Issues of confidentiality; Skip telling Mumford his secret and Mumford affirming Skip by confessing his own story—of degradation and deceit, of rehabilitation and conversion, a story about using gifts for others.

- Mumford empowering his clients to take responsibility for their lives, to see through their problems, and to find strength to change their lives; the reaction of his clients and his friends who support his new, converted life after it is discovered he really is not a psychologist.

FOR REFLECTION AND CONVERSATION

1. Is Mumford a person, a place, or a collection of anonymous people who don't even know who they are? Perhaps it is all the above. Today's feast is about change of heart and change of life. How do the characters in the town of Mumford change? How does the pseudo-psychologist Mumford continue to change? What is

the catalyst for the transformations that take place because of Mumford's practice in Mumford? After watching this film, why can Christians say that conversion is not a one-time event, but something we are called to renew every day?

2. Ananias was a disciple who lived in Damascus and was sent to help Saul recover his sight. How do the other two psychologists in town become the means for Mumford, who has fallen into deceiving others, to regain his sight once again? What other ethical issues about helping professions are explored in the film? Does *Mumford* have an explicit message for anyone? If so, what is the filmmaker trying to say? How much does the interpretation of the film depend on the audience's experience? Is Mumford all things to all people? Why or why not?

3. *Mumford* does not seem to have so much a story line as an ensemble cast of fine actors who really inhabit their characters. Though some of the characters are eccentric, there is a wide variety of burdens and worries for viewers to identify with. Which character speaks most to your own experience? Recall someone who took the time to listen to you and encourage you so that you could change and grow as a Christian. In the same way, can you speak to those with problems or difficulties, to encourage them on their journey?

Prayer

Paul, you show us how, no matter what our lives have been like, it is possible to be touched by God, to be invited to say yes to conversion, and to be an instrument of grace for others. We ask this grace through your intercession. Amen.

Chazz Palminteri and Lillo Brancato in *A Bronx Tale*.

St. Joseph, Husband of Mary

2 Samuel 7:4–5, 12–14, 16; Romans 4:13, 16–18, 22; Luke 2:41–51

A Bronx Tale

U.S.A., 1993, 121 minutes
Cast: Robert De Niro, Chazz Palminteri, Lillo Brancato, Joe Pesci
Writer: Chazz Palminteri
Director: Robert De Niro

A Bronx Tale

Searching for a Father

On the streets of the Italian, 1960 Mount Carmel neighborhood in the Bronx, Sonny, the local Mafia boss, kills a man. Nine-year-old Calogero Anello witnesses the murder, but tells the police that he didn't see anything. Calogero, nicknamed "C," lives with his quiet father Lorenzo, a bus driver, and his mother Rosina, in a walk-up tenement. Sonny appreciates C's loyalty and offers his father a job with a generous salary that he refuses. Lorenzo also makes C return money he made serving drinks for Sonny.

By 1968, C seems to be more under Sonny's influence than that of his father, though both offer words of wisdom to guide the young man. The area around the neighborhood is changing. African-American families move in, and Hells Angels and hippies appear. C and his friends pass the time beating up African-American kids who ride through the neighborhood on their bikes. Sonny wants to protect C from life on the street and he continually offers him advice. Lorenzo quietly resents this influence and refuses the ringside seat at a boxing match that C and Sonny offer him.

SYNOPSIS

One day C is riding his father's bus. He sees a young African-American girl named Jane, and is attracted to her. He learns that they go to the same school, and they become close. C asks his father and Sonny for advice about his relationship with Jane by presenting a hypothetical scenario. On another occasion, Lorenzo had already said that he thinks different races should stay among themselves. But this time, while neither Sonny nor Lorenzo is enthusiastic, they each tell him in their own way that he has to do what he thinks is right.

C gets caught up in violent racial activities with his peers, which pit him against Jane's family. He is almost killed, but Sonny pulls him from a car just in time to save his life. C goes to thank Sonny just in time to see him gunned down. Lorenzo and C go the funeral parlor to pay their respects, and Sonny's successor introduces himself.

COMMENTARY

A Bronx Tale is based on a successful one-man autobiographical play written by Chazz Palminteri. The film also marks the directorial debut of Robert De Niro. Both are cast in the film, De Niro as Lorenzo, Calogero's father, and Palminteri as the Mafia boss, Sonny. It is an affectionate and realistic look at the East 187th Street, Mount Carmel, Arthur Avenue-Fordham section of the Bronx in the 1960s, a "neighborhood" populated by first and second generation Italians. The Mafia and their violent activities exist side by side with families that try to raise their children to be law-abiding citizens.

A Bronx Tale is very convincing and well acted, especially by De Niro and Palminteri. Lillo Brancato is a non-professional, first time actor in the role of Calogero, and he makes an impressive debut. Joe Pesci appears in a cameo at the end of the movie. *A Bronx Tale* shows the Mafia as a rather benign presence in the midst of changing times. It is a reaffirmation of more traditional values, rather than those of "easy" success, Mafia style.

Focus: Joseph is a loving father who searched Jerusalem to find Jesus. In A Bronx Tale, *Calogero has both a father and a father-figure. Both men want the best for Calogero who longs for a father's love.*

Today's readings emphasize a tradition that highlights the significant role and status of a father. In the tradition of the Hebrew Scriptures, fathers achieve immortality through their children. In the first reading, God promises David that he, the Lord, will be a father to his son after David's death. Paul reflects that God fulfilled his promises to Abraham and made him the father of many nations because of Abraham's fidelity.

Joseph can be considered within this enduring tradition. As foster-father of Jesus, his duty was to instruct him and ensure that his son was on the right path toward his God-given destiny. When we come to Joseph in Luke's Gospel, he is the protector and the quiet father-figure. The story of the finding in the Temple has a deep religious significance, because it points to Jesus' special call and mission from God. It also has a human dimension; through Mary and Joseph we can experience the distress of parents who love their children, worry about them, teach them, and then have to let them go.

The role of a father is a key theme of *A Bronx Tale*. Young Calogero is influenced by two father-figures. Lorenzo, whose life lacks excitement and glamour, is usually ignored by his son. Lorenzo has some values, but he is also limited, for example, by his racial bias. From the outset, it is clear that Sonny is a gangster and a murderer. His human values are questionable, yet he protects Calogero, cares for him, gives him advice, and saves him from death. Sonny is an ambiguous father-figure. Both men love Calogero and want the best for him, but both have dark and light sides to their characters.

Today's feast of St. Joseph, Husband of Mary, and today's Gospel reading invite us to reflect on the role of a father, especially in the complex situations of contemporary families.

KEY SCENES AND THEMES

- The streets of the Bronx; the song on the streets, streets in the life of the Italians, of the African-Americans, the bars, school, apartments.

- Calogero's voice-over narration, his perspective as a boy on his life, his father, Sonny, and the Mafia types; Calogero as a teenager, the gang mentality, peer pressure, tough stances, watching Sonny and the men at the street corner, in the bars, the way they dress and talk; Calogero moving away from his father and toward Sonny.

- Riding on the bus with his father, his father's advice about honesty; the boxing match and Lorenzo refusing Sonny's seats despite the pressing invitation; Lorenzo's prejudice; Lorenzo's visit to the funeral parlor, paying his respects to Sonny, appreciating what he had done for Calogero; Calogero having to learn the hard way how to trust his experience and people, apologizing for hurting his father.

FOR REFLECTION AND CONVERSATION

1. This poignant story is full of fatherly wisdom. Lorenzo is actually talking about himself, and could be talking about St. Joseph, when he tells Calogero, "You want to see a real hero? Look at a guy who gets up in the morning and goes off to work and supports his family. That's heroism." Is there anything truly heroic

about the ordinary, humdrum dimensions of life? Why or why not? From what we know from the Scriptures, and what we might imagine, what is the significance of the "ordinary" in St. Joseph's role as Jesus' foster father?

2. Life in the Bronx neighborhood was insulated, as was life in the bus or in the Mafia. It was difficult for the characters in the film to see beyond the roles that seemed to have been chosen for them. The sweeping events of the 1960s changed all that, and as Calogero's father and father-figure tell him, he will have to choose to do what he thinks is right, or to live with the consequences of doing what he thinks others expect of him. What can fathers and sons learn from a film like *A Bronx Tale?*

3. Compare *A Bronx Tale* with *Billy Elliot, Rain Man, The Truman Show, Moonstruck, Dead Poets Society, Finding Forrester,* or other films and stories about fathers and father-figures. How are the characters alike or different? What commentary do these films and characters make about the relationship between fathers and sons? What is your relationship with your father like? Is it ever too late to strengthen or rebuild it?

Prayer

Jesus, you knew and loved Joseph as your father. Give your guidance to those who struggle with their role as parents. Help them to be worthy of their children's love. Amen.

Sommersby

U.S.A., 1993, 113 minutes
Cast: Richard Gere, Jodie Foster, Bill Pullman,
James Earl Jones
Writers: Nicholas Meyer, Sarah Kernochan
Director: Jon Amiel

Sommersby

Heritage of Hope

SYNOPSIS

As the Civil War comes to an end, the troops return home. It takes Jack Sommersby two years to arrive back at Vine Hill to rejoin his wife, Laurel, and their son. Because Sommersby was not a local man and went off to war early in his marriage, the people in the town are not certain that this man really *is* Jack Sommersby. Even Laurel is not sure: he looks like Jack, but he is kinder. She suppresses her own doubts and accepts him as her husband. Eventually, most of the townspeople accept Jack as well, with the exception of Orin who helped Laurel maintain the estate during the war. Laurel is soon pregnant again.

Jack is not only a loving husband, but also a hard worker. He energizes the demoralized citizens by convincing them to plant tobacco instead of cotton, to rebuild the town, and to rediscover a sense of civic pride. Before the war, Sommersby was a slave owner; now he lets a Negro sharecropper buy a parcel of his land.

Some time later, Sommersby is arrested for the murder of a gambler during the war. This presents a dilemma for Jack and Laurel. If he really is Sommersby, then he has to go to trial and will be executed for his crime. If he acknowledges that he is not Sommersby, then he proclaims himself a fraud, makes his new child a bastard, humiliates Laurel and her son, and loses all claim to the land. The townspeople, who had put such faith in him, would also be disillusioned. We learn that the man's real name is Horace Townsend and that he spent time in jail with the real Sommersby, who actually did kill the gambler. Except for assuming Sommersby's identity and living with Laurel, Townsend is innocent. But rather than admit to fraud and accept all its consequences, Townsend allows himself to be convicted and executed for a crime he did not commit. Laurel visits his grave as the people continue to rebuild the town and place a steeple on their church.

COMMENTARY

Sommersby is an adaptation of the 1982 French film, *The Return of Martin Guerre,* written and directed by Daniel Vigne. Screenwriter Nicholas Meyer *(Star Trek, Fatal Attraction, The Seven-Per-Cent Solution, Time After Time)* has transferred Vigne's plot to the period immediately following the American Civil War. Director Jon Amiel directed the celebrated television version of Denis Potter's *The Singing Detective,* and his movies include *Queen of Hearts, Tune in Tomorrow, Copycat,* and *Entrapment.*

The film recreates the atmosphere of post-Civil War Virginia and shows the impact of the soldiers' return home, the uncertainties about the future, racial tensions, the reality of the Ku Klux Klan, and the rebuilding of farms and towns.

Richard Gere is sympathetic as Jack Sommersby, as is Jodie Foster as Laurel. The cinematography is beautiful and the Virginia locations are attractive. The interiors are filmed in sepia shades to suggest old period photographs. *Sommersby* is an emotionally satisfying romantic drama.

**DIALOGUE WITH
THE GOSPEL**

Focus: The Ascension is the final event of Jesus' life on earth. The story of Jack Sommersby, who made it possible for the towns-people to build a new and fuller life after his death, evokes an Ascension-like image.

The final verses of Mark's Gospel have been chosen for this feast. The theme of this reading is the meaning of Jesus' life and how he proclaimed the good news of forgiveness and redemption. At his Ascension, Jesus leaves a heritage of hope for his disciples and future followers, promising salvation to those who believe. He asks them to continue his mission. The disciples know that Jesus will stay with them because he promises to accompany their preaching with signs and wonders.

Jack Sommersby comes mysteriously into the town and changes the life of a poor and war-weary community. He shows the people a new way of life and encourages them to take pride in rebuilding their community. Though certainly flawed, Horace Townsend/Jack Sommersby resembles the Jesus of the Gospels in the "new life" he brings to the people.

As Jesus came into our world and was not immediately recognized, so Horace Townsend comes among the people, intending to find a new opportunity for his life. Although not the person he says he is, he becomes the "savior" of the town, empowering Laurel and the people to start a new and hopeful life. Just as Jesus had to pay a price and endure people's hostility, Horace/Jack has to pay a price. But unlike Jesus, it is a price of his own making. By impersonating Sommersby, he takes on the burden of the real man's sinfulness. He dies as Jack so that people's hopes and aspirations would not be dashed. In this self-offering, he is a limited but real Christ-figure.

Significant for our reflection today is the small hint of Jesus' living on in his disciples that can be imagined in Sommersby's legacy to the people: he is not forgotten.

- Jack Sommersby's long trek home and arrival, his knowing all the details about the people, their welcome and greeting, the six years' absence; Horace Townsend taking on Jack Sommersby's character, persona, and credibility; his genial character.

- Jack's plan for the town, his hard work, the crops, his treatment of the African-Americans and allowing them to own the land; the people trusting him with money for the tobacco seeds; planting the seeds, the hard work, watching the crop grow, the fruitful harvest.

- The trial, his chance to save himself; accepting Sommersby's guilt, the farewell; Laurel at his execution, his love for her and the people of the community; the rebuilding of the town, the steeple, and Laurel walking to Sommersby's grave.

KEY SCENES AND THEMES

1. Lloyd Baugh's 1997 book, *Imaging the Divine: Jesus and Christ-figures in Film* (Sheed & Ward), distinguishes between film characters that suggest the person or story of Christ through metaphor or analogy to greater or lesser degrees (Christ-figures), and films that deal explicitly with the person of Jesus, (Jesus-figures), for example, *King of Kings,* or Pasolini's masterpiece, *The Gospel According to St. Matthew.* To what extent does Jack Sommersby work as a Christ-figure for you? Why?

2. Former Confederate Army soldiers began the Ku Klux Klan in Pulaski, Tennessee during the winter of 1865–1866. At first it was a kind of social organization, but by 1867 it was directing its activities against Reconstruction in the South. By 1868, some of its founding documents already revealed the Klan as a secret, rac-

FOR REflECTION AND CONVERSATION

ist society, opposed to Negro equality with the white man, and in favor of the white man's governance of the United States. What role does the Ku Klux Klan play in the film? How is it important to the story, to our understanding of this period in American history and of the KKK's presence in our culture today?

3. In broad strokes, this tale of Jack Sommersby/Horace Townsend can be paralleled to aspects of Jesus' life and to the way his memory endures in the hearts of those who believed in him. However, the story is wrought with problems. Despite the good that comes from his actions, Horace is an imposter. Do the ends ever justify the means? Is there a kind of poetic justice in Sommersby being executed? Why or why not?

Prayer

On this feast of your Ascension, Lord Jesus, we celebrate the completion of your earthly life through your gift of self in your passion, death, and resurrection. We rejoice that you are one with the Father and the Spirit. Amen.

Hosea 11:1, 3–4, 8–9; Ephesians 3:8–12,
14–19; John 19:31–37

The Omega Man

U.S.A., 1971, 94 minutes
Cast: Charlton Heston, Anthony Zerbe, Rosalind Cash,
Paul Koslo
Writers: John William Corrington, Joyce Hooper Corrington
Director: Boris Sagal

The Omega Man

Life Blood

SYNOPSIS

Dr. Robert Neville drives through the empty streets of Los Angeles. He seems to be the last man on earth. Neville discovers a mysterious woman named Lisa in a bombed out store. They leave together.

As night falls a group of albino creatures that call themselves the Family prowls the city. They attack Neville and Lisa on their way to his apartment. Flashbacks reveal that Neville was a scientist working on vaccines against the germ warfare that has annihilated the population of the United States. He sees his role now as the exterminator of the Family and chronicler of the devastation.

After Lisa and Neville escape, she asks Neville to cure her son, Richie, who has been affected by the Family and has almost become one of them. She also leads Neville to a young man, Dutch, who lives with a small group of healthy children in the countryside.

Neville takes Richie back to the city and gradually heals him. While Lisa is out "shopping," she is captured by the Family's leader, Matthias. Matthias then kills Richie and waits for Neville. The Family captures him, but before they have a chance to kill him, they destroy his apartment, his scientific apparatus, and his works of art.

Neville escapes with Lisa, but Matthias wounds him and he falls into a fountain, his blood mingling with the water. In the morning, Dutch finds him, retrieves the serum that will heal all the infected people, and rescues Lisa. The young people drive away as Neville lies dead in the fountain, arms outstretched.

COMMENTARY

The Omega Man was a small-budget movie released in 1971. However, it has stood the test of time and found its place among classic science-fiction films. Audiences were accustomed to seeing Charlton Heston in biblical, epic, and historical roles, but at this period of his career he appeared in several significant futuristic movies, including *Planet of the Apes* in 1968 and *Soylent Green* in 1973.

The Omega Man is based on *I Am Legend,* an original story by Richard Matheson published in 1954. Matheson was a writer for Rod Serling's television series *The Twilight Zone* and Steven Spielberg's 1971 television thriller *Duel.* Matheson's novels, *The Shrinking Man* and *What Dreams May Come,* were also made into films. *I Am Legend* was first filmed in 1964 as *The Last Man on Earth* with Vincent Price, in which the Family was made up of vampires.

DIALOGUE WITH THE GOSPEL

Focus: The Feast of the Sacred Heart is a celebration of the ways in which Jesus loves us with a human heart. In The Omega Man, *Neville parallels Jesus. Both are loving, even to the point of shedding their blood so that others might live.*

When *The Omega Man* was released, some reviewers were quick to comment on the finale and point out the similarities between Charlton Heston's character and Jesus. Neville's side is pierced with a lance, his blood flows out into the water, and he takes the phial with the healing serum from the pocket near his side. At the end, his wide-spread arms give an impression of the crucifix.

The principal images and references of the screenplay echo themes of St. John's writings. Jesus is the original Alpha and "Omega" man, the first and the last, the Creator and the fulfillment of all creation. Robert Neville's experience of this is in reverse order. He seems to be the end of all human creation, but then discovers that he has the means to be a new life-giver, a re-creator, and a healer of illness. Neville is not merely a survivor, he is asked to be a savior, to give his lifeblood to save others.

John's Gospel draws on the symbols of light and darkness, as does the movie. The humans are able to live in light; in fact, it is the light which protects Neville. The "Family" is literally cloaked in darkness. Matthias tells us that they refuse the light. They do not want to be healed and return to their former life. As John's Gospel says of those who refuse God's revelation in Jesus, they have preferred darkness rather than light.

Lisa is reminiscent of the widow of Naim, whose son Jesus brings back to life. Richie, who hopes to bring light to the darkness, becomes a figure of betrayal when he leads Neville into an ambush. The children are what the prophets call the "Remnant," those who remain faithful and experience God's saving power.

The first reading from Hosea speaks of God as a loving father who rescues his beloved children—as Neville does in the film. The Letter to the Ephesians is a hymn to the love of God, which is what we celebrate on the feast of the Sacred Heart. *The Omega Man* is a movie full of the implicit hope that a new and loving world can emerge from the darkness.

KEY SCENES AND THEMES

- Neville surviving in the empty city, staying in the light; the Family appearing only in the darkness; their need to stay in the dark; their cruelty and vindictiveness; the war they wage on Neville, and the rampant destruction of his possessions.

- Neville's career as a doctor and his immunity from infection; his healing of Richie, using his own blood to prepare the life-giving serum; his hopes for the children, and his inability to save Lisa.

- The movie's use of biblical images and themes to establish and develop the parallel between Neville and the Jesus of John's Gospel; Neville's role as the savior who gives his blood and life; Richie's betrayal, the attack by the powers of darkness; Neville's side pierced by a lance, his blood flowing into the water.

FOR REFLECTION AND CONVERSATION

1. As far back as St. Francis de Sales (1567–1622) and St. Ignatius of Loyola (1567–1622), there has been a devotion to the Sacred Heart of Jesus based on the Gospel of John and the teachings of the Fathers of the Church. St. John Eudes (1601–1680) composed a Mass and Office in honor of the Sacred Heart, but the actual practice of the devotion developed following the apparitions to St. Margaret Mary Alacoque (1647–1690) in France between 1673 and 1675. This devotion emphasized acts of reparation and consecration, and was interpreted for modern times in the 1956 encyclical of Pope Pius XII, *Haurietis Aquas.* How is the film *The Omega Man,* with all its elements, a meeting place between faith and culture when considered in the context of today's readings for the feast of the Sacred Heart?

2. The heart is considered the center of a person's inner life, both natural and spiritual. What kind of a

man was Neville? What elements in the film symbolized his inner life and showed him to be a man with a heart, capable of self-sacrificing love? How is love, and the lack of love, demonstrated in the film? What do the biblical symbols of water, light and darkness, and the religious symbolism of the monks' hoods and the cross mean? How might *The Omega Man* be seen as a kind of biblical film?

3. Science fiction is a genre that allows speculation on the consequences of contemporary life, a way of exercising the moral imagination. The film says that a scientist is a man who understands nothing until there is nothing left to understand. What does this mean? In the film, how does the devastation of the plague parallel the interior devastation of humanity? What was the message of *The Omega Man* for its own day, and what does it mean today?

Prayer

Jesus, you know our joy and pain, because you shared our lives and loved us with a human heart. When we are desperate, come quickly to our aid. Amen.

Steel Magnolias

U.S.A., 1989, 118 minutes
Cast: Sally Field, Shirley MacLaine, Dolly Parton,
Olympia Dukakis, Julia Roberts, Tom Skerritt,
Daryl Hannah, Dylan McDermott
Writer: Robert Harling
Director: Herbert Ross

Steel Magnolias

Ark of the Covenant

SYNOPSIS

In Louisiana, the Eatenton family prepares for their daughter Shelby's wedding. Shelby is a diabetic and her family, especially her mother M'Lynn, is concerned that Shelby's precarious medical condition will be threatened if she becomes pregnant. She warns Shelby about this danger. M'Lynn and her friends, the eccentric Ouiser and the caustic Clairee, regularly discuss their problems at the beauty parlor, run by Truvy and her new assistant, Annelle.

Though her husband is prepared not to have children for Shelby's sake, Shelby knows how much a son would mean to him. Shelby becomes pregnant and is jubilant. Shelby's father does not seem to realize the danger the pregnancy poses for Shelby. Her mother is angry, concerned, and anxious. A son is born.

When the baby is still a toddler, Shelby's kidneys fail and M'Lynn donates one of hers to save her daughter. Shelby's condition does not improve, and she dies with only her mother by her side. M'Lynn experiences a crisis at the funeral, but is consoled and challenged by her friends. Annelle becomes pregnant and says that she will name her child in honor of Shelby, whether it is a boy or a girl.

Robert Harling wrote the screenplay for *Steel Magnolias*, adapting it from his successful stage play. The movie is a close look into the lives of a group of six women, their friendship, families, marriages, illnesses, and death. Much of the action and interaction takes place in the beauty parlor. Under the direction of Herbert Ross, who also directed *The Turning Point* and *Nijinsky* (1980), the movie becomes a vehicle for some very smooth entertainment. The combination of wisecracks and the eccentric personalities of the characters create a sure recipe for success. Dolly Parton is the humorous and genial personification of the South. Shirley MacLaine plays a widow who has been in an over-the-top bad mood for forty years. Olympia Dukakis has many of the good lines as a rather cynical Southern widow. Daryl Hannah is almost unrecognizable as the gawky, religiously scrupulous hairdresser. Sally Field has the more serious role as Shelby's mother. The movie gave Julia Roberts her first major role and Oscar nomination.

Steel Magnolias captures the atmosphere of the deep South. Though the characters are somewhat caricatures of human nature, the movie's most forceful message is full of hope: women who support one another in adversity have hearts of gold and backbones of unbreakable steel.

COMMENTARY

Focus: The Assumption of Mary is celebrated with the Gospel of the Visitation that commemorates Mary's own pregnancy and her visit to her pregnant cousin Elizabeth. Like today's Gospel and feast, Steel Magnolias *celebrates new life.*

DIALOGUE WITH THE GOSPEL

The Visitation is an important part of Luke's infancy narratives. The focus is principally on Mary and what she does after the Annunciation. The liturgy both exalts Mary and her Assumption in the apocalyptic images of Revelation and presents her as the humble woman who undertakes an arduous journey to visit her cousin.

The traditional Litany of Loreto invokes Mary as "Ark of the Covenant." This title has long been associated with Mary's visit to Elizabeth. Just as the Hebrew Ark of the Covenant contained the Ten Commandments and was revered wherever it was taken, so Mary, holding Jesus within her, is the new Ark of the Covenant. In ancient times, anyone who touched the Ark died at once; Mary, on the other hand, is full of life, blessing her cousin Elizabeth who feels her son leaping in her womb.

The focus of *Steel Magnolias* is a young mother, her pregnancy and the support that her own mother and her friends give her. The pregnant Shelby, like Mary, is a great giver of life and enthusiasm to those around her. She wants her child and successfully gives birth.

The Gospel is one of joy, though we know that Mary will one day experience the death of her son. The movie's emotional power comes from the viewer's becoming part of the tightly knit group of women. We feel the tragic loss of this loving mother and yet the touching joy that her child lives.

Just as Mary's memory lives in the words of her Magnificat prayer, Annelle allows Shelby to be remembered by promising to name her child after her. This is an evocation of the hope of resurrection described in the reading from First Corinthians. Today, we celebrate the moment of Mary's union with her Son in new life, just as we hope to experience this union one day.

KEY SCENES AND THEMES

- Shelby's diabetic incident and M'Lynn's skillful response to the emergency; her love and care for her daughter; the difficulties involved in a possible pregnancy for Shelby, the news of the pregnancy, M'Lynn's reaction, her concerned anger, their argument; the women at Truvy's and their discussion of the issue, their humor and support of one another.

- The birth of the baby, M'Lynn's love for him; the first birthday celebration, reconciliation with Shelby.

- Shelby's illness, the kidney transplant, playing cards, the jokes, helping Shelby to live; Shelby going into a diabetic coma; M'Lynn urging her to fight; taking Shelby off life support; the funeral, M'Lynn at the cemetery; her outburst of anger and her demands, the support of the women, Annelle's promise to call her baby "Shelby."

FOR REFLECTION AND CONVERSATION

1. *Steel Magnolias* is one of those movies with a BK rating: Bring Kleenex. It is a quintessential women's movie. Many of the films chosen for this movie lectionary are from a male perspective (e.g., *A Bronx Tale, Billy Elliot, Thirteen Days, A Simple Plan*), but credible films that deal with life from a woman's perspective are rare in the film industry. Studies show that, while women will usually watch what men watch, men will only rarely watch what women watch. What accounts for this phenomenon in our culture? Why are fewer women's stories held up as examples of the universal human experience in film in the way that men's stories are?

2. Elizabeth and Mary share the common bond of a first pregnancy. Elizabeth is advanced in age, and we think that Mary was very young. Despite the dangers of which she must have been aware, Elizabeth rejoiced to find herself with child. Shelby, too, rejoiced to find herself pregnant: neither prevention nor termination was an option for her. The film raises important questions, though not explicitly, regarding life issues, among them: the fecundity of marriage, artificial contraception, natural family planning, responsible parenthood, and the preservation of life. Shelby set out to deliberately have a child despite her knowledge of

the danger to her life. Was this virtue? Why or why not? Talk about this moral dilemma and how the teachings of the Church respond to it (cf. *Catechism of the Catholic Church*, especially nn. 236ff).

3. Today's feast of the Assumption of Mary into heaven is a mystery of our faith. Tradition also presents this event for our contemplation as the fourth Glorious Mystery of the Rosary. How does the reading from Revelation help us to contemplate Mary's role in our redemption today? Why do we believe that Jesus would honor his mother by taking her up into heaven after her earthly pilgrimage? How does the joyous canticle of Mary, the Magnificat, help us to meditate more deeply on the events and mysteries of our faith presented in Luke's Gospel?

Prayer

On this celebration of your Assumption, Mary, may we share your joy and spirit of thanksgiving. May we also share as you did in the grace of Jesus, your risen Son. We ask this in his name. Amen.

ALL SOULS DAY

Wisdom 3:1–9; Romans 14:7–12;
Matthew 25:31–46

Flatliners

U.S.A., 1990, 114 minutes
Cast: Kiefer Sutherland, Julia Roberts, Kevin Bacon,
William Baldwin, Oliver Platt, Hope Davis
Writer: Peter Filardi
Director: Joel Schumacher

Flatliners

Death and Judgment

SYNOPSIS

Nelson Wright and a group of fellow Chicago medical students conduct a series of experiments to try to test the assertion that a near-death experience is one full of light and euphoria. The students induce death by stopping the heart; a monitor indicates the moment of death when its signal "flatlines." After a short time, they revive the person who has "died."

Nelson does not tell the students that during his "death experiment" he had nightmare visions of Billy, a child whom Nelson bullied as a boy. The others successively undergo the death experience, and each one tries to outdo the other by lengthening the duration of death. They panic when Rachel, a more serious researcher, is "dead" for five minutes. They manage to revive her.

Each of the students discovers a secret of the past in their death experience. Joe, a womanizer, is haunted by the women he has videotaped in bed without their consent; Rachel relives her father's suicide, which she had been blamed for; David meets an African-American girl he attacked at school. After the medical students have been revived, these experiences somehow carry over into their lives. The boy from the past attacks Nelson, Rachel has visions of her dead father, David visits the adult woman he had victimized, and Joe sees past conquests displayed on public video screens.

Nelson finally undergoes death again as a means of atonement for what he did to Billy, and Billy forgives him. Each of the students comes to terms with his or her past, and is reconciled and forgiven.

COMMENTARY

The writer of *Flatliners,* Peter Filardi, said that human experience is the last frontier for innovative filmmakers. His screenplay reflects the yearning that many people have for some understanding of the afterlife as well as themes of responsibility, sin, guilt, forgiveness, atonement, and reconciliation. The movie is a reminder of other stories about scientists like Dr. Frankenstein, who defied the laws of nature.

The movie was directed by the prolific Joel Schumacher, who completed eight films in the 1990s, including *Falling Down, Batman Forever, Batman and Robin, The Client,* and *A Time to Kill.* Shot in pastel colors and shades, the dilapidated buildings, echoes of monuments and churches, and dramatic flashback and fantasy sequences give *Flatliners* a Gothic feel. The movie has a popular cast led by Kiefer Sutherland as the passionate initiator of the experiments and Julia Roberts as the serious Rachel.

The film is pop science for a mass audience, but useful as an entry point for the exploration of deeply human issues.

DIALOGUE WITH THE GOSPEL

Focus: All Souls Day focuses on life after death, our judgment in the eyes of God, and on repentance, atonement, and praying for the deceased. The students in Flatliners *attempt to discover whether there is life after death and, in so doing, they discover sin, judgment, and repentance.*

The late twentieth century was a time when many people were interested in exploring the afterlife. Near-death experiences were frequently reported, and *Flatliners* draws on that relentless human preoccupation with what comes after death.

What the medical students discovered in their death experiences was not a bright light at the end of a tunnel. They did not see God. Rather, they experienced what Christians would call a "particular judgment." They saw past experiences about people they had victimized in some way that awakened feelings of guilt. When they were resuscitated, they carried these visions of sin and judgment with them and were "haunted" until they acknowledged their guilt, sought forgiveness, and attempted some kind of "purgation" and atonement.

As Paul says to the Romans, the life and death of each one of us has influence on others. The students learned something about the truth that we will all have to stand before the judgment seat of God and give an account of ourselves.

Matthew's Gospel gives us a very down-to-earth description of God's judgment and God's criteria for salvation and damnation. In their flatline experience, the students are graced with an opportunity to see their lives for what they are. What the students experience from beyond gives them time to repent and to undergo purgation and atonement while still on earth. They learn the Gospel lesson that by doing good to others, we do good to Christ and, hence, we can be found worthy of eternal life.

- Nelson's passion for science, his arrogance, how he approaches the other students, motives, speeches, the experiment itself; the effect on him: sensitive hearing, Billy, the physical attacks, being bruised and hurt,

KEY SCENES AND THEMES

trying to hide, Billy attacking him within the room; the fight with Billy in the truck; the cemetery, atonement.

- Rachel interviewing the people about their death experiences and her death experience; being five again, the presence of her father in the photo and in her memory; her mother, the father's return from war, going upstairs to the bathroom, her father killing himself, her mother blaming her; the appearances of Rachel's father, realizing that he was a drug addict, his asking forgiveness, and the reconciliation.

- David and Joe and their death memories; David's decision to go back and see Winnie Hicks, his apology, her acceptance; Joe's cavalier manner, haunted by the images of the women.

FOR REFLECTION AND CONVERSATION

1. *Flatliners* brings to mind other films about the medical profession and the afterlife and their deeper themes: *The Doctor* (pride versus humility), *Gross Anatomy* (humility and kindness), *The Sixth Sense* (the supernatural, reparation and atonement), and *After Life* (the best memory we can take with us when we die). What are some intertextual elements or themes of these films that enrich the meaning of a movie like *Flatliners*? What do you think about the accounts of people who have had near-death experiences? Why are people so interested in finding out what life will be like after death?

2. What Gospel parable could have been the model for this film and why? (Hint: The poor man in this story is the only one in the parables to whom Jesus gives a name—cf. Luke 16:19–31).

3. *Flatliners* is a film full of moral and ethical issues far beyond the audacity of medical students risking their lives while searching for truth. They also want to become famous for their "discovery." They break the rules and put their lives and the lives of their colleagues at risk. Was their risk worth what they learned? Were their actions ethical? If the film is a "place" where we can exercise our moral imagination and test the conclusions, what might we have done in the students' place? What might we want to know about the life to come?

Prayer

Lord, on this day help us examine our consciences, acknowledge our sins, experience your forgiveness, and find ways to make atonement. May we meet you at the judgment with great trust in your mercy. Amen.

Thanksgiving Day
1 Kings 8:55–61; Colossians 3:12–17;
Mark 5:18–20

What's Cooking?

U.S.A., 2000, 110 minutes
Cast: Joan Chen, Mercedes Ruehl, Alfre Woodard,
Kyra Sedgwick, Julianna Margulies, Lainie Kazan,
Denis Haysbert, Maury Chaykin, Estelle Harris
Writers: Gurinder Chadha, Paul Mayeda Berges
Director: Gurinder Chadha

What's Cooking?

Thanks-Giving Not Thanks-Taking

SYNOPSIS

Four American families living in Los Angeles prepare their Thanksgiving Day dinner. One family is Hispanic, another African-American, one Jewish, and the other Vietnamese.

The Vietnamese family owns a video store, and the oldest son, James, is away at college and cannot make it for dinner. The second son, Gary, has failed his exams, and his sister finds a gun hidden under his bed. All three generations of the family help with the preparation of the dinner. During the upsets of the day, the turkey is burned and the family eats a takeout dinner. James brings his Hispanic girlfriend, Gina, home. Some harmony is restored.

James had, in fact, gone to his girlfriend's home for Thanksgiving dinner. Gina is the daughter of the Hispanic family. It is a jovial, macho household where the women cook and the men watch football on television. The parents are divorced because of the father's infidelity. The son, Anthony, meets his father, Javier, in the supermarket and impulsively invites him to dinner. His mother, Lizzie, reluctantly allows it. Javier arrives and confronts his wife, Lizzie. He wants her to take him back and she refuses.

Rachel arrives home for the Jewish family celebrations. She brings her lesbian partner, Carla. Her parents make valiant efforts to be tolerant of their relationship. When the rest of the family arrives, they try to be discreet, but an elderly aunt keeps asking questions and giving advice, seemingly clueless about Carla and Rachel. Finally, an exasperated Rachel announces that she is pregnant and that the donor father is a gay friend. Despite their initial consternation, the family accepts Rachel and Carla.

As Audrey meticulously prepares dinner for the African-American family, she has to go to the airport to meet her intrusively critical mother-in-law, Grace. Ronnie, Audrey's husband, is in charge of security for the governor. It emerges that their son, Michael, was involved in a protest the day before and threw paint on the governor. Ronnie is critical of his son's African-American courses of study and wants him to do something more substantial. When the angry Michael makes it public that his father has had an affair, Grace rebukes her son. He expresses his regrets to Audrey who forgives him.

COMMENTARY

What's Cooking? is directed by Gurinder Chadha who co-wrote the screenplay with her husband, Paul Mayeda Berges. Chadha, an Indian with Punjabi and Kenyan roots, grew up in London, and her husband is an American with some Japanese ancestry. Chadha's films include *Bhaji at the Beach* and *Bend It Like Beckham.*

During the movie's celebratory dinners, diverse family problems are set before us in lively ways. As an audience, our beliefs are tested and we are made to consider why we empathize with one character rather than another. The issues in the Jewish household are the most controversial. Kyra Sedgwick plays the daughter, Rachel, who is in a lesbian relationship with Carla, Julianna Margulies. The other issues are expected from a movie dealing with ethnicity and culture in the United States: racial identity, prejudice, mixed-race marriages, infidelity, and forgiveness.

The women in the cast, Mercedes Ruehl, Joan Chen, Alfre Woodard, and Lanie Kazan, are the strongest of the characters, reinforcing the cultural connection between mothers, home, family, and Thanksgiving in America.

DIALOGUE WITH THE GOSPEL

Focus: In today's Gospel Jesus tells the man he cured to "Go home to your family and make it clear to them how much the Lord in his mercy has done for you." What's Cooking? *shows us that Thanksgiving can be a joyful and painful time for family, as well as an opportunity to acknowledge blessings and grow in love and forgiveness.*

The reading from First Kings introduces the theme of cultural identity, blessing, and our call to live life according to God's commandments in love. Living by the rules and expectations of religious, human, and cultural values is the struggle each of the families in *What's Cooking?* must confront. The characters vocalize these tensions and struggles when they say grace before the meal. Their stories and prayers highlight particular issues of cultural identity experienced by different ethnic groups, which have existed in the United States since the first Thanksgiving. The cantankerous Monica, remarking on the Native American Indians and the various settlers occupying their land, says that Thanksgiving is more of a "Thanks-taking."

The reading from Colossians holds up the ideals of love, kindness, and self-giving as the distinguishing signs of a Christian family, whatever its culture. The text is almost a program for goodness to guide any family struggling—like those in Paul's time—to live the Gospel message in today's world. Despite the difficulty, pain, moral issues, and betrayals, each family in the movie is able to offer some thanks for the blessings in their lives. They search for and find some unity and reconciliation.

Perhaps the passage from Mark does not appear an obvious choice for a Gospel to celebrate Thanksgiving. However, a man possessed by evil is liberated by God's grace through Jesus. He wants to go with Jesus, but Jesus tells him to stay with his own people and acknowledge what God has done for him. This can serve as an image of the spirit of Thanksgiving: God has cast out evil from his people and has set them free to live in gratitude.

KEY SCENES AND THEMES

- The preparations for the Thanksgiving Day meal; supermarket shopping, unexpected invitations; Gina bringing home her Vietnamese boyfriend, Jimmy; the preparation of the food with the different cultural approaches; the extended family helping in the preparation; the collage of food, cooking, and serving.

- The range of problems in each family, especially concealment, lies, betrayals, and the possibility of forgiveness; various sexual tensions, issues, and infidelities; the children; interracial, intercultural, and intergenerational relationships; the lesbian couple.

- The four prayers of grace before the meal, the petitions, the concerns; Grace asking each guest at the table to express something for which they are thankful; the final images of family unity and reconciliation.

FOR REFLECTION AND CONVERSATION

1. Beyond its North American history, Thanksgiving is probably rooted in ancient feasts celebrating the end of harvest time. But in an increasingly non-rural North America, the Thanksgiving holiday is about thanking God—each in his or her own way—for

blessings received. Thanksgiving has also become a time for family, football, and cultural assimilation, as seen in *What's Cooking?* Is this a good thing? Why or why not?

2. Some say that the Thanksgiving holiday is the one celebration in the United States that has not been exploited by commercialization. It is a federal and bank holiday, and schools and most major stores are closed. People travel great distances to be with their relatives, because, as Paul describes in today's second reading, they believe family is the most important part of life. The day after, however, is usually the biggest shopping day of the year and the "official" start of the Christmas retail season. How does a Christian negotiate the tension between family, the religious, and the secular? What answers can be found in today's readings?

3. How do the family dynamics in *What's Cooking?* make Thanksgiving what some people call "the holiday from hell"? What aspects also make this cinematic vision of Thanksgiving very realistic? Talk about the four families: their cultural heritage, the cinematic device of looking inside the homes of four families living on four corners of one intersection—and the fact that they don't even know each other. What does the film show us about male and female roles in the United States, same-sex partnerships, intercultural and intergenerational problems of communication? What is the Christian response when cultural, moral, and religious values clash in life and in the movies?

Prayer

We celebrate, Lord, your gifts to us, and we ask you to be patient with our faults. Help us to forgive those who have offended us, as you forgive our offenses. May this be a time of unity and reconciliation. Amen.

Appendices

Contents By Movie Title

Contents By Movie Title

Movie Title	Sunday/Celebration	Gospel Text	Page #
House of Mirth, The	Week 22	Mk 7:1–8, 14–15, 21–23	271
Jesus of Montreal	Lent Sunday 3	Jn 2:13–25	75
Joy Luck Club, The	Mary, Mother of God	Lk 2:16–21	346
Judas	Good Friday	Jn 18:1—19:42	101
Keeping the Faith	Week 31	Mk 12:28–34	315
Kundun	Epiphany	Mt 2:1–12	50
Last Valley, The	Week 29	Mk 10:35–45	306
Legend of Bagger Vance	Easter Sunday 3	Lk 24:35–48	121
Life is Beautiful	Week 25	Mk 9:30–37	286
Lilies of the Field	Baptism of the Lord	Mk 1:7–11	55
Little Women	Christmas Dawn	Lk 2:15–20	27
Long Walk Home, The	Week 32	Mk 12:38–44	320
Lord of the Rings, Part 1	Christmas Day	Jn 1:1–18	32
Magnificent Seven, The	Week 15	Mk 6:7–13	235
Mass Appeal	Easter Sunday 4	Jn 10:11–18	127
Matrix, The	Easter Sunday	Jn 20:1–9	111
Mighty, The	Easter Sunday 5	Jn 15:1–8	132
Mission, The	Easter Sunday 7	Jn 17:11–19	142
Molokai: …Fr. Damien	Week 6	Mk 1:40–45	184
Moonstruck	Body and Blood of Christ	Mk 14:12–16, 22–26	159
Mr. Holland's Opus	Week 23	Mk 7:31–37	276
Mumford	Conversion of St. Paul	Mk 16:14–20	351
My Left Foot	Week 7	Mk 2:1–12	189
Omega Man, The	Sacred Heart of Jesus	Jn 19:31–37	367
Patch Adams	Week 5	Mk 1:29–39	179
Rain Man	Holy Thursday	Jn 13:1–15	96
Remains of the Day, The	Advent Sunday 1	Mk 13:33–37	1
Romero	Week 14	Mk 6:1–6	229
Savior	Holy Innocents	Mt 2:13–18	340

Contents By Movie Title

Contents By Sunday/Celebration

Contents By Sunday/Celebration

Contents By Sunday/Celebration

Contents By Gospel Text

Contents By Gospel Text

Contents By Gospel Text

Gospel Text	Movie Title	Sunday/Celebration	Page #
Mk 5:18–20	*What's Cooking?*	Thanksgiving Day	382
Mk 5:21–43	*Test of Love, A*	Week 13	222
Mk 6:1–6	*Romero*	Week 14	229
Mk 6:30–34	*Dances With Wolves*	Week 16	240
Mk 6:7–13	*Magnificent Seven, The*	Week 15	235
Mk 7:1–8, 14–15, 21–23	*House of Mirth, The*	Week 22	271
Mk 7:31–37	*Mr. Holland's Opus*	Week 23	276
Mk 8:27–35	*Simple Plan, A*	Week 24	281
Mk 9:2–10	*Billy Elliot*	Lent Sunday 2	70
Mk 9:30–37	*Life is Beautiful*	Week 25	286
Mk 9:38–43, 45, 47–48	*Second Best*	Week 26	291
Mt 2:1–12	*Kundun*	Epiphany	50
Mt 2:13–18	*Savior*	Holy Innocents	340
Mt 25:31–46	*Flatliners*	All Souls Day	377
Mt 28:16–20	*Black Robe*	Trinity Sunday	152
Mt 6:1–6, 16–18	*Chocolat*	Ash Wednesday	60

Movie Ratings Chart*

Movie Title	MPAA (1)	BBFC (2)	OFLC (3)	USCC (4)
2001: A Space Odyssey	G	U	—	A-II
A.I.: Artificial Intelligence	PG-13	12	M 15+	A-II
Absence of Malice	PG	PG	PG	A-II
Agnes of God	PG-13	15	PG	A-IV
Alive	R	15	M 15+	A-II
Angela's Ashes	R	15	M 15+	A-IV
At First Sight	PG-13	12	M 15+	A-III
Beautiful Mind, A	PG-13	12	M 15+	A-III
Bed of Roses	PG	PG	G	A-III
Billy Elliot	R	15	M 15+	A-III
Black Robe	R	15	M	A-III
Bram Stoker's Dracula	R	18	M	O
Bronx Tale, A	R	18	M 15+	A-III
Brother Sun, Sister Moon	PG	U	PG	A-II
Burning Season, The	R	15	MA	——
Cast Away	PG-13	12	M 15+	A-II
Chocolat	PG-13	12	M 15+	O
Dances With Wolves	PG-13	15	M	A-III
Daylight	PG-13	12	M	A-III
Dead Poets Society	PG	PG	PG	A-III
Disney's The Kid	PG	PG	PG	A-II
Edward Scissorhands	PG-13	PG	PG	A-II
End of the Affair, The	R	18	MA 15+	A-IV
Exorcist, The	R	18	R 18+	A-IV
Finding Forrester	PG-13	12	M 15+	A-II

* Information regarding the rating codes may be found on each organization's Web site.

(1) MPAA: Motion Picture Association of America, United States; www.mpaa.org

(2) BBFC: British Board of Film Classification, United Kingdom; www.bbfc.co.uk

(3) OFLC: The Office for Film and Literature Classification, Australia; www.oflc.gov.au

(4) USCC: United States Catholic Conference, www.nccbuscc.org

Movie Ratings Chart

Movie Title	MPAA (1)	BBFC (2)	OFLC (3)	USCC (4)
Firm, The	R	15	M 15+	A-III
Flatliners	R	15	M	O
Godfather, The	R	18	M	A-III
Harry Potter...Sorcerer's Stone	PG	PG	PG	A-II
House of Mirth, The	PG	PG	PG	A-II
Jesus of Montreal	R	18	M	A-IV
Joy Luck Club, The	R	15	M	A-III
Judas	——	——	——	——
Keeping the Faith	PG-13	12	M 15+	A-IV
Kundun	PG-13	12	PG	A-II
Last Valley, The	PG	15	——	A-III
Legend of Bagger Vance, The	PG-13	PG	PG	A-II
Life is Beautiful	PG-13	PG	M 15+	A-II
Lilies of the Field	NR	U	——	A-I
Little Women	PG	U	G	A-I
Long Walk Home, The	PG	PG	PG	A-II
Lord of the Rings, Part 1	PG-13	PG	M 15+	A-III
Magnificent Seven, The	PG-13	PG	PG	A-II
Mass Appeal	PG	15	——	A-II
Matrix, The	R	15	M 15+	O
Mighty, The	PG-13	PG	M 15+	A-II
Mission, The	PG	PG	——	A-III
Molokai: The Story of Fr. Damien	PG	——	PG	——
Moonstruck	PG	PG	PG	A-III
Mr. Holland's Opus	PG	PG	PG	A-II
Mumford	R	15	MA 15+	A-III
My Left Foot	R	15	M	A-III
Omega Man, The	PG	PG	——	A-III
Patch Adams	PG-13	12	M 15+	A-III

Movie Ratings Chart

Movie Title	MPAA (1)	BBFC (2)	OFLC (3)	USCC (4)
Rain Man	R	15	M 15+	A-III
Remains of the Day, The	PG	U	G	A-II
Romero	PG-13	15	M	A-II
Savior	R	18	MA 15+	——
Second Best	PG-13	12	PG	A-II
Seventh Sign, The	R	15	M	O
Simple Plan, A	R	15	M 15+	A-III
Simply Irresistible	PG-13	PG	PG	A-III
Sommersby	PG-13	12	M	A-III
Spitfire Grill, The	PG-13	12	M 15+	A-II
Stanley & Iris	PG-13	15	M	A-II
Steel Magnolias	PG	PG	M	A-III
Test of Love, A	PG	PG	——	A-II
Third Miracle, The	R	15	M 15+	A-III
Thirteen Days	PG-13	12	M 15+	A-II
Titanic	PG-13	12	M 15+	A-III
To Kill a Mockingbird	NR	PG	PG	A-II
Truman Show, The	PG	PG	PG	A-III
Unbreakable	PG-13	12	M 15+	A-II
What's Cooking?	PG-13	12	M 15+	A-III

Recommended Reading on Movies and Religious Themes

Baugh, Lloyd, *Imaging the Divine: Jesus and Christ-Figures in Film.* Kansas City, MO: Sheed and Ward, 1997.

A thesis-based study of the Jesus movies and some selected Christ-figure movies; defines what Christ-figure means; extensive and thorough, if somewhat controversial in interpretation.

Belknap, Bryan, *Group's Blockbuster Movie Illustrator.* Loveland, CO: Group Publishing, 2001.

Over 160 film clips are presented according to theme. Includes Scripture references, cue times to start and end clips, and reflection questions. Suitable for teenagers.

Blake, Richard A., *After Image: The Indelible Catholic Imagination of Six American Filmmakers.* Chicago: Loyola Press, 2000.

An exploration of imagination and its religious dimension in the movies of six Catholic-educated directors: Capra, Coppolla, De Palma, Ford, Hitchcock, Scorsese.

Eilers, Franz-Joseph, *Church and Social Communication, Basic Documents.* Manila: Logos Publications, Inc., 1993.

The texts of nine Vatican documents from 1936 to 1992, with the addresses for World Communications Day and quotations on communication from other official documents. Eilers provides introductions and some structure outlines of the documents.

Fields, Doug and Eddie James, *Videos that Teach.* Grand Rapids, MI: Zondervan, 1999.

Fields, Doug and Eddie James, *Videos that Teach 2.* Grand Rapids, MI: Zondervan, 2002.

"Teachable movie moments" from modern film classics suitable for use with teenagers. Offers clip selection, reflections, and Scripture references to spark discussion.

Fraser, Peter, *Images of the Passion: The Sacramental Mode in Film.* Westport, CT: Praeger Publishers, 1998.

Selected movies are examined to illustrate how they implicitly dramatize aspects of the Gospel and the sufferings of Jesus.

Fraser, Peter and Neal, Vernon Edward, *ReViewing the Movies: A Christian Response to Contemporary Film.* Wheaton, IL: Crossway Books, 2000.

An application of the theory in Fraser's *Images of the Passion* to contemporary popular cinema in a wide-ranging survey.

Jewett, Robert, *Saint Paul at the Movies.* Louisville, KY: Westminster/John Knox Press, 1993.

A New Testament scholar writes an enlightening book about the Greco-Roman world of Paul. A movie enthusiast, Jewett has chosen ten popular movies to illustrate the virtues that Paul holds up to the Roman Empire.

Jewett, Robert, *Saint Paul Returns to the Movies.* Grand Rapids, MI: William B. Eerdmans, 1999.

A sequel which is as good as, perhaps better than, the original.

John Paul II, *Giovanni Paolo II e il Cinema, Tutti i discorsi (John Paul II and the Cinema: All the Talks).* Rome: Ente dello Spettacolo, 2000.

A collection of 8 speeches by the Pope on cinema. Texts in Italian and in English with commentary articles on the Church and cinema.

Johnston, Robert K., *Reel Spirituality: Theology and Film in Dialogue.* Grand Rapids, MI: Baker Academic, 2000.

A theologian from Fuller Theological Seminary who loves cinema asks basic questions about the religious dimension of movies, opening up the spirituality implicit in so many mainstream movies. It has a wide range of film references.

Maher, Ian, *Reel Issues: Engaging Film and Faith.* Swindon, UK: The Open Book, Bible Society, 1998.

Maher, Ian, *Reel Issue: Five More Films to Engage Film and Faith.* Swindon, UK: The Open Book, Bible Society, 2000.

Produced for the Open Book program of the British Bible Society, these booklets are designed for use with Christian groups.

Mahony, Roger M., *Film Makers, Film Viewers: Their Challenges and Opportunities.* Boston: Pauline Books & Media, 1992.

The text of Cardinal Mahony's pastoral letter to the diocese of Los Angeles, his synthesis of a contemporary Catholic approach to cinema.

Malone, Peter, *Movie Christs and Antichrists.* New York: Crossroads, 1990. (Originally, Sydney: Parish Ministry, 1988.)

A study of movies and meanings, focusing on the Jesus-movies (the Jesus-figures) and the movies of characters who resemble Jesus (Christ-figures); also chapters on movies and antichrist symbols.

Malone, Peter, *Myth and Meaning: Australian Film Directors in Their Own Words.* Sydney, Australia: Currency Press, 2001.

Fifteen interviews with Australian film directors such as Bruce Beresford, George Miller, Fred Schepisi, Scott Hicks, Gillian Armstrong on the values and spirituality underlying their films.

Malone, Peter, *On Screen.* Manila: Daughters of St Paul, 2001.

An introduction to the study of movies and meanings.

Marsh, Clive and Ortiz, Gaye, eds, *Explorations in Theology and Film.* Oxford: Blackwell, 1997.

A collection of theological essays exploring specific contemporary popular movies like *The Terminator, Groundhog Day, The Piano, Edward Scissorhands.*

May, John R., *New Image of Religious Film.* Kansas City, MO: Sheed and Ward, 1997.

A collection of theological essays which examine theoretical aspects of religion, society, and cinema.

May, John R., *Nourishing Faith Through Fiction, Reflections on the Apostles' Creed in Literature and Film.* Franklin, WI: Sheed and Ward, 2001.

An American pioneer in the studies of cinema examines stories that evoke the presence and images of the Trinity, the Creator, the Savior and the Holy Spirit, the Life-giver. Classic movies and novels are considered in reference to many contemporary movies.

McNulty, Edward, *Films and Faith: Forty Discussion Guides*. Topeka, KS: Viaticum Press, 1999.

As the title indicates, discussion material for forty films. They are designed for the non-expert in cinema and provide detailed information about each film as well as some theological background. There are extensive questions for reflection.

McNulty, Edward, *Praying the Movies: Daily Meditations from Classic Films*. Louisville, KY: Geneva Press, 2001.

A collection of thirty-one devotions that connect movies and the spiritual life of moviegoers.

Romanowski, William D., *Pop Culture Wars, Religion and the Role of Entertainment in American Life*. Downers Grove, IL: InterVarsity Press, 1996.

A wide-ranging study of entertainment, including cinema, noting the hostile U.S. religious tradition as well as the movements to find the religious values in media and entertainment.

Rosenstand, Nina, *The Moral of the Story: An Introduction to Ethics*. Mountainview, CA: Mayfield Publishing, 2000.

This popular textbook uses film stories in particular to explore ethics and ethical theories.

Schreck, Nikolas, *The Satanic Screen: An Illustrated Guide to the Devil in Cinema*. London, UK: Creation Books, 2001.

A book that documents the devil's twentieth-century celluloid history and locates 300 or so films in the culture of the years in which they were made.

Scott, Bernard Brandon, *Hollywood Dreams and Biblical Stories*. Minneapolis: Fortress Press, 1994.

The author brings his scriptural background to modern, popular movies and highlights the links between the biblical stories and the new cinema stories to draw out their meanings and their myths.

Short, Robert, *The Gospel from Outer Space: The Religious Implications of E.T., Star Wars, Superman, Close Encounters of the Third Kind, and 2001: A Space Odyssey*. San Francisco: Harper and Row, 1983.

The author of *The Gospel according to Peanuts* and *The Parables of Peanuts* offers the text of a multimedia presentation of Gospel parallels in popular science fiction and fantasy movies.

Solomon, Gary, *The Movie Prescription: Watch This Movie and Call Me in the Morning: 200 Movies to Help You Heal Life's Problems.* New York: Lebhar-Friedman Books, 1998.

Solomon, Gary, *Reel Therapy: How Movies Inspire You to Overcome Life's Problems.* New York: Lebhar-Friedman, Books, 2001.

Dr. Gary Solomon has registered "Cinema Therapy" and "The Movie Doctor" as his trademarks and blends a popular approach to movies along with the academic. Though these two books are not specifically religious, he has selected a great number of films that can be used for "cinema therapy," that is, healing and inspiration.

Stern, Richard C., Clayton N. Jefford, and Guerric Debona, *Savior on the Silver Screen.* Mahwah, NJ: Paulist Press, 1999.

The authors have run courses on the principal Jesus movies from Cecil B. De Mille to *Jesus of Montreal.* This is the expanded course with a thorough rationale for studying these movies.

Stone, Bryan P., *Faith and Film, Theological Themes at the Cinema.* St. Louis: Chalice Press, 2000.

The framework for examining a range of generally well-known movies is the Apostle's Creed, enabling the author to highlight religious themes in movies in a context of faith and the exploration of faith.

Vaux, Sara Anson, *Finding Meaning at the Movies.* Nashville: Abingdon Press, 1999.

The author wants to encourage study groups in schools, universities, and parishes by taking a range of popular movies and showing how they can be fruitfully discussed.

Voytilla, Stuart, *Myth and the Movies: Discovering the Mythic Structure of 50 Unforgettable Films.* Los Angeles: Michael Wiese Productions, 1999.

The author draws on the culture of referring to and using myths, especially the hero's journey, to look at a number of popular screen classics.

Film Websites

(Some websites which may be of interest. Please apply your own criteria when visiting these websites. They are listed here as references only.)

Film and Spirituality

www.signis.net

> The international Catholic association for communications includes current jury prizes for film festivals and reviews by Rev. Peter Malone, MSC, President of SIGNIS.

www.paulinecenterformediastudies.org

> Media literacy in faith communities, includes some in-depth movie reviews and links, sponsored by the Daughters of St. Paul.

www.nationalfilmretreat.org

> Information on the National Film Retreat, an annual interfaith gathering that screens and prays several films over a weekend (Friday evening to Sunday noon).

www.HollywoodJesus.com

> This ecumenical website is dedicated to finding Christian spirituality in movies, with a searchable archive.

www.catholic.org.au

> Four film reviews a month beginning in 2001 from the Australian Conference of Catholic Bishops.

www.chiafilm.com

> This site is named for *Chiaroscuro,* the interplay of light and shade in an image, and seeks to move beyond the culture wars and encourage a conversation between the cinema and Christian spirituality. Contains new reviews, retrospectives, and essays.

www.cityofangelsfilmfest.org

> Interfaith film festival site with reviews, resources, and events.

www.spiritualityhealth.com

Fred and Mary Brussat offer an e-course, "Going to the Movies as a Spiritual Practice," as well as current film and video reviews with a searchable database.

www.FilmClipsOnLine.com

Hollywood filmmaker Michael Rhodes and industry colleagues and educators offer clips from popular films to use in educational settings.

www.christianitytoday.com/ctmag/features/columns/filmforum.html

Christian film reviews that integrate and analyze commentaries from several sources, both from religious and from the mainstream press.

www.unomaha.edu/~wwwjrf

Articles and reviews by the Journal of Religion and Film, University of Nebraska at Omaha.

www.christiancritic.com

The Christian critic's movie parables.

www.textweek.com

Sermon-helps with a movie concordance for the Catholic and Anglican lectionaries.

www.visualparables.com

Visual Parables is a monthly review of films, videos, and the arts with lectionary links.

www.udayton.edu/mary

This site features the videos on Mary and Marian subjects archived by the University of Dayton's Marian Library/International Marian Research Institute.

Cineandmedia@yahoogroups.com

E-group for those interested in cinema, spirituality, and theology.

Film/Media Education

www.bravo.ca/scanningthemovies

Canada's BRAVO! Channel presents a media education perspective based on the television program, "Scanning the Movies," hosted by Neil Anderson and Rev. John Pungente, SJ, with study guides.

www.filmeducation.org

> This U.K. film-education site is provided for secondary school teachers to encourage and promote the study, evaluation, and analysis of a wide range of media, including film, within the curriculum. Free online study guides and resources.

www.udayton.edu/~ipi

> *The Pastoral Communication and Ministry Institute (PCMI)* of the University of Dayton is an annual summer program to prepare leaders to proclaim the Gospel using all the means of pastoral communications available today. The program includes courses on film, theology, and spirituality.

Film and Families

www.daughtersofstpaul.com/myfriend

> Movie and video reviews by kids for kids.

www.americancatholic.org

> *St. Anthony Messenger's* "Entertainment Watch—Movies" section and the *Every Day Catholic* newsletter's "Media Watch" feature movie reviews and articles.

www.moviemom.com

> "Helping families share great times, great movies, and great conversations."

www.screenit.com

> Entertainment reviews for parents with a searchable archive.

Film Review Sites

www.usccb.org

> The United States Catholic Conference site includes current film reviews, searchable archive, and "information for guidance."

www.imdb.org

> The Internet Movie Databases is the largest movie archive on the web and includes industry information and a multitude of links to sources and reviews.

www.suntimes.com/index/ebert.html

> The index on this website contains famed movie critic Roger Ebert's film reviews since 1985, along with a searchable database of these reviews.

www.movie-reviews.colossus.net

> Film reviews since 1996 by James Bernardelli.

Film Ratings

(Please note: while all of these sites list film ratings, only a few list their criteria for judging films.)

www.mpaa.org

The Motion Picture Association of America (U.S.A.) film ratings.

www.ccr.gov.on.ca/ofrb

Ontario Film Review Board.

www.media-awareness.ca/eng

Film rating links for all other provinces of Canada.

www.bffc.co.uk

The British Board of Film Classification.

www.oflc.gov.au

The Office for Film and Literature Classification, Australia.

Index

H

S

T

ABOUT THE AUTHORS

PETER MALONE, MSC, is a Sacred Heart Father from Australia currently living in England. In 1998, he was elected president of the International Organization for the Cinema (OCIC), an appointment which received immediate Vatican approval. He is currently president of The World Catholic Association for Communications (SIGNIS).

Peter is known worldwide for his pastoral approach to integrating film, faith, and life. He has served as juror at film festivals throughout the world and is currently a consultant to the Bishops' Committee for Film in the Philippines.

Father Malone is the author of *Myth and Meaning: Australian Film Directors in Their Own Words, On Screen, Movie Christs and Anti-Christs, The Film, Films and Values,* a co-author of *Cinema, Religion and Values,* and a regular columnist in *The Universe* Catholic newspaper in the U.K.

ROSE PACATTE, FSP, is a Daughter of St. Paul and the Director of the Pauline Center for Media Studies in Boston. She has an MA in Education in Media Studies from the University of London and is a frequent speaker at conferences throughout the U.S. and abroad.

Sr. Rose is an active member in several Catholic and ecumenical communications and film organizations, including the U.S. affiliate of SIGNIS. She has been a jurist at the Venice Film Festival, and a panelist at the City of Angels Film Festival and Boston's Faith & Film Festival. She is one of the founding directors of the annual National Film Retreat and is the author of *A Guide to In-House Film Festivals in Ten Easy Steps.*

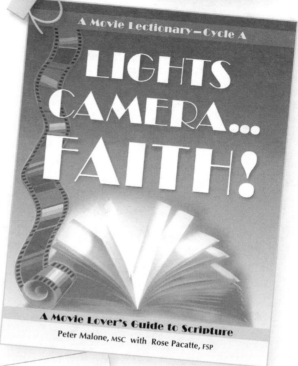
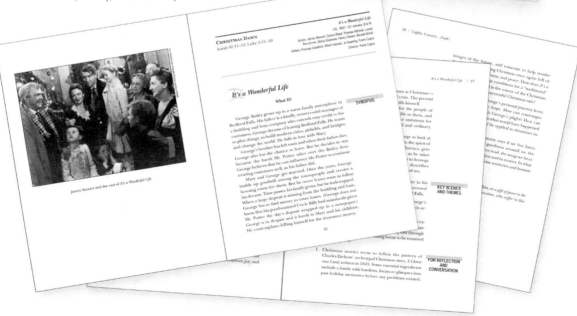

Pauline
BOOKS & MEDIA

The Daughters of St. Paul operate book and media centers at the following addresses. Visit, call or write the one nearest you today, or find us on the World Wide Web, www.pauline.org

CALIFORNIA
3908 Sepulveda Blvd, Culver City, CA 90230   310-397-8676
5945 Balboa Avenue, San Diego, CA 92111   858-565-9181
46 Geary Street, San Francisco, CA 94108   415-781-5180

FLORIDA
145 S.W. 107th Avenue, Miami, FL 33174   305-559-6715

HAWAII
1143 Bishop Street, Honolulu, HI 96813   808-521-2731
Neighbor Islands call: 800-259-8463

ILLINOIS
172 North Michigan Avenue, Chicago, IL 60601   312-346-4228

LOUISIANA
4403 Veterans Memorial Blvd, Metairie, LA 70006   504-887-7631

MASSACHUSETTS
885 Providence Hwy, Dedham, MA 02026   781-326-5385

MISSOURI
9804 Watson Road, St. Louis, MO 63126   314-965-3512

NEW JERSEY
561 U.S. Route 1, Wick Plaza, Edison, NJ 08817   732-572-1200

NEW YORK
150 East 52nd Street, New York, NY 10022   212-754-1110
78 Fort Place, Staten Island, NY 10301   718-447-5071

PENNSYLVANIA
9171-A Roosevelt Blvd, Philadelphia, PA 19114   215-676-9494

SOUTH CAROLINA
243 King Street, Charleston, SC 29401   843-577-0175

TENNESSEE
4811 Poplar Avenue, Memphis, TN 38117   901-761-2987

TEXAS
114 Main Plaza, San Antonio, TX 78205   210-224-8101

VIRGINIA
1025 King Street, Alexandria, VA 22314   703-549-3806

CANADA
3022 Dufferin Street, Toronto, Ontario, Canada M6B 3T5
    416-781-9131
1155 Yonge Street, Toronto, Ontario, Canada M4T 1W2
    416-934-3440

¡También somos su fuente para libros, videos y música en español!